MARTIN LUTHER

KNOWLEDGE AND MEDIATION
IN THE RENAISSANCE

JAN LINDHARDT

Texts and Studies in Religion

Volume 29

The Edwin Mellen Press
Lewiston   Queenston

Library of Congress Cataloging-in-Publication Data

Lindhardt, Jan.
  Martin Luther : knowledge and mediation in the
renaissance.

  (Texts and studies in religion ; v. 29)
  Bibliography: p.
  Includes index.
  1. Luther, Martin, 1483-1546--Contributions in
Christian doctrine of man. 2. Luther, Martin, 1483-
1546--Contributions in Christian doctrine of
communication. 3. Man (Christian theology)--History
of doctrines--16th century. 4. Communication (Theology)
--History of doctrines--16th century. I. Title.
II. Series: Texts and studies in religion ; 29.

BR333.5.A5L56 1986   128'.092'4   86-17940
ISBN 0-88946-817-6 (alk. paper)

This is volume 29 in the continuing series
Texts and Studies in Religion
Volume 29 ISBN 0-88946-817-6
TSR Series ISBN 0-88946-976-8

The Edwin Mellen Press
Box 450
Lewiston, New York
USA 14092

The Edwin Mellen Press
Box 67
Queenston, Ontario
L0S 1L0 CANADA

Printed in the United States of America

To Cæcilie

Rhetoricatur igitur Spiritus sanctus iam,
ut exhortatio fiat illustrior.

(May the Holy Spirit become rhetorical in order
that the vocation may become more illustrious.)

M. Luther, WA XL/3, 59f.

TABLE OF CONTENTS

1. **Renaissance and Reformation**   1

2. **The Tripartite Man**   17
   Plato   18
   Aristotle   20
   Our Own Times   24
   St. Augustine   25
   Two Types of Love   27

3. **The Undivided Man**   29
   Mysticism   31
   The Will   37
   Astrology   40
   Humanism   43
   Luther and Rhetoric   61

4. **From Accidia to Melancholy**   66

5. **Luther's Understanding of Faith**   86
   The Transmitter - God   87
   The Word as the Source of Understanding   89
   "Oralness"   94
   What it Means to Believe   101
   Faith is a Sentiment   105
   Faith as Experience   112
   Justification of Faith   114
   Faith and Works   116

6. The Enslaved Will 119
The Freedom of the Will 120
Free Will and Theology 123
The Conflict Between Erasmus and Luther 130
Luther on the Enslavement of the Will 134
The Exemplum 143
Guilt and Responsibility 144
Both Justified and a Sinner 150

7. Use of the Bible 156
The Translation of the Bible into German 159
Only Through the Scriptures 163
Can We do Without the Tradition 165
Scripture is its own Interpreter 171
Luther's Relationship to Allegorical
   Interpretation 172
Symbol Instead of Allegory 178
What is Allegory? 180
Adolf Jülicher's Understanding of Parables 184
Language and Reality 189
Luther and the Scholars 191
Luther's Understanding of Language 193
Synechdoche 199
The Five Senses 203
The Clarity of Scripture 205
Where is the Holy Spirit? 207
Textual Intentionality 209
No to the Quadriga 212
The Battle with the Serpent 248

Conclusion 225

Notes 228

Literature 250

Index 256

Preface

This book was published in Danish in 1983 in Copenhagen. The same year I defended my thesis on the basis of this book and two others, Retorik, Copenhagen 1975 (a Danish presentation of the fundamental concepts and philosophical and psychological implications of rhetorics) and Rhetor, Poeta, Historicus. Studien über eine rhetorische Lebensanschauung in der Renaissance, Leiden 1979 (a presentation of the rhetorical philosophy of the Florentine Chancellor of State, Coluccio Salutati, died 1406).

The present book deals with Luther and his fundamental ideas. It is, however, still more a book about the Renaissance, since Luther is here seen as a genuine representative of renaissance humanism. And to a still higher extent it is an analysis of what rhetorical anthropology, psychology and philosophy really are.

The greater part of the references will probably be unknown to Anglo-Saxon readers, since the sources are German and most of the secondary literature Danish and German. The problem is, however, so general that it will hopefully be of interest beyond the limits of the chosen field.

I could thank many people for having inspired me in this work. I shall confine myself to mention dr. theol. Johannes Sløk, professor of Ethics and Philosophy of Religion at the University of Aarhus, whose studies of the Renaissance have influenced me decisively and whose support has never failed. Furthermore, I should like to thank the Edwin Mellen Press for publishing the book and the Danish Research Foundation for the Humanities for having paid the translation into English. Thanks to the translater, Fred. Cryer, who has without difficulty grasped the intentions of the book, and to Karin Nielsen for typing it.

MARTIN LUTHER

KNOWLEDGE AND MEDIATION
IN THE RENAISSANCE

1. Renaissance and Reformation

In recent years there has been much discussion as to
the degree to which our knowledge is determined by our
language. Is it, for example, the case that words are
merely audible designations for things or concepts, or
is it more correct to say that the very process of knowing requires words? In short, that our words determine
what we "know", "believe", "know of", and so forth? The
ancient Israelites were of this opinion; they believed
that to know or acknowledge something was the same as
to have a word for it. And this was held to be the same
as to have power over the thing in question, or at least
to be able to control it. Thus it was incorrect to ut-
ter the name of God, since it would be an abomination
to claim that one was thoroughly familiar with God, or
that one had power over him. This position has for quite
some time been regarded as naive, but in modern times
the philosophy of language has broached similar ideas.
It seems to be the case that language indeed creates
what it designates.

Historical research seems to confirm this impression.
An important tool in this connection is the division
of the past into periods or epochs. Such terminologies
generally contain both a description and an evaluation.
Some periods are more fortunate than others. The span
from 400 to 1400 AD has been exceptionally unfortunate,
as far as its title is concerned: the Middle Ages. The
term itself implies only middling qualities at best,
as well as the fact that as a period it is situated between two others, antiquity and the Renaissance. The
term was plainly not invented by those who lived during
the Middle Ages; rather, it was proposed by the denizens
of the Renaissance, who regarded it as a mediocre age,
and who wished to lay it to rest once and for all.

The Renaissance was more fortunate, but then, so it should have been, since this period, like the Enlightenment, managed to baptize itself.[1] The magics of these names still retain their power to conjure. No matter how many scholars attempt to revise our estimate of the myth of the dark Middle Ages, or to challenge the phrases which suggest that the Renaissance was the period in which modern man, or the modern age, was born, this has no effect on the general consciousness (which exercizes its influence on historians as well) of the distinction between the two ages. According to this distinction, one of these ages was dull and dark, a time in which society either stagnated or even regressed, whereas the other, as the term "Renaissance" itself suggests, implies something like sunrise and progress. Moreover, this is the case in spite of the fact that the Middle Ages were probably more closely related to the 20th century in terms of philosophy, psychology, and science. Such objections are, however, to no avail, since our very language informs us that the Renaissance must have been a much more exciting and significant period than the Middle Ages.

Now, while it may be the case that language is our master, we should note that it is not a single language which has this distinction. More accurately, our linguistic horizon offers us many possibilities, so that if we discover that something is a myth, or, to use modern terminology, that it is an example of "false consciousness", we are able to turn against it. One of the main purposes of this study is in fact to demonstrate that we have been entirely too prone to regard the Renaissance as contiguous with our time. We have been overly ready to assume that there is common ground between the 16th and the 20th centuries with respect to the understanding of knowledge, man, approach to life, and so forth. It is possible that the Renaissance is actually far more foreign than we tend to think was the case.

We shall additionally consider whether language does not imprison us within yet another illusion when it associates two other terms with the Renaissance period, namely "renaissance" and "reformation". Would it not, for example, be better to limit ourselves to a single term? In this instance, too, we encounter a reflexive habit of mind with which language has equipped us. Of course, it may be objected that we have here to do with two completely different things, since one of the phenomena in question was a scientific, cultural, and political breakthrough, while the other term signifies the ecclessiastical breakthrough which Luther introduced with his reformatory writings and his break with the Pope. The consequence of the latter, as is well known, was that several new protestant churches arose alongside of the Catholic church. Thus, one might conclude, it is only natural that we have two separate terms, since they point to two distinct phenomena, namely a secular and an ecclesiastical evolution.

Closer examination, however, reveals that it is by no means natural to term the two movements mentioned previously "renaissance" and "reformation", respectively. The actual meaning of the terms themselves, that is, "rebirth" and "reshaping" (usually rendered: "back to the original form") does not entitle us to conclude that one has a particular religious significance, while the other does not. Furthermore, during the Renaissance itself both terms were used synonymously and indiscriminately together with other terms of similar content, such as regeneratio (rebirth), resurrectio (resurrec-

tion), renovatio (renewal), restauratio (restoration),
and resuscitare (awakening). Konrad Burdach has noted
that all of these expressions have been derived from
Christian usage.[2] The word "Renaissance" itself, used
as a term describing the period in question, first appears in vol. 7 of Michelet's "Histoire de France", the
subtitle of which was simply "Renaissance", and which
appeared in 1855.[3] Taking his point of departure in the
work of Hegel, Michelet regarded the Renaissance as the
time when modern reason was born, that is, as the last
stage on the passage of the Spirit towards liberation.
Thus the concept of the "Renaissance" was created, and
in this connection it is useful to consider that in actuality we have to do with a child of the 19th century.
For the present we shall ignore the question as to
whether this child could not equally well have been
born in the 14th or 15th centuries. Finally, we should
observe that the terms equivalent to "Renaissance",
that is, "renascentia" (Latin), and "rinascita" (Italian) first came into currency in the 16th century in the
works of such figures as Erasmus of Rotterdam, Machiavelli, and Melanchthon.[4]

    Thus the ways in which the various words received
their significance in later times and so became specific designations for a spiritual and cultural breakthrough and an ecclesiastical renewal (or, for that
matter, for a place to eat - restaurant - or for the
removal of litter - renovation) were in reality fairly
accidental. The fact that the period itself lacked a
terminology for distinguishing between "secular" and
"ecclesiastical" renewal ought to provide us with some
food for thought. This lack of precision in the language
of the time is to be taken as an indication that people
simply did not distinguish sharply between ecclesiastic-

al and secular renewal. But why did they not so distinguish, when there is such a great difference between
these two phenomena? At least one obvious explanation
could be that at the time in question people did not
feel that there really was any great difference. If we
are to grasp this possibility, it will be necessary to
abandon our own views and attempt to see the past in its
essential foreignness.

Today, historians are increasingly tending to realize the untenability of the distinction in question.
Renaissance humanism was by no means irreligious. Very
much to the contrary, most of the humanists were in fact
deeply rooted in Christianity, and one of the questions
which concerned them most, from Petrarch (died in 1374)
to Erasmus (died in 1536) was precisely how it was spi-
ritually possible to re-erect the Church and re-form
it back to its situation in the time of the Early
Church. The humanists did not regard the Church as an
opponent. To the contrary, they understood the internal
crisis of the Catholic Church as the main reason for
the nationalist separatism of the time, as well as for
the degeneration of both art and philosophy. This applies to scholars in both Germany and Italy.

Now, for her part, the Catholic Church was by no
means hostile to the artists and humanists of the Renaissance. Of course, the most grandiose evidence of
this ecclesiastic patronage was the assistance extended
to artists and architects. The examples of Michelangelo
and the church of St. Peter's are the best known proofs
of this, but it is important to recall that these are
merely the high points in a truly massive effort on the
part of the Church.

It is much less often recognized that literary efforts, too, were supported by the Church, both di-

rectly, in the form of the commissioning of works by humanist artists and scholars (resulting in various publications and in translations) and indirectly, in the form of providing countless humanists with their daily bread by securing them positions as papal secretaries or the like. Naturally, such collaboration was not entirely without its problems. The Church was frequently concerned as to the possibility of reawakening heathendom, while the humanists were often critical of many ecclesiastical practices.

Nor were the great Reformers, Luther, Melanchthon, Zwingli, and Calvin, hostile to the humanists or the Renaissance. To the contrary, all of these figures supported the humanistic program of liberal arts education, in connection with which the humanists placed especial emphasis on language learning and language use, and thus on the three disciplines which have to do with language: grammar, dialectics, and rhetoric. Furthermore, the Reformers did what they could to insure that these efforts were realized in the form of schools, universities, curricula, and so forth. All of these features have only recently been stressed by modern scholarship.

Our way of dealing with the past frequently leads us to compress our understanding of it in a few, easily understandable symbols or symbolic events. Thus, it is too often the case that the relationship between the Catholic Church and science is represented by the burning of Giordano Bruno and the persecution of Galileo Galilei. In the same fashion, Luther's controversy with Erasmus is all too often used as a metaphor for the relationship between the Reformation and Renaissance humanism. I have no intention in these pages of warning against the dangers of using these sorts of compact individual events as symbols of complex historical developments or problems. This pitfall is probably unavoidable, as is indicated by my earlier remarks about the terms historians choose to designate specific periods. It is simply the case that our historical understanding is aided by the use of such symbolic examples. Of course, this does not compensate for the fact that they are invariably concise and therefore only crude representations of our knowledge. In the examples mentioned previously, the matter is even more unfortunate than one might suppose. The examples are not only crude, they are simply incorrect and useless. For example, the friendship between Luther and Melanchton provides us with a much better illustration of the relationship between the Reformation and humanism than does Luther's (rather late) enmity to Erasmus.

In recent years, scholarship has become aware of this. An impressive series of recent studies has contributed to the piecemeal destruction of the old picture. These works have shown that the relationship between the Reformation and humanism was in reality vastly different from what was once supposed. Actually, however, I do not believe that our change in attitude is primarily the result of new research, since the knowledge that was available 50 or 100 years ago was sufficient to destroy the impression that these phenomena were directly opposed to one another.

The explanation is more likely to reside in the fact that we are now somewhat better at examining the past because we have by now lost some of our "blinders". How has this come about? Hans-Georg Gadamer has said that we comprehend history with the aid of our prejudices.[5] By this he means that if we did not in advance have some knowledge or opinion as a basis, that is, as a

horizon for framing our questions, then we would get
no answer from history, for the simple reason that we
would have no questions to pose. But then, what is the
horizon of our questions in this instance? In order to
understand this, it will be necessary to consider what
has transpired in the years between our times and the
Renaissance. The most important phenomenon is that of
secularization. It is usually maintained that with the
18th century Enlightenment the spiritual sovereignty
of the Church was destroyed, so that science and ethics
and philosophy were freed from ecclesiastical bondage
and thus went their own way. The proponents of these
disciplines sought independence, and maintained that
each had its own autonomous basis. This process may be
studied from a number of points of view, but irregardless of one's approach to it, at least one of its consequences was that the internal coherence of European
culture was lost. Ecclesiastical speech about an omnipotent God who created the world, and about Christ as
the Savior of mankind was no longer experienced as
speech derived from plausible descriptions of the way
of the world or of the task of humanity. The proclamation of the Church was no longer universal, whether
understood in the sense of norms which were acknowledged to apply everywhere, or in the sense that all men
regarded the Church and its message as true. The sequence of these two features also corresponds to the
chronology of secularization. The reason for all this
was not that something else had arrived on the scene
and replaced the Church's claim to universal validity.
To a very large extent, the process of secularization
may be seen as the collapse of the concept of universal
validity in general. This collapse did not have dire
consequences for the various sciences, since these man-

aged to retain their claim to validity independently of each other, that is, within their own domains. On the other hand, the loss of universal validity and thus of universal intelligibility was particularly cata- strophic for the Church, and in the end disastrous.

Naturally, the Church did not go along with these developments voluntarily. If one happens to possess the truth as to heaven, earth, and man, it is obvious that one cannot allow others to raise doubts as to this fact. Conversely, the new sciences, philosophies, and ideol- ogies were by no means content to allow themselves to be gagged by a Church which was a survival from the past, and which had outlived its day. In other words, the struggle for the human soul had begun, and the com- petition for the lion's share of the market was vicious. All means were considered to be fair.[6]

One of the means in question was the study of his- tory. By presenting oneself and one's activities in an extended perspective, it is possible to illustrate that the battle one wages is necessary and just. The implic- ation is that generations both prior to and, presum- ably, after ours have fought and will continue to fight the good fight. Legitimation occurs by depicting one- self as a humble soldier in that army which is called the necessary evolution. The past has many uses; not merely to ordain what is to be done in future, but also to explain how and why we have arrived at the present impasse. I should like to emphasize that this is not intended in a critical spirit, but only as an obser- vation. It is a useful insight, since it prompts us to seek changes in a realistic spirit in our understand- ing of history, not primarily in history itself, but in the historian.

Up to our times the histories of the Renaissance and

Reformation have mainly been written by two sorts of historians, both of which have adhered to the model of confrontation. One of these tendencies takes the part of the Renaissance. Scholars have acknowledged that an ecclesiastical breakthrough took place, but they maintain that from a humanistic point of view this was practically a retrograde development. Thus emphasis is placed on Luther's diatribes against Erasmus, on his reactionary position during the Peasant Revolt, the spiritual intolerance and absence of religious freedom of the newly arisen confessional states, on witch-burnings, and so forth. Seen from this point of view, it is regarded as fortunate that evolution has left the Reformation with the status of an enclave in history, since democracy and enlightenment eventually won the day. This approach holds that the humanistic initiative had its beginnings in the Renaissance, and that it is the duty of our time to keep the torch on high and bear it to ultimate victory.

Against this we have an ecclesiastical approach which admits that the Renaissance represented a breakthrough, but one which is held to be only superficial. It was first the Christianity of the Reformation which was a major breakthrough and which opened men's eyes for new dimensions of human existence. It is possible that the humanists were good philologists, but in spiritual terms they had little to offer except a certain flat optimism on behalf of man. The superficiality (a few generations ago scholars claimed: immorality) of the humanists was such that it was completely correct of Luther to flagellate their most eminent representative, Erasmus. The moral to be derived from this viewpoint is that just as Luther was unimpressed by the secularity and humanism of his times, so should we also fail to be impressed by ours.

This approach is often further developed with a specifically theological consideration, which is easily accomodated to the argument, namely the view that Christianity is not based on human presuppositions. It is necessary for God to condescend to meet with us, since we can achieve nothing on our own. The human ("humanistic") is lost in sin, and can only hope for grace. Thus the humane sciences often lead to an arrogant self-understanding; this is humanism in one form or another, to be treated with great circumspection. Seen from this point of view, humanism is easily understood as a metaphor for man's revolt against God. Did not Luther himself reject the value of human reason?

These are various ways of legitimating the contemporary fact that the Church and culture have been divorced from one another, since it is claimed that this is the way things must inevitably go with true Christianity, and, it is said, this is how things have actually been since the Reformation, when true Christianity emerged. This is the basic tendency underlying the Luther studies of the 20th century, as exemplified by such scholars as Karl Holl and Otto Scheel, and which has persisted up to the studies of Paul Althaus and Gerhard Ebeling, not to mention in contemporary Danish Luther research. The Danish theological movement known as Tidehverv ("the labor of time"), has, for example, sharply distinguished between reflective reason, which attempts to control its experience, and a life in obedience to and respect for the given terms of our existence. The Gospel assists us in the latter effort, since it commands us to abandon our speculations and "be faithful to the earth". Danish scholars have attempted to demonstrate this opposition in the 16th century; thus, for example K.E. Løgstrup has allowed Erasmus to

represent the reason, while Luther represents the unreflective and immediate understanding of life. "Erasmus
thinks that it is possible to get some idea of what it
is to be human by reflectively abstracting from that
existence which both exists and which exists as a particular type of existence, independently of any reflect-
ions as to what existence itself really is."[7] Indeed,
it is a peculiar facet of many investigations of Luther
that his differences from or hostility to the main
tendencies of his day are simply taken for granted, so
that there is practically no reason to mention them at
all; they are merely touched on en passant. This procedure has had the astonishing result that scholars
have been prone to allow Luther, unlike any other historical figure, to exist without context or presuppositions. Thus his originality and genius are endowed
with superhuman dimensions.

This situation, however, is no longer completely the
case. The frontlines as described previously have been
softened at a number of points. Indeed, secularization
has gone one step farther, with the result that the
Church and Christianity are no longer the Beast of Revelations for humanistic historians. Non-ecclesiastical
circles and scholars with no ecclesiastical affiliat-
ions now approach the phenomenon of the Church in a
manner that is both more relaxed and more curious than
before. In addition to this is the fact that our times
have been characterized by an increasing interest in
religious phenomena in general, an interest which includes all sorts of prophets from the exotic religions,
to astrology, to healthfoods, and so on,[8] and which accordingly also applies to the Church. Of course, one
of the contributory reasons for this development is the
fact that science and philosophy are no longer as am-

bitious as they once were with respect to producing absolute truths. Curiosity and openness have to some degree replaced the earlier cocksureness. No one is any
longer inclined to accept the native myth of the individual who disentangles himself from a past mired in
myth and superstition on his way to an enlightened and
rationalistic future.

For her part, the church has begun to accomodate
herself to secularization and the pluralistic society,
with their attendant free market for opinions and fish-
ers of men. The task is no longer seen as a merely conservative one, but also as the duty to proclaim the
message to a non-Christian society. To this end it is
important to conduct one's mission by, like St. Paul,
being as a Jew among Jews and a Greek among Greeks,
that is, to speak to one's audience on its own terms.

Of course, this is only a very short and general
sketch. Nevertheless, I feel that it provides at least
part of the explanation as to why it is no longer
necessary to distinguish so sharply between the Reformation and the Renaissance as we once did. Thus we now
have a new chance to study Luther in connection with
numerous new developments which occurred in his time
in many areas. It should now be possible to discard the
mistaken set of alternatives which make of Luther either
a reactionary bogeyman or a divinely sent and inspired
Reformer.

But what does it mean, to say that the Reformation
and the Renaissance are to be examined together? If
this claim is to have any significance, it must entail
that in one or another fundamental way Luther must be
seen to be dependent on the understanding of life and
the thought in general of his times. It is a banal observation that Luther was a contemporary of the great

artists and thinkers of the Renaissance, but it is nevertheless the case that scholars have frequently stopped at this mere observation. Some have gone a little further and mentioned such things as Luther's interest in the visual arts or in philology. I do not mean that philology is unimportant, but it should be obvious that it was not this or Luther's interests which prompted his religious breakthrough. The publication by Erasmus of his Greek edition of the New Testament in 1516, that is, before Luther decided to translate it into German, was an important event, and particularly with respect to the northern European familiarity with Greek and Latin in succeeding centuries. Nonetheless, no one would maintain that this event, no matter how important it was, awakened any sort of reformatory knowledge in Luther. He had already arrived at clarity in this respect, and for completely different reasons.

On the other hand, to claim that Luther was a Renaissance man in the fundamental sense of the term is the same as to claim that his religious breakthrough itself is unthinkable unless seen against the background of the intellectual developments of the time, which are best reflected by Renaissance humanism. In short, it is suggested that Luther's thought and such aspects of his theology as his conception of faith, for example, are to be understood as further extensions of ideas that were current in his day.

To determine whether this conclusion is correct, it will be necessary to ask what features were characteristic of the Renaissance. It is obvious that the answer to this question can hardly consist in a mere recitation of various developments within the areas of philosophy, politics, or the arts. If a fruitful result is desired, it will be necessary to dig somewhat deeper, and thus to inquire as to whether there is some sort of lowest common denominator capable of unifying various phenomena of the Renaissance. Could we discover this by inquiring as to the understanding of man current in the period, that is, its philosophical or psychological anthropology? We have to pose this fundamental question, if we are to deal with the concept of an epoch which is called "renaissance". If we instead merely have to do with a long series of individual phenomena without some sort of common factor, then the very distinguishing of a period and the determination of it as an "epoch" is meaningless or, at best, a false declaration of contents.

On the other hand, one might object, posing such a general question runs the risk of being speculative and trivial, with the result that we may only get a trivial answer. By the same token, this procedure has a tendency to oversimplify one's account, since the subtleties are difficult to maintain alongside of the generalizations.

Against this, I would emphasize the necessity to clarify one's thinking as to the general framework within which one intends to conduct his investigations.

A great deal of historical research commits the blunder of operating within an all too narrow area, so that one runs the risk af failing to see the forest for the trees. It happens to be the case that we understand things in relation to their context, and that the wider the context, the better we understand. Ignoring this wider perspective does not solve the problem, since it will be there anyway, if only in a concealed or unconscious form. Thus one becomes the victim of the presuppositions and prejudices of one's own time, perhaps much more than need be the case.

In what follows we shall accordingly pose the following question: what sort of anthropology was characteristic of the Renaissance? In order to answer this question we shall further be forced to pose a second one: what understanding of man was dominant in the preceding period?

2. The Tripartite Man

There is a deeply-rooted tradition in European thought according to which man is not merely a something, but also a someone. Thus we say that an individual has an "I", that is, a personality, an identity. It may be difficult for us to describe more closely just in what this identity consists. Whenever we attempt to define the "I" in question, it tends to slide through our fingers, which is why modern philosophy has very perceptively spoken of "the elusive I".

Nevertheless it would seem necessary to stress the fact that man has a fixed center; it seems inadequate merely to characterize him as an aggregate of various parts and qualities. In one way or another, the individual is more than the sum of his attributes, although in practice it may be very difficult to specify just what this "more" is.

A survey of the long historical course of ancient Greek culture allows us to determine what the most likely reason was which compelled us to utilize the concept of the ego or soul. Simply put, man has not always done so; thus, for example, Homer knows nothing of this "I". For Homer man consists of a series of functions, that is, various ways of sensing, knowing, and acting. Man is subdivided into forces or attributes; he has no unifying "I". This fact is related to a lack of ability to generalize: there were countless different words signifying "to observe, to look calculatingly at, to look measuringly at," and so forth, but no single, general term meaning simply "to see".[1] In the same way there was no word for body or soul, but only for a number of individual phenomena which in our usage would fall under the rubric of "soul" or "body". The ability

to generalize is possibly related to one's ability to
look objectively at one's self. Thus at some point one
discovers that the various ways of "seeing" entail not
only an object that is seen, but also an act of seeing,
that is, one sees something. This corresponds to the
difference between "a bird is flying" and the statement
that "I see that a bird is flying". It is difficult to
say with certainty just when this potential for observ-
ing one's own actions (that is, for reflection) was
first realized, but it is at least clear that this occurred with the poetess Sappho (b. 612 BC). Sappho is
namely aware that in her imagination - or with her soul
- she is able to be together with her loved one on a
far distant island, in spite of the fact that her body
remains in a different locale. To put the matter differently, she is able to look at herself from without,
and to distinguish between soul and body. Of course,
the "self" in question is the soul, while the body is
its external form. From this point onwards, men began
to speak of a self which has a body. Later they spoke
of one which possesses feelings, and eventually they
spoke of a soul with a full retinue of attributes.

Plato

The Orphaeans and Plato elevated this distinction between soul and body to the status of a postulate, one
which has persisted in the Western cultural tradition
until the present. This distinction has been so much
taken for granted that it is difficult for us to read
and understand texts which do not share it. This fact
has inhibited our understanding of Luther, since scholars have proved to be virtually unable to imagine that
he did not share the traditional view of the distinction between soul and body.

In a famous passage in his Republic, Plato allows

Socrates to remark that it would not be unreasonable "if
we were to claim that there are two quantities different from each other, such that we term that part of the
soul by means of which it thinks the rational part, and
the part by means of which it feels lust and hunger and
thirst or in other ways is mired in desire the irrational and desiring part, that which craves to be filled in
one way or another and is a friend of pleasures." (439D).
Shortly afterwards, however, it occurs to Socrates that
this subdivision is insufficient, since the will is
probably better characterized as an independent part
of man: "by nature and aid to the reason, if uncorrupt-
ed by bad upbringing" (441A), since it is the province
of the "reason to lead, it being wise and making provi-
sion for the entire soul, whereas the will is subordinate to it and sustains it in battle..." (441E).

In short, man is composed of three distinct parts,
namely the sensual appetites, reason and the will.This
prompts the question as to whether it should not be
possible to point to a single one of these features as
especially characteristic of man. Naturally, the sensual appetites are out of the question, since they bind
man to the external, material world, which in the last
analysis is only a shadow world. Thus Plato would prefer to opt for the reason. In the Republic Plato illustrates how he conceives of the human situation and of
the role played by the reason in it. Unenlightened men
are like prisoners chained in a cave with their faces
turned towards the rear wall of the cave. Behind them,
a bonfire is burning, and various types and shapes of
wooden figures are carried back and forth between the
prisoners and the fire. Thus shadow-pictures are cast
on the wall, and these images are all that the prisoners can see, so that they imagine the shadow images to
comprise the whole of reality. According to Plato, we

committt the same error if we imagine the visible world to be identical with the real world. However, suppose with a little luck one of the prisoners manages to free himself from his bonds and turns about, thus discovering that it is the fire and the wooden figures which enable him to see shadow-pictures on the rear wall of the cave. However, according to Plato, such a prisoner would still possess only imperfect knowledge, since he would have yet to realize that the wooden figures are mere imitations of real objects outside of the cave, and that the fire in question is also only a pale imitation of the sun, which is not visible in the cave, but which is behind everything.

It is the function of reason to enable the prisoners to turn around and find their way out of the cave. However, the thoroughly "lost" individual would prefer to remain seated with his back to the fire. Thus man is a divided entity who participates in two worlds, the sensual and the ideal.

It would also be more or less correct to claim that the will is man's character; this claim would not change the total picture definitively. The will is able to be guided by both the sensual appetites and the reason; in this fashion it expresses man's dual potential. In other words, we have not only to do with a description of man's nature or psychology, but with an account of his purpose. However, the potential for self-reflection, that is, the ability to observe oneself and to describe oneself in generalizing categories is only part of Plato's characterization of man's identity. What is additionally described is the path along which man not only can, but must, wander.

Aristotle

We encounter a similar tripartition of man in the work of the second of the two greatest philosophers of antiquity. Aristotle presupposes the existence of a part

which has to do with man's drives (threptikon-capacity
to seek nourishment/drive). In this connection Aristotle distinguishes between the ability to perceive via
the senses and to feel pleasure or aversion as a result.
This layer is called the aisthetikon (the ability to
feel or perceive). Finally we have the nous or noetikon
(the ability to know), which is man's preeminent function, and the only one of them that is immortal. Reason
is the faculty which recognizes the nature of things,
things which are not merely visible, but also invisible
ones such as principles, laws, and concepts. In fact,
there are two kinds of reason, practical and theoretical. The former explores the good and advises us as to
how to achieve it in the ordinary conduct of our lives.
The goal is to make decisions and to initiate actions.
On the other hand, the theoretical reason functions
"theoretically", that is, it observes and analyzes. Its
goal is to discover the fundamental structure of existence and thus to answer such questions as what is unity, being, substance, and so forth.[2]

The difference between these two types of reason may
in a certain sense be said to consist in the fact that the
practical reason addresses itself outwardly, while the
theoretical reason confines itself to analyzing the
data it receives.

Aristotle is decidedly the father of the distinction
between the understanding of man's being which asserts
that he has two aspects, one which actively addresses
itself to externals, and one which is receptive. He extends this distinction to apply, in addition to the
reason, to the feelings and the sensual appetites. Aristotle distinguishes between passion (pathos), understood as something which affects or seizes one, and
feelings (hexis), with which, in a manner of speaking,

we are equipped in advance. Love and hate, fear and confidence, shame and shamelessness, and so forth, belong to the first category. It is the receptive aspect of man which is characterized by these things. On the other hand, man is master of his virtues and vices thanks to his will; they may be conceived of as a movement from the individual out into his environment. If one allows oneself to be led by one's passions, this necessarily leads to an irrational existence. On the other hand, if one permits the will - following the directions of the reason - to rule over the passions, the result is both an ethical and a rational existence.

If we descend into the sensual part of man, which is determined by his drives and impulses, then we discover a force which ineluctably seeks to be satisfied, for example, with respect to such matters as hunger or sex. In short, a movement which passes from the individual outwards. Aristotle has no desire to deny man's physical basis, but he does insist that it cannot be one's point of departure for seeking true knowledge or real happiness.

This philosophical description of man enables Aristotle to extend the Platonic tripartition of man. In this connection he seizes upon one particular aspect which has played a vast role in European thought. This is the distinction between feeling and reason. Aristotle regards the former as a quantity which is or ought to be subordinate, while he regards the latter as man's really essential characteristic. This distinction may be taken to suggest that there is no knowledge in one's feelings. Both quantities are the results of impulses or inductions coming from without. The feelings (pathos) are either influenced by or simply arise out of the confrontation between the individual and his environment.

For example, another individual is able to awaken in
one feelings of hate or love, but the appropriateness
of this hate or love cannot be determined on the basis
of one's feelings alone. It is essential that the reason should also be involved, and a truly qualified relationship to the other is first established when the
reason has confirmed one's feelings, whereby the relationship becomes one of virtue.

Furthermore, the way the reason perceives is different from that of the feelings, in that it is neither
arbitrary nor unaccountable; it reflects reality as it
is, for which reason we may rely on the objectivity of
its impressions. Just as a good mirror reproduces objects correctly, so the reason represents the world and
nature as they actually are. This is why the highest
type of reason was termed during the Middle Ages specu-
latio, that is, reflection. By way of contrast, the
feelings or passions are unreliable, a judgement which
applies to both the affective states of the soul (pathe)
and the bodily drives.

This psychology or anthropology became normative
during the Middle Ages, when theologians reckoned Aristotle to be almost as authoritative as the Bible itself. More than any other figure, St. Thomas Aquinas
was responsible for this development. Also in Aquinas'
works we encounter the tripartition of the faculties;
moreover, he states even more clearly than Aristotle
had done that the function of the reason is to guide
the will, which in turn is to govern the passions and
drives. Thus, if we are to be concerned in future with
the tripartition of man, there is no need to confine
ourselves to Aristotelian tradition, since the entire
Christian tradition appropriated this concept from
Greek thought and made it its own.

Our Own Times

Even today the tripartite individual is a more or less
conscious or unconscious presupposition for both psychological science and quotidien understanding. Moreover, this tripartition still has the same implication
for us, namely that the passions are unreliable and
that they must be guided and governed by the reason.
We resist the notion of allowing our feelings to "run
away with us", since we, too, have difficulty imagining
that the passions have any value as a source of knowledge.

However, there may be a single issue on which modern
thought differs from that of Aristotle. This is in our
description of the feelings, since to a far greater degree than Aristotle was prone to do we tend to regard
them as the property of the individual. We regard them
more as a facet of individual drives than as something
caused from without. In a strict sense the passions
have become disobjective, that is, we do not regard
them as arising in response to an external event, since
we see them as coming from individual subjectivity. We
may possibly recognize the character of the passions
in such a way that we are aware that they may assume
control of us, but to us the external cause is only admitted the role of external occasion of the "awakening"
(a metaphorical expression which emphasizes that they
are always present and are activated by external influences from time to time) of our passions. Since the
time of Rousseau and the Romantics, the emotions have
been regarded as something internal to the individual.
We tend to describe the passions as an ability; thus,
for example, we may say of someone that he is even-
tempered or credulous. Alternatively, we may describe
them as needs; thus, for example, we all acknowledge

that we have a need to be accepted or loved by someone
else. In both cases we tend to seek the origin of the
feelings involved in the self of the individual rather
than in his surroundings.

One might occasionally be led to suspect that our
language not only accompanies our knowledge and understanding; it may sometimes actually precede them. We
are prone to allow our language to convince us to accept nouns as things which refer to independently existing realities. When we have such terms as "joy" or
"hate" we are easily convinced that these terms conceal
independent phenomena or forces which must accordingly
be located within man. The furnishing of the human spiritual existence with a number of independent forces
began already in antiquity. Its clearest expression was
the spiritual dramas of the Middle Ages, of which the
Psychomachia (soul battle) is the best known. In these
allegorical dramas we encounter a number of persons
with names like Ira (anger), Caritas (love), Odium
(hate), and so forth, and a complicated intrigue develops in which they participate. Of course, one might
object to this that such examples are merely easily
penetrated allegories. Nevertheless, D.W. Robertson is
surely right to maintain that this sort of drama is
nevertheless a step on the way to giving man an independent spiritual life with his own feelings.[3]

St. Augustine

The modern view of these matters was also prepared for
in other ways far back in the tradition. St. Augustine
(d. 431) determined, in extension of the Platonic tradition, that a man was identical with his love. He defined love itself as concupiscentia (desire). This love
was able to adopt two different forms, namely a posi-

tive and a negative one. If the soul aimed its desire towards corporeal things, then it was seeking below its own level, that is, in the direction of the lusts of the flesh. In this event, such desire was negatively characterized as cupiditas (greed). However, or so Augustine held, it is also possible for the soul to set its sights on spiritual matters, namely on God and the eternal. In this event Augustine chose the term true love, that is, caritas. In both cases it is the same concupiscentia or amor which is active, but the satisfaction (delectatio) of them is quite different. If one seeks satisfaction in the pleasures of the flesh, then one discovers that such desires can only apparently be appeased. In reality, one will continue to be plagued by a useless desire. On the other hand, if one chooses to pursue spiritual happiness, then one ultimately discovers that the intuitive observation of the eternal will fulfil all desires. In this way the great father of the Church was the spiritual forefather of modern psychologies based on human needs. Thus he was also the ultimate author of the notion that needs, feelings, and drives are synonymous concepts, and that all of them are anchored within the individual man.

Thus we may conclude that from antiquity until today a conceptual tradition has persisted which regards man as tripartite, and which additionally separates reason and the passions. It might be added that this view, which looks at the individual from within, examines the environment from the viewpoint of the individual subject. This is a psychology which attempts to answer the question as to how the self understands the world around it and acts within the context of .it. It is an understanding of man in which the will plays a major part, both as a mediator between the various parts of man, and as the active agent with respect to the individual's environment. At the same time, this view attempts to explain and interpret the fact which was mentioned by way of introduction, namely, that one is able to stand in relationship to oneself.

Two Types of Love

However, there were other features in the Augustinian philosophy which entail that, rightly or wrongly, it was interpreted during the Renaissance as representing a completely different view of man. I have mentioned that St. Augustine regarded man more as a unity than as a creature subdivided into various departments. In this respect Augustine was really only concerned with the role of the will. It was not the distinction between body/soul/reason, which occupied his attention, but the direction adopted by the soul or will, or drive. The human will (or love, or urge: for St. Augustine these were all synonyms) may take one of two possible forms. Augustine distinguishes between an uti-love and a frui-love. "Uti" refers to that type of amor in which one cares for something or someone as a means, that is, for the sake of something else. For exemple, one may care for horses, because they can transport one from one place to another. In contrast, "frui" refers to the sort of love in which one loves some one or thing for its own sake, as for example, when one loves a girl, not for her money or for her looks, but for her own sake. In this connection, Augustine's point is that there is really only one thing that ought to be loved for its own sake, that is, frui-love, and that one thing is God, since everything else in Creation are merely things which He has created, and so it is only proper to admire and love their author, God. Unfortun-

ately, man does not realize this; he is instead prone
to regard the created world with all its goods with a
frui-love; but in so doing, one forgets that these are
only relative goods which have no worth in themselves.

The notions of the two types of love underlines the
view of man as a unity. It implies that the decisive
feature of a man is not his psychological structure,
but his love. "A man is his love", as a famous quotation
from Augustine has it. This view proved to be of decisive importance during the Renaissance, when this aspect
of St. Augustine's thought was made much of. For this
reason he became the favorite Church father of the
theologians and humanists of the day. In what follows
we shall seehow this came about.

3. The Undivided Man

The way of describing man which was presented in the preceding chapter is essentially characterized by the fact that it takes its point of departure from inside of man. In a manner of speaking, it has arisen in answer to the question, who am I?

When one studies oneself, one of the things one discovers is that one is affected by influences over which one has no control. One has a particular social status one cannot dispense with without more ado, and one possesses a body which, with its limbs, needs and drives defines its owner in a particular way. One also has a soul and an ability to reason which further help to delimit the functions of the individual within the available framework.

On the other hand, one also seems to discover a feature which may well be decisive with respect to the others mentioned, namely the fact that one is not merely determined by one's environment or one's physical or social equipment. The self seems to be able to undertake initiatives and make decisions which it subsequently carries out. One discovers the very elementary fact that one is able to consider a case from a number of vantage points and make one's decision accordingly. It is possible to develop one's reason and sharpen one's will or reason and thus reduce the extent of foreign influence upon the self. Indeed, it is conceivable that our conception of freedom is to be understood on the basis of the possibilities of the self to develop itself without hindrance. Admittedly, we are, by way of example, forced to submit to illness; nevertheless, we also have a say in the matter as of how we shall relate to the fact of illness, that is, how we are to suffer it. In spite of all of the factors which influence the subject from without, he nevertheless experiences the fact that he is an active being, both with respect to the external world and himself. As we have seen, this way of thinking leads to the plotting and mapping of the personality into various departments such as reason, soul, and body, with the will located in the midst of the soul, that is, in a central position as a decisive indication of the fact that the starting point is taken in man, in the self-sufficient and willing subject. I shall not undertake in these pages to attempt to discuss just how realistic this way of thinking may happen to be. I am inclined to believe that it has its limitations,[1] but these are not germane to our present concern with Luther's historical presuppositions. In our investigation it is sufficient to note that during the late Middle Ages there were a number of forces which opposed the notion of man as tripartite and independently acting. A variety of positions led to the development of a different sort of anthropology, one in which man was not conceived of as an active subject, but as a receptive object.

It should be noted parenthetically that this insight has begun to make itself felt again in our own way. The essential presupposition of the social sciences is a concept of man as influenced and governed by various forces; otherwise it would be quite impossible to formulate theories about such things as the behavior of voters or prospective shoppers. Also, rather a lot of contemporary behavioral psychology tends to regard the individual on the basis of his observable behavior. Thus this form of psychology confines itself to stimulus-and-response explanatory models which make nonsense of the notion of a free self. Indeed, in this connect-

ion the more basic philosophical question has been
posed as to whether it is at all meaningful to postulate such internal entities as soul, or mental states
such as excitement or joy. We shall not deal with these
matters more thoroughly here; it is sufficient merely
to call attention to the fact that during the late
Middle Ages there were parallel phenomena to the tendency of contemporary science to raise questions as to
the self and its tripartite structure.

There were no doubt more than four factors active
in this questioning process of the Middle Ages, but at
any event it is at least certain that <u>mysticism, astrol-</u>
<u>ogy, the renewed interest in the will, and above all,</u>
<u>the emergence of Renaissance humanism</u> were all active at
the time and in fact expressed a completely different
understanding of man than the one we examined in Ch.
2.

Mysticism

Until af few years ago, Luther scholarship had to con-
tend with considerable difficulties because scholars
lacked fixed landmarks which would enable them to relate Luther to his own times. As a rule, though, this
was not felt to be problematical, since the tendency
was also to regard Luther as representing so radical
a departure that it would be strictly speaking meaningless to attempt to seek his intellectual pedigree in
his historical context. To many scholars, Luther's way
of reading the Bible, and particularly St. Paul, was
a sufficient explanation of his reformatory breakthrough.

Nevertheless, recent scholarship has discovered that
mysticism provides a fruitful way of viewing Luther in
relation to his own time. In recent years, especially

since it was made the main theme of the 3rd International Luther Congress in 1967, mysticism has achieved considerable importance in Luther research. This development signified a radical change with respect to all
previous German, Anglo-American, and Scandinavian Luther studies, since until recently it was customary to
attempt to keep Luther and mysticism quite separate,
and for two reasons. In the first place, it was held
that mysticism was a feature of Catholic and Latin culture, and thus was both unprotestant and non-germanic.[2]
In the second place, the nature of mysticism itself
seemed to be in stark contradiction to Reformation
Christianity. It was held that the mystical union between God and the believer (unio mystica) tended to
break down the distinction between God and the individual, which would appear to be entirely non-evangelic-
al. According to the usual protestant view, the proclamation of the Gospel inevitably entails that man be
seen as a sinner in relation to God. Furthermore, the
mystical experience seems to presuppose that the personality is eradicated and replaced by a completely
wordless and motionless condition of peace, a situation
which would seem to be a complete contradiction of the
theology of call and regiment which has come to be Luther's trademark.

It is well known that Luther himself was very interested in mysticism, particularly in the years around
the breakthrough of the Reformation. Thus in 1518 he
published the mystical treatise Theologia Deutsch with
his own rather enthusiastic preface.[3] Of course, this
fact requires explanation (or perhaps it must be explained away). A fruitful line of inquiry would be to
acknowledge, as Erich Vogelsang[4] did already as early
as in 1937, that there are numerous types of mysticism,

and that Luther did not regard them as a single phenomenon.

In general terms, it is possible to divide the mystics of the Middle Ages into two groups. The first of
these maintains that one achieves the unio mystica (i.
e., the mystical union with the deity) by means of thorough and energetic preparations in the form of meditation, various types of asceticism, and so forth. In
the sixth century a number of tracts appeared which
were wrongly assigned to Dionysios the Areopagite, a
Greek nobleman whom St. Paul is supposed to have con-
verted in Athens, (Acts 17,34). These tracts depict a
heavenly hierarchy of forms and spirits, each of which
represents a particular level of being. The earthly parallel to this phenomenon was seen as the hierarchical
structure of the Catholic church. By means of, among
other things, the mystical fellowship achieved through
prayer the individual is able to penetrate the symbols
and attain direct access to God, who can only be comprehended negatively, that is, by leaving all humanly-de-
rived conceptions behind one. These writings were of
great significance for the theological and mystical
thought of the Middle Ages. A less complex expression
of the same notion is to be found in St. Augustine's
conversation with his mother in Ostia: "And when our
conversation had arrived at that point, that the very
highest pleasure of the carnal senses, and that in the
very brightest material light, seemed by reason of the
sweetness of that life not only not worthy of comparison, but not even of mention, we, lifting ourselves
with a more ardent affection towards "the Self-same",
did gradually pass through all corporeal things, and
even the heaven itself, ... yea, the very soul be silenced to herself, and go beyond herself by not think-

ing of herself, - silenced fancies and imaginary revelations, every tongue, and every sign, and whatsoever exists by passing away, since, if any could hearken, all these say, "We created not ourselves, but were created by Him who abideth for ever." If, having uttered this, they now should be silenced, having only quickened our ears to Him who created them, and He alone speak not by them, but by Himself, that we may hear His word, not by fleshly tongue, nor angelic voice, nor sound of thunder, nor the obscurity of a similitude, but might hear Him - Him whom in these we love - without these, likeas we two now strained ourselves, and with rapid thought touched on that Eternal Wisdom which remaineth over all."[5]

In our time it has proved possible to achieve states similar to that described by St. Augustine, and which has many parallels in the religious experience of the East, via the use of LSD or other hallucinogens.

As a sort of rough and ready characterisation, one could describe this type of mystical experience as something which is eagerly desired by those who attempt to achieve it. They strive purposefully towards it, and yet all the while the experience itself is quietistical by its very nature: one undertakes nothing at all. Thus it would perhaps be hairsplitting to attempt to say whether the practitioner is unconscious, or whether his consciousness has been expanded enormously, since in the course of the mystical experience consciousness does not contain concepts and thoughts as we usually conceive of these.

There is also another sort of mysticism; it is one which may to a large extent be described with the same phrases, but which is nevertheless distinct from the Dionysian-Augustinian variety. Here, too, a species of

unio mystica is experienced, but the pathway to its a-
chievement is quite different. There is no question of
progressing up a ladder to the heights; rather, God,
or the divine, comes to meet one. This is perhaps too
weak a description, for in reality the experience is
more like being kidnaped or assaulted. The German mystic
Tauler[6] (d. in 1361), of whom Luther greatly approved
and whose sermons he published, used the expression
"raptus" (i.e., stolen, kidnaped). As a phenomenon, it
approaches ecstasy (lit. to stand outside of one's
self). In English one still speaks of "rapture", a term
which continues to retain some sense of being "trans-
ported away" by an experience (cf. Concise Oxford Dic-
tionary).

What is important for our purposes is that it is
true of both types of mystical experience that they
tend to regard the individual as a unity. The mystical
experience renders the distinction between soul and
body irrelevant; one's entire person is involved, even
though this occurs in different ways. While St. Augustine seems to renounce all of his human qualities,
Tauler concentrates on the feeling, that is, the affectus, which is not merely a part of the individual.
Rather, it represents all of him.

Yet another important feature is the fact that Tauler's
mystical experience is not something one approaches or
strives to achieve. On the contrary, one is struck down
right where one happens to be; one experiences an assault
or a type of possession. This also entails a transformation
of one's identity, in that one is no longer what one was
before. One loses one's former identity, because one has
been possessed by yet another. After having been conquered and occupied by a foreign power, one is obliged to
follow it, come what may. "And when this one, this Being,

appropriates a creature to itself and makes it its own, and when it joins itself to Him, so that He may know himself through it, then the creature also acknowledges light here and revelation there, and desires nothing else than existence. Thus only the good will be desired and loved, and that in virtue of the fact that it is the good and not like one thing or another, like loved or unloved, beneficent or painful, sweet or sour. Nothing of this sort is sought for, nor is there any self or I, for all selfhood and I-ness and I and me and mine are surrendered and have disappeared."[7]

One more distinctive difference deserves to be mentioned. As we have characterized it with the aid of Dionysios the Areopagite and St. Augustine, the mystical experience itself is by nature world-remote. In other words, external things no longer exist for the subject. One has dispensed with all desire and activity, and, in extreme cases, with all forms of consciousness. What reigns is the absolute peace and rest of the soul, which is why the phenomenon has also been termed quietism (from lat. "quietas", rest). With respect to this feature, Tauler's sort of mysticism greatly encourages action, since neither thought nor body is brought to rest: both are forced into activity and purposive action.

All of these features of the German mysticism of the late Middle Ages, that is, the understanding of man as a unity which is in turn determined by an affective state, the experience's character of assault, the renewal of identity and the tendency to compel personal action, are features which may be discerned in Luther's thought. All of these features suggest an understanding of man as a unity. Among other scholars, Oberman and Hoffman have emphasized the features common to Luther and mysticism, and I have drawn upon their observations.

Finally, it should be mentioned parenthetically that during the Middle Ages in Holland a movement of laymen arose which aquired considerable influence and popularity throughout Europe. This was the so-called <u>devotio moderna</u>; it was a type of piety which had numerous features in common with Tauler's mysticism, not least in its emphasis on the affective aspect. Luther was probably right in not distinguishing sharply between these two types of spirituality.[8]

The Will

During the Late Middle Ages, a variety of types of spirituality were concerned with the will as the distinctive faculty of man, that is, it was held to be vastly more important than both the reason and the body. As we have seen, the existing philosophical tradition characterized man as tripartite by nature, and emphasized that the will was an important and central aspect of human structure. However, this emphasis may be considered a matter of degree. It is possible to limit the role of the will to that of assenting to the recommendations of the reason. Alternatively, as we saw was the case with St. Augustine, the will can be held to be man's real nature. "A man is his love", and, to St. Augustine, will and love were identical.

This is interesting for our investigation, since St. Augustine enjoyed a renaissance during - the Renaissance. The Italian humanists, Petrarch (d. in 1374) being preeminent among them, enthusiastically harked back to Augustine. Indeed, Petrarch allows St. Augustine to participate in a dialogue entitled "On the Secret Conflict Between my Efforts".[9] We shall presently return to Petrarch's struggles with himself in his dialogue with St. Augustine (see below, pp. 71ff). In brief, the

problem is that Petrarch finds himself to be torn between his need for virtue and his tendency towards vice.
He refuses to regard this situation as a sign that the
will is thoroughly evil, that is, because the will seeks
to commit evil, since it also seeks the good. St. Augustine, however, adheres to the opposite view: the
will is a unity, and one cannot will two things at the
same time. As mentioned, we shall return to this discussion at length. In this connection what is important
is to recognize that the will is held to be the real
aspect of man.

With St. Augustine's help, Petrarch discovered that
man is identical with his will. This discovery became
the common property of Italian humanism, and it is reflected in the works of such figures as Coluccio Salutati and Lorenzo Valla. What separates Petrarch and St.
Augustine in the previously mentioned dialogue is not
the significance of the will, but its character.

Voluntarism, that is, the stress upon the will as
man's most essential characteristic, also came into
prominence in the philosophy and theology of the time.
William of Occam (died 1349), for example, distinguished between faith and reason. What is true in terms of
the reason is not so in terms of faith. According to
Occam, the reason has only limited capabilities. In
fact, he assigns to it only the ability to determine
what is the case. Concepts and abstractions are things
we invent for ourselves, and they are not present in
reality. It is possible to say that Socrates is a man,
but not that Socrates possesses "humanity". After all,
"humanity" is not a determinable thing (res), for which
reason the latter expression is, strictly considered,
meaningless.[10] The same applies to all theological concepts, and thus we have no knowledge of God which can

be grounded in the reason. Accordingly, the truth of
Christianity cannot be rationally arrived at; instead,
it must be conferred by means of mediation or revelation. The result of Occam's having more or less expelled
the reason from the discussion is that more room was
created for the will. The will is thus the sole determining instance, however absurd its decisions may appear from the vantagepoint of the reason.

Anthropology (in the sense of a view of man) and
theology usually accord with one another, and this is
also true of Occam: just as man is characterized as
will, so, too, is God, who sovereignly elects for whatever he pleases. Or, to put it another way, God's absolute will is synonymous with incalculability and un-
predictability. The most forceful statement of this
notion is the concept of predestination, that is, the
notion that everyone's fate has been determined by God
from birth to grave, and indeed even beyond the grave,
since even one's salvation or condemnation has been determined in advance. Moreover, all this occurs in a manner
which we humans have no possibility of comprehending,
since the fact of God's free will insures that no principles or logical insights would ever enable us to de-
duce the course of the future.

Strangely enough, this Late Scholastic concept had
many parallels in the humanism of the Renaissance, although their roots did not lie in a philosophical criticism of the reason, but in St. Augustine's severe
teachings about predestination.[11] Thus Coluccio Salutati (d. 1406) used St. Augustine to combat the astrology
which was becoming so popular in his day. He maintained
that if God determines everything sovereignly and in-
scrutably, then astrological knowledge is worthless.
Calculations of the respective positions of planets and

stars will invariably be rendered nugatory in the face
of God's omnipotence. In this manner the idea of predestination was used to guarantee the unfathomableness
of God's will, and thus his omnipotence. Any God who
was intelligible, or whose actions one could predict,
would speedily come under man's control, since men
would of course be prone to utilize their knowledge of
God in order to calculate and control their own lives.
Therefore an omnipotent God must also be an inscrutable
one. Furthermore, or so Salutati maintained, God's
freedom and free will are paralleled in man's own will.
We shall not be concerned in these pages with the paradoxical idea that both God and man enjoy unlimited
self-determination. Instead, it would be appropriate
to concentrate on the fact that on Salutati's view God's
free will is the presupposition which insures that man,
too, has free will, for if this were not the case, then
man would not have been created in the image of God.[12]
This tendency to localize the specifically human to the
will reveals yet another aspect of the anthropology of
the late Middle Ages which seems to imply an understanding of man as a unity.

Astrology

"This is the excellent foppery of the world, that when
we are sick in fortune - often the surfeits of our own
behaviour - we make guilty of our disasters the sun,
the moon, and stars, as if we were villains on necessity, fools by heavenly compulsion, knaves, thieves, and
treachers by spherical predominance, drunkards, liars,
and adulterers by an enforced obedience of planetary
influence; and all that we are evil in by a divine
thrusting-on. An admirable evasion of whoremaster man,
to lay his goatish disposition on the charge of a star.

My father compounded with my mother under the Dragon's tail, and my nativity was under Ursa Major, so that it follows that I am rough and lecherous. Fut! I should have been that I am had the maidenliest star in the firmament twinkled on my bastardizing."[13]

This sceptical view of astrology, which Shakespeare has placed in the mouth of Edmund, the bastard son of the Earl of Gloucester, was by no means considered a matter of course during the Renaissance, in spite of the fact that it was supported by both churchmen and humanists. It was precisely during the Renaissance that astrology, as well as many other types of magic, achieved recognition as a significant spiritual power in a way we should today find incredible. One reason for this was the fact that in general no sharp distinction was made between astrology and astronomy, which meant that the former, too, enjoyed the status of a science. It was first much later that astronomy succeeded in disentangling itself from astrology, much as chemistry eventually managed to emerge from alchemy.

The difference between the position of astrology now and then is that in the late Middle Ages and the Renaissance astrological learning had nothing esoteric about it; its presuppositions were to be found among those generally acceptable to science. All educated people assumed that the universe consisted of two parts, the lunar (from "luna", i.e., the moon), within the orbit of which the stars, sun, moon, and planets were located, and the sublunary realm, which was comprised of the four elements of earth, air, fire, and water. The heavenly world brought these four elements in continual contact with one another by influencing them with cold, heat, dryness, and moisture. This causal relationship was held to underlie all physical changes

which took place on the earth. This applied not only
to the mineral and vegetable kingdoms, but also to the
living creatures, which were influenced by the stars.[14]
The physiological theory of antiquity was revived; according to it, man consists of four fluids, choler
(warm), phlegma (wet and cold), sanguis (blood, warm
and moist), and melancholy (dry and cold). As a rule
the four fluids are not in balance with one another.
Thus one or another influence is dominant, so that the
individual - perhaps in his various ages of development
- could be described as a choleric, phlegmatic, sang-
uinic, or melancholic person.[15] It was accepted as a
matter of course that the motions and internal relations
of these various fluids were governed by the heavenly
powers, the influence of which was thought to be especially great at the moment an individual was born. These
insights were not the property of a narrow élite; rather,
thanks to the art of printing they were matters of general knowledge. In fact, it is strange to consider that
one of the reasons why so many printers were prepared
to publish the works of the great humanists and theologians was that their incomes were in any case assured,
thanks to the publication of the annual almanacs which
resembled astrological calendars, containing as they
did predictions as to the course of the year, tables
of lucky and unlucky days when it would be appropriate
or inappropriate to conclude business agreements, attempt to cure illnesses, and so forth.[16]

Our very language still retains some vestiges of this
fascination with astrology. Consider, for example, the
English "lunatic" (lit. "moon-sick"), which still reflects the belief that the moon influenced, particularly in its full and old phases, the human psyche. Alternatively, we have the illness called "influenza",

which is simply the Italian term signifying the "influence" of the heavenly powers.

We shall not be further concerned with the flowering
of astrology during the Renaissance or with its subsequent decline in the 17th and 18th centuries (one of
the causes of which was the abandonment of the Aristot-
elian-Ptolemaic worldview, which included the division
of the world into lunar and sublunary regions). Here
it will be sufficient merely to point out that astrology emphasizes an understanding of man as ruled by external forces, and thus ultimately as a unity. The need
to describe man's internal structure diminishes when
one no longer has to seek explanations of his behavior
in himself, but in causes external to him.

Humanism

I do not intend to assert that the spiritual ancestors
of Luther's ideas are to be traced directly to the topics mentioned above: mysticism, voluntarism, astrology.
Admittedly, scholars are still disputing Luther's as-
sociation with mysticism, just as others have probed
the issue of his relations with Late Scholastic philosophy. Moreover, it is obvious that Luther's theological education is dependent on the tradition descend-
ing from William of Occam. However, it is at least
equally clear that much of the form of Luther's theology represents a break with this Late Scholastic theology on important issues.[17] Nor do I wish to suggest
that astrology and magic had any influence on Luther's
theology, even though there are numerous indications
that Luther, too, adhered to the popular superstitions
of his time. Indeed, had he not done so, it would be
quite surprising.

In short, I am not attempting to depict the genetic

parentage of Luther's theology in my description of the phenomena dealt with above. Instead, I am attempting to characterize a way of thinking which was quite general during the Renaissance. A variety of traditions, some of which are mutually contradictory, as far as their implicit anthropology is concerned, all point in the same direction, namely, the tendency to look at man from the outside, as a unity which is determined by affective states. As I shall presently attempt to suggest, the same characteristics apply to the political, literary, and artistic movement we call Renaissance humanism. But in addition to this - and this is one of the major emphases of this work - I shall argue that there is a close relationship between humanism and Luther.

One's first impulse is to say that this would be only natural, if Luther was a child of his times, and in fact, we should require quite special argumentation if we were to reject this notion. On the other hand, it requires no argumentation at all to support it, for the simple reason that it is quite obvious. Nevertheless, it is surprising to discover that Luther research has not been significantly concerned with this connection between Luther and humanism.

Perhaps one of the reasons for this was, as mentioned previously, Luther's feud with the leading humanist of the time, Erasmus of Rotterdam. Scholars seem to have had a somewhat undifferentiated understanding of humanism; thus they supposed that the only variety of importance was that to which Erasmus' treatise "On the Freedom of the Will", which all Luther scholars appear to have read, bears witness. Erasmus, however, was a multi-faceted individual of much greater complexity than is evident in his debate with Luther. In "Praise of Folly" and the methodological treatises dealing with

the publication of the Greek edition and the new Latin
translation of the New Testament all contain quite a
different approach than is evident in Erasmus' polemics
against Luther.[18] This also applies in part to Erasmus'
reply to Luther, "Hyperaspistes", which is unfortunately never dealt with in the literature on Luther.

For the present I shall merely make the bold claim
that Erasmus and Luther are in fact in agreement as to
many fundamental features. Thus their discussion of the
freedom of the will takes place within a framework of
broad agreement. We shall return to this presently (pp.
119).

At this point it would be appropriate to attempt a
general description of humanism. This might at first
sight appear to be a hopeless undertaking, since humanism seems to branch off in a welter of directions and
to be distributed over a number of periods. There is
the early poetical humanism in Italy, with which such
names as Mussato, Petrarch, and Boccaccio are associated. Alternatively, one could mention the political
humanism of the Italian republics, in which connection
the figures of Coluccio Salutati and Leonardo Bruni
were preeminent. These writers occupied key offices
from which they attempted to fuse together their literary and political horizons. Related to this was what
might be termed "secretarial humanism", a category consisting mainly of papal or ecclesiastical secretaries
who, by virtue of personal connections and countless
journeys were able both to collect and publish great
quantities of previously unknown manuscripts by ancient
authors. Poggio Bracchiolini and Lorenzo Valla are representative of this branch, which was also concerned
with problems related to the interpretation of texts.
Their views on such matters would be a worthwhile ac-

quaintance also for Luther scholars. The Platonic academy which assembled in the 1480's and 90's around the Renaissance prince par excellence, Lorenzo the Magnificent (d. 1492), is most prominently represented by Marsiglio Ficino and Pico della Mirandola. The mere mention of these "schools" by no means exhausts the humanistic landscape of Italy. One could also mention the architect Leon Battista Alberti, or, of course, the political theorist, Niccolo di Machiavelli (d. 1527). Although he was an opponent of humanism, Machiavelli's political analyses would be unintelligible unless seen against the background of humanistic insights.

If we proceed north of the Alps, we find a distinguished list of humanists towards the close of the 15th century and the beginning of the 16th. These included such figures as Agricola, Reuchlin, and Melanchton, to mention only those who were close to Luther. But towering above all these was, naturally, Erasmus of Rotterdam. The northern variety of humanism has somewhat unjustly been termed "Biblical humanism" - a rather sizable inaccuracy, when we consider that the Italian humanists, too, had the Bible as their most revered text.

We have cursorily mentioned some names of important figures who were prominent within humanism, and to whom others paid attention. This must not be allowed to obscure the fact that humanism was in actuality a popular movement, perhaps not one which was disseminated among the common people, but which was patently present at all institutions of learning, including the universities, as well as the courts and among princes, in ecclesiastical circles and among the leadership strata of the towns and cities. If one were to mention a pertinent modern analogy, it would be tempting to point to - cum grano salis - the vogue for Marxist or left-wing

ideas in general in western Europe since 1968. Both movements are comparable in terms of the extent of their
social penetration. Like humanism, Marxism has made head-
way among the young, among the middle classes, and in the institutions of higher learning. In this fashion it has also
made itself felt in both the political and the cultural
debate of our time. Although the numbers of actual Marxists
are no doubt rather small, the understanding of problems in
both school and society at large has been influenced by
them, either because people have sought to embrace Marxist ideas to a greater or lesser degree, or because they
have preferred to combat them. In Denmark the so-called
bourgeois parties even tend to define themselves in
terms of their opposition to Marxism or socialism.

Of course, I do not mean to suggest that humanism
and Marxism are identical, or even that they have other
parallels than the superficial ones mentioned here. The
point is that one can get some idea of the quantitative
influence of humanism by comparing it with this modern
parallel phenomenon. And this brings us to the decisive
point in the parallel in question, namely the fact that
whereas in the future it would be impossible to describe
a citizen of the 20th centure and his religious or
political views without reference to Marxism (construed
either broadly or narrowly), it would be similarly impossible to discuss Luther without investigating his
relationship to humanism.

But what is this humanism? If one replies that it
consisted of people who desired to revive antique culture and literature, then one has answered wrongly. There
have probably never existed individuals who wished to
recreate the past. Of course, the word "Renaissance"
(rebirth) has often been understood in this way, but
in reality it means something quite different, since

the idea was not to help antiquity to be born again,
but the Renaissance itself. A metaphor which was current at the time was that of a giant who bore a dwarf
on his shoulders. The giant symbolized antiquity, while
the dwarf signified the times. The point of this metaphor was that the dwarf was thus in a position to see
farther than the giant could do, because he sat on the
giant's shoulders. The humanists desired in an analogous way to use the lore of antiquity to raise themselves to a higher level. In short, the rebirth or renewal in question had to do with themselves and their
own times. But why, then, was antiquity so essential
to the humanists? There may have been a number of factors, but there is at least one which linked humanists
- possibly with the exception of the Florentine Platonists[19] - both north and south of the Alps throughout
the period, namely, the interest in rhetoric. Rhetoric
was not unknown in the Middle Ages, since at that time
it was part of the elementary university curriculum,
the so-called artes liberales, a sort of high school
training which every university student was obliged to
take.[20] During the Renaissance rhetoric became independent from the universities and was no longer part
of the university curriculum. It had instead become a
living reality which was the very heartbeat of all political propaganda and activity. It had also become a
way of reading and interpreting texts, both ancient and
modern, and preeminent among these, the Bible. In fact,
we may also expand the concept of "text" to include the
figural varieties of art, as these were also understood
on rhetorical principles, and, in their execution, the
demands which were made of them were based on rhetorical
criteria.[21]

     And furthermore: in the period in question rhetoric

had not only to do with the means of expression; rather,
it had acquired the status of a philosophy or an understanding of life. Thus it left its mark on all human
achievement of the time, in the disparate fields of
art, law, science, and theology.

Thus there is good reason to investigate the nature
of rhetoric. Superficially, the term has to do with the
"science" (if we may be permitted so grand a term) of
giving a presentation of something a beautiful and convincing form. This is a very good description, except
for the fact that on reading this definition modern
people would automatically supply it with an understood
"just" or "only" as far as the reference to "form" is
concerned. We would be inclined to regard the contents
as by far the most important part. Of course, no one
would deny this, and yet, it was precisely one of the
main emphases of the rhetorical tradition that form and
content were intimately attached to one another. However, before we examine the nature of rhetoric, let us
briefly examine the social developments which had produced a need for rhetorical abilities.

During the late Middle Ages the European societies
suffered comprehensive changes. Economic development
accelerated and became international in character. The
economy was no longer limited to the confines of the
isolated feudal society. Already the Crusades had contributed to expand the traderoutes to the east. This
naturally also entailed that more traffic appeared on
the European traderoutes, since the increasing supply
of goods had to find markets. The great Italian trade
centers in Venice and Florence and, in the north, in
the Hansa states were no longer satisfied with the
local markets, so that all of Europe became the basis
of trade. Furthermore, production, and textiles in

particular, became more systematic, so that productivi-
ty increased, which again led to an increase in trade.
Since all of these developments had produced something
resembling the modern economics of the marketplace, a
natural need also arose for an equivalent to the modern
advertising industry. During the late Middle Ages the
art of composing, among other things, letters of trade,
developed in such a way as to make an impression on
their recipients in order to persuade them to purchase
the recommended goods. The so-called ars dictaminis[22]
was this science of writing the best possible letters.
Thus it was very rapidly discovered that the technology
of communication which was stored in the ancient science
of rhetoric was applicable for these and similar purposes.

The economic changes in question also brought about
political changes. This is especially evident in Italy,
and to some degree also in Germany, where a number of
small independent states began to conduct foreign policy
in their own right. This in turn produced a need for
a political ars dictaminis. Furthermore, within these
small states, or, as they came to be called in Italy,
commune, leadership also became more democratic. The
ascendant bourgeoisie often declined to tolerate further the local prince, so that he was deposed in favor
of a council, with a mayor as chief of state. This development signified that power was no longer stable,
as it had been in dynastic principalities. Power had
as a result to be won, rather than inherited, and to
this end the aid of the people, whether narrowly or
broadly construed, was essential. This situation made
political propaganda important also inside the petty
states in question.

These economic and political developments influenc-

ed the course of artistic and literary innovation. Many
poets were themselves trained in the ars dictaminis
tradition, so that it was natural for them to apply
rhetorical norms to their poetry. One could also draw
parallels between the economic market structure and the
new reading public which arose in this period. In Italy
the three giants, Dante, Petrarch, and Boccaccio achieved national popularity in a manner unknown during the
Middle Ages. Crowning the poet with laurel became a popular event,[23] a fact which illustrates the extent to
which people were aware that a man could first be called
a poet once he had achieved recognition and a sizable
public. Rhetoric was accordingly rediscovered as the
literary norm.

    Then what is rhetoric? Let us begin by regarding it
"only" as a matter of form, even though, as noted above,
this is not wholly just. To a businessman who wants to
unload his goods, a politician seeking influence, and
a poet in search of a public it is of the utmost importance to master the art of getting people to listen.
Towards the close of the Middle Ages, people began to
realize that the works of a number of ancient authors
contained systematic knowledge of the ways one could
get people to listen. These works contained rules for
the shaping of a message so as to achieve the best
chance of penetrating the public consciousness. For
example, it was maintained that a speech ought not to
be merely a collection of sentences or arguments or
statements, no matter how correct they happened to be.
Considered in isolation, the truth is infinitely insig-
nificant, unless it has been understood by the person
to whom it is addressed. Accordingly, one's presentation had to be prepared with great care by, for example, bringing it into accord with the following five-

part scheme: a) One has to introduce it in such a way that one immediately makes contact with the hearer or addressee, who is to be favorably inclined towards the speaker or sender of the message in question (exordium). Especially in the ars dictaminis of the late Middle Ages, great emphasis was placed on the use of the correct introductory formulas. Nor is this strange, since if the introduction does not manage to "hook" the recipient, he will never be open to the actual contents of the message, and the entire message will be wasted. b) Next a short address as to the purpose of the communication is in order (narratio). c) It is also often appropriate to account for the circumstances underlying the matter in hand, and which has produced the need for the discourse in question. Also, one announces how one's argumentation will proceed, so that the recipient is prepared for what is to come (partitio). d) The argument itself follows at this point, in the course of which one - using among other things, a number of rhetorical questions - anticipates actual or imagined objections, which are naturally rebutted (confirmatio). e) Finally, one draws the threads together in one's conclusion, so that the hearer has a clear impression of what he has heard. Here, too, it is important that one has the benign attention of one's audience, so that a handy quotation or bon mot would not be inappropriate as a concluding remark (peroratio).

Of course, this scheme may be broken up. It may be reduced to a three-part one, or even revised entirely. Nevertheless, every departure from the scheme must be faithful to its intention, that is, to retain the attention of the audience.

For reasons of space it will not be possible here to examine the widely ramified analytical apparatus of

of rhetorical doctrine. Interested readers are invited
to immerse themselves in Lausberg's massive handbook,
which records the thousands of rhetorical phenomena,
terms, and distinctions.[24] For our purposes, it will
be sufficient to examine only two features, namely the
questions of style and stylistic level.

The rhetorical style is an embroidered one. It contains attractive phrases, striking metaphors, and impressive cadences. It is probably this aspect of the
rhetorical art which, more than any other, has served
to discredit it. It has been accused of seeking to de-
corate a presentation without reference to merit, so
that the audience is fooled into accepting something
they would not have accepted, if they had seen things
as they really are. In reality, this is the same accusation that is usually directed against one of the modern heirs of rhetoric, namely advertising, which is
also frequently accused of giving a false impression
of the product in question.

Of course, a good deal of such criticism is accurate. People have always been tempted to represent themselves or their goods or their views as better than
they actually are. However, such criticism ought not
to be allowed to overshadow the fact that the actual
intention behind the rhetorical concept of ornatus
(decoration) is to inform about and illustrate a matter
so that it is completely clear to the audience. Thus
one employs images and metaphors from the everyday world
of the senses so that the audience will be able to
picture the object in question to itself. For this
reason it is important to utilize a language which is
as natural and close to the senses as possible. Concepts and technical expressions may have some limited
value, but if one intends for people to grasp what

really lies behind them, one is forced to translate them into things which can be sensed. Abstractions are difficult to understand, for the good reason that they are remote from the senses. Furthermore, it is important to recognize that this is not just a matter of pedagogical effort, but a result of an epistemological theory. According to this theory, only that which is perceived by the senses is capable of captivating our reason, will, and feeling. This point has further implications for the understanding of the rhetorical concept of clarity (perspicuitas). This concept entails not only that one intellectually understands a given subject, but also that one grasps what that subject means to me, that is, how it concerns me. Thus both feeling and reason are involved in rhetorical understanding.

But clarity entails more than that one is obliged to find the appropriate sensual expressions, since in reality it is only possible to comprehend the intelligible by means of the senses. Aristotle's dictum that a poem has to have a beginning, middle, and end[25] applies to rhetoric as well, as, for example, to the previously adumbrated description of a rhetorical address. Also, not only the message as a whole, but its individual sections must be rythmical, if they are to be correctly understood. The rhythm must further penetrate to the way the words are linked together, for it can only penetrate to the mind of the hearer and make an impression if this is the case. According to a common figure of speech, it is possible to get an idea "pounded into one's head". The figure may derive from the pedagogical techniques of earlier times, but it is possible that it also points to a rhetorical phenomenon: that one understands something by resonating with

it in the same rhythm. This is especially obvious in
the case of melodious poetry, songs, and psalms, where
the melody helps to eludicate the text. This occurs in
a similar fashion, although perhaps using slightly different tools, in a thoroughly prepared prose presentation. The concept of rhythm joins both form and content together.

There is also reason to discuss the classical teaching about the stylistic levels, or, simply, the styles.
Rhetoricians distinguished between three different
styles, low, middle, and elevated. In the first of
these, one teaches, that is, one represents a matter
plainly and to the point (docere). In the second style,
it is important to dissolve the distance between the
speaker and his audience by, among other things, using
humor as a tool (delectare, to please). Finally, there
is the elevated style in which one addresses the audience directly and aims to bring about a change of attitude or immediate action. One's goal is to activate
one's audience (movere).

It is clear that a presentation becomes increasingly
"rhetorical" the higher one progresses through the
hierarchy of styles. One could also say that the feelings become increasingly involved as we approach the
highest stylistic level. In the low style one is at
some distance from the object in question, and concerning which one is being instructed. The informational
instructions as such are not overly important. In the
middle style, it is a question of evaluation, although
it is still possible to approach things in all their
complexity, that is, from a number of points of view.
But it is evident that the things under discussion are
of greater importance than are those dealt with under
the first style, as is revealed by the use of humor,

which is the special trademark of the middle style. The
humor involved may be defined as the ability to maintain opposed views, or phenomena which are mutually
contradictory,but which may nevertheless be encompassed
by the same framework or the same frame of mind. In
Greek this style is termed ethos, which actually means
custom or usage, which points to the connection between
this stylistic level and ethics. The question of moral
rules is usually dealt with in the middle style, since
norms are the result of an evaluation of what one con-
siders to be reasonable. A sense of proportion is important if one intends to discover a middle term, which
is what most laws and regulations in reality represent.

In the elevated style the level of emotion is cor-
respondingly increased. This is the case because one's
feelings are no longer mixed, as is the case with ethos.
In the elevated style, appeal is made to some all-con-
quering passion which sweeps away all other considerations and feelings; one attempts to arouse a passion
which possesses one's hearer and compels him to act.
Therefore this level of style is called pathos (passion).

One important aspect of the theory of the stylistic
levels deserves to be emphasized. Content and stylistic
level have to accord with one another. If it is a question of relatively unimportant matters, they are to be
dealt with in the humble style (genus subtile), important matters are discussed in the middle style, while
very important issues are reserved for the elevated
style. In other words, one has no choice as to one's
selection of style: one has instead to make sure that
there is close agreement between form and content. If
one breaks this rule, the result is either parody
(trifles which are dealt with in the elevated style),

or travesty (in which truly important matters are depicted in the low style).

As I suggested previously, rhetoric is not merely
a question of pedagogical form which may be used or not
at one's discretion. Like most practical procedures,
rhetoric, too, has theoretical consequences, and those
which are of interest for our purposes are the consequences for anthropology, the understanding of man. We
accordingly conclude this chapter with an examination
of some of the consequences of rhetorical practice,
with a view to determining later whether these have
parallels in Luther's theology.

1) As a matter of course, rhetoric concentrates attention on the phenomenon of language. Today a great
deal of rhetorical theory is subsumed under a variety
of categories, such as stilistics. Nevertheless, the
subject matter of the discipline is the function and
application of words, sentences, narratives, and expos-
itions. This preoccupation would appear to be in vain,
if its practitioners felt that language is an imperfect
and inappropriate epistemological tool, as was generally asserted by many of the linguistic theorists of the
Middle Ages. Indeed, it was frequently maintained that
the acquisition of knowledge could be divorced from
language, a position which can hardly be said to provide an incitement for concerning oneself with ordinary
language to any significant degree.[26] Rhetoric in fact
encourages confidence in the word as the basis of all
understanding and knowledge. This also implies, as we
shall see subsequently (see ch. 7), a different understanding of the concept of "text" from that which predominated during the Middle Ages. The latter was mainly
a symbolic view of language which held that every individual word or sentence in some manner pointed beyond

itself to a different sort of reality. The rhetorical emphasis on rhythm, composition, and structure indicates an insistence on reading a context, that is, in which the context makes up the basis for understanding.[27]

2) The rhetorical interest in language also implies the tendency to regard man as a passive recipient. This is indicated already by the situation of the hearer in the situation in which he is addressed. Of course, one takes up one's discourse in order to say something to someone, that is, to convey new knowledge to the recipient, or to awaken him to action or to a new emotional reaction. If one has no desire to change anything in the situation of one's hearer, one has no reason for speech. The audience is regarded as receptive, impressionable, and malleable.

A lawyer may serve as an example.[28] According to Quintillian, the lawyer's audience is the judge, who must be motivated to judge in favor of the lawyer's client. The lawyer does not share the previously mentioned understanding of man as tripartite; he does not distinguish between the reason, will, or emotions of the judge. In fact, if he felt that the judge was master of his own will, he would probably regard his defense of his client as superfluous. The judge has to be regarded as a single individual, since the lawyer is interested in his verdict, and, in this connection the many psychological distinctions are irrelevant. It is both sufficient and more rational, to the extent that it empirically arrives at the desired results, to assume that reason, will, feeling, and action make up a unity which is receptive to a variety of arguments. This applies to both unimportant information and to the truly weighty facts and views, the import-

ance of which is identical with the feelings they arouse
(see above p. 55ff.). In short, the judge is a single individual, and he is subject to influences from without.

In this connection it could be mentioned that, like
the scholars of antiquity, Renaissance rhetoricians
emphasized that the sense of hearing was "compliant"
(K.E. Løgstrup), in spite of the fact that, as mentioned previously, the original point of departure was the
ars dictaminis, which depended on writing. The spoken
and living word was held to be man's most important
access to reality; and this dictum rends intelligible
the fact that the hearer is a passive recipient. In
whatever is heard, one's reception is namely governed
by the voice employed, and by the rhythm and sequence
of the words and thoughts which the hearer has no possibility to alter. Vision, on the other hand, is much
more difficult to control in any mediatory situation.

3) In the example of the lawyer, the rhetorician's
goal is not merely to get the judge to will or believe
something, but also to act, that is, to find in favor
of the accused. All the efforts of the lawyer are wasted if the appropriate action does not follow his words.
But this will inevitably occur, it should be noted, in
the event that the judge has really understood the
nature of the case. By "understanding" is meant not
merely getting the point, but also becoming involved
in the issue. This in reality renders quite problematical the distinction between soul and body. The idea
is that if one has really arrived at a particular understanding of a matter, then one will also perform the
actions appropriate to that understanding. In a manner
of speaking, one's actions provide a criterium for
evaluating the extent of one's understanding. If the
judge does not rule the way the lawyer desires that he

should, then all the latter's efforts have been in vain.

There is no reason to expatiate further on the nature of rhetoric. Instead, I shall at this point summarize the understanding of man implicit in it. Rhetoric presupposes an undivided individual. There is no sharp distinction between the reason, the soul, and the body. In this, rhetoric resembles certain types of mysticism. Man is regarded as receptive to the things offered him by his senses and by language. Moreover, this is the case to the extent that the individual is in the power of his environment and his language. Particularly the latter feature is of interest for our purposes.

A direct line leads from the rhetorical understanding of life implicit in Renaissance humanism back to one of the forefathers of Greek rhetoric, the sophist Gorgias. In his defense of the lovely Helen who journeyed to Troy with prince Paris, Gorgias mentions the possibility that she may have been the victim of persuation, against which one cannot defend oneself: "But if it was speech which persuaded her and deceived her heart, not even to this is it difficult to make an answer and to banish blame as follows. Speech is a powerful lord, which by means of the finest and most invisible body effects the divinest works: it can stop fear and banish grief and create joy and nurture pity. I shall show how this is the case, since it is necessary to offer proof to the opinion of my hearers: I both deem and define all poetry as speech with meter. Fearful shuddering and tearful pity and grievous longing come upon its hearers, and at the actions and physical sufferings of others in good fortunes and in evil fortunes, through the agency of words, the soul is wont to experience a suffering of its own."[29] When the possib-

ilities of language are exploited to the full, one is
unable to resist. This was the presupposition of rhetoric and the Renaissance. Furthermore, it is the foundation upon which humanistic philosophy, psychology, and
theology must build.

Luther and Rhetoric

Up to this point I have been concerned to offer a
general characterization of the Renaissance and its
various facets on the assumption that if one knows a
period, then one also knows its inhabitants. If rhetoric was a keyword of the time, then Luther must also
have been influenced by rhetoric in his thought and
praxis.

It would nevertheless be interesting to see if this
hypothesis could not be confirmed through concrete
studies of Luther's authorship. Was he familiar with
the basic concepts of rhetoric, and did he employ them
himself? Was he conversant with the use of ancient texts
in the humanism of his day, and did he share the then-
current enthusiasm for antiquity?

I have not personally undertaken an intensive investigation of these questions, but I have been able
to draw on a considerable literature on the subject.
In what follows I shall briefly summarize the findings
of five scholars who have dealt with it. I could have
chosen others, but in my opinion these five names represent a variety of types and approaches to the topic.

In a monographic treatment Helmuth Junghans has
dealt extensively with the influence of humanism on
Luther until 1518.[30] After a thorough summary of the
history of research on the subject Junghans particularly concentrates on the university in Erfurt, where hu-

manism had already manifested itself as early as in 1460 in the form of an intensive preoccupation with rhetoric. Around the time Luther was admitted as a student at the university in 1501 a new and far more distinctive generation of humanists had appeared on the scene; not the least of their emphases was devoted to breaking with scholastic philosophy.

As a matter of fact, ever since the days of Petrarch Luther's own order of Augustinian monks had enjoyed close relations with humanism. This applies above all to Luther's immediate superior, the General Vicar Johannes von Staupitz, who introduced the study of the Bible into the order under the influence of humanism.

It is fully apparent that in this context humanism was identical with the revival of the old "trivium", consisting of grammar, dialectics, and, above all, rhetoric. Thus, by virtue of his environment Luther could not have avoided a first hand knowledge of these matters, which he was later to insure that the students at Wittenburg also studied. For this reason he introduced a course on rhetoric there in 1518.

A number of scholars have dealt with the fact that Luther was influenced by his surroundings. In these pages I shall confine myself to the work of Lewis W. Spitz.[31] Spitz emphasizes Luther's broad knowledge of and enthusiasm for the classics, and above all for Cicero and the Latin poets, among whom he held Vergil to be pre-eminent. Spitz also demonstrates the value Luther assigned to rhetoric, a subject which he found more important than dialectics. Luther regarded St. Paul and Moses as great rhetoricians, and he stressed that they were to be read with this in mind.[32] Both were capable of appealing to the will rather than the reason. Furthermore, Luther praised the rhetorical theoreticians

Cicero and Quintilian because they showed how to avoid
ambiguity and how to speak to the heart. Ulrich Nembach
has studied Luther's dependence on Quintilian in his
homeletical writings from a more theoretical point of
view.[33] According to Nembach, Luther's study of Quintilian, and the fruits it bore, lasted throughout his
life.[34] He also shows that Luther makes use of the rhetorical teaching about status, the various disciplines
of rhetoric, structure (dispositio), elaboration (ornatus), and the fact that he utilizes Quintilian's analyses of allegory and metaphor and other "figures" whose
function was to create tension and to gain attention
(which Nembach calls "eloquente Textverfremdung").

A very important bit of fieldwork has been carried
out by the Swedish scholar Birgit Stolt. Dr. Stolt has demonstrated that a superficially simple and popular sermon of Luther which seems to be direct and to the point in
reality attains its clarity, simplicity, and ability
to win conviction by living up to the classical rhetorical rules in even the most minute details.[35] Close
examination shows that such sermons are a finely calculated lacework of stylistic elements which are structured according to all the rules of the art. She further
demonstrates the way Luther employs the rhetorial
styles, and in particular the two highest ones, delectare (to please) and movere (to activate), in order to
achieve the right impact on his audience's feelings
(affectus), so as to compel them to accept his insights.

In a major monograph Birgit Stolt compares the Germ-
an and Latin editions of Luther's work entitled "On
Christian Freedom". Her study illustrates the fact that
Luther transferred the structural rules of classical
Latin to the German version of his work.[36] In a final
chapter entitled "Luther and Rhetoric", Dr. Stolt offers

an insightful survey of Luther's understanding and use
of rhetoric. At the same time she draws up the consequences of the analysis in her work and martials them
so as to make a clean break with earlier studies of
Luther's use of language. Previous scholars had spoken
of Luther's "casualness with respect to linguistic
formalities"; they had also asserted that "the inner
involvement is, in Luther's works, the force underlying
his style." In other words, Luther was held to be a
natural talent as far as language was concerned, newly
emerged from the Teutonic forests, "quite uninfluenced
by foreign models and rules" (Petsch). Dr. Stolt's analyses of Luther's language show that nothing could be
further from the truth. It was not without reason that
Luther was both proud and pleased to be called "the
German Cicero". Thus the claim that Luther was a great
linguistic innovator may be summarily dismissed. To the
contrary, he was rooted solidly in the existing tradition.

In conclusion, I should like to mention one of Germany's most eminent students of rhetoric, namely Klaus
Dockhorn, who perhaps more than any other scholar has
stimulated my interest in Luther and his relationship
to rhetoric. In an article dealing with "Luther's Concept of Faith and Rhetoric"[37], Dockhorn claims that
Luther's faith is determined by affective states. Luther's variety of faith is a pathetic feeling which is
transferred and mediated in the ways prescribed by
rhetoric. He argues somewhat surprisingly for this
point by comparing texts in which Luther describes the
communication of the Holy Spirit with the human heart
with Quintilian's descriptions of the use of emotion
as a means of mediation in the 6th book of his <u>Institu-
tio oratoria</u>. To use Dockhorn's phrase, the similari-

ties, even as far as the details of language are concerned, are "fast bestürzend" (quite astonishing).

Having accomplished this much, Dockhorn has paved
the way for a step beyond linguistic and stylistic analysis, so that we may proceed to the fundamental analysis of contents, as such, that is, from Luther's hu-
manistic-rhetorical background to his theology. It is
this step which I propose to take in the main chapters
of the present work.

The same number of <u>Linguistica Biblica</u> in which
Dockhorn's article appeared also contains a bibliography of works dealing with Luther's use of and relation
to rhetoric. The list consists of 77 titles. In terms
of size and number, scholarship from before 1800 makes
up the main part of these works. Perhaps better than
any other evidence, this fact illustrates the extent
to which a dimension of our culture has been lost.[38]
In modern times rhetoric has been forgotten to such a
degree that it has been possible to overlook both the
theory and practice of it, even in texts in which it
has determined both the form and the content. This has
been greatly detrimental to our understanding of the
Renaissance and its people, not least among them being
Martin Luther.

4. From Accidia to Melancholy

Before concerning ourselves more closely with Luther's
"Renaissance theology", it would be appropriate to pause
briefly in order to examine and exemplify more closely
the differences between the Middle Ages and the Renaissance with respect to their views of man. Some perspective on this issue may be achieved by a concrete investigation. We shall attempt to follow how it changes
its character as we approach the Renaissance.

During the Middle Ages (in the Catholic Church it
has remained valid doctrine until our times) the teaching was that there were seven "deadly sins"; these received their title because it was obligatory to have
confessed to them prior to one's death. These were sins
worthy of capital punishment, and thus of eternal damn-
ation. Anyone guilty of them could not expect a stay
of indeterminate length in Purgatory in order to atone
for them. Rather, the appropirate punishment was the
eternal agony of Hell. The better known of these sins
were such things as arrogance, wrathfulness, gluttony,
and greed. Accidia, that is, sloth, is less well known.
It may perhaps appear peculiar to the modern sensibility that sloth or dullness should be characterized as
a vice. We would instead be more inclined to describe
it as an inborn aspect of the human character, or else
as an illness, for example, in the form of dementia
praecox (schizophrenia). The matter was understood quite
differently in the Middle Ages and in antiquity.

In ch. 2 of his Second Letter to the Corinthians,
St. Paul speaks of an individual who has caused both
himself and the congregation of Corinth much "pain",
for which reason he offers the following caution: "For
such a one this punishment by the majority is enough;

so you should rather turn to forgive and comfort him,
or he may be overwhelmed by excessive sorrow" (2 Cor
2,6-7). In St. Jerome's Latin translation of the Bible,
the so-called Vulgate, the Greek word lypē, which the
RSV renders "sorrow", is translated by tristitia, sadness. The word was soon to be related to yet another
Greek expression, akedia (later spelled accicia), which
means sloth.[1]

It was probably not an accident that led heaviness
of heart to be identified with sloth. This evolution
presupposes an understanding of man as something active,
striving, enterprising and so forth, that is, as a being who manifests his essence through a variety of
activities. Preeminent among these were the spiritual
variety: contemplation and devotion to the divine. It
was thought that these "abilities" or possibilities
were weakened or undermined by sloth; the spiritual
energy of the slothful was seen to reside on a level
lower than that of the healthy or normal individual.

The understanding of sloth as a vice seems to have
manifested itself concretely for the first time in the
eastern monastic movement. Here sloth, under the designation akedia, was referred to as the "midday demon"
which makes languor settle upon people when the sun
is at its highest (and perhaps also after one has enjoyed a glass of something with one's lunch). However,
it was not merely during the middle of the day that the
monastic life was threatened by creeping slothfulness,
and which caused the monks to daydream and look out the
window instead of being preoccupied with their prayers.
The monotonous life of the cloister, in which one day
was virtually inseparable from another, was sufficient
to make monks break down psychically.[2]

In connection with his exegesis of an Old Testament

psalm, presbyter Origen mentioned that sin entails a weakening of our rational perspective and thus produces accidia. In the 4th century, Cassian remarked that the heart could be attacked by an "anxietas sive taedium", that is, anxiety or boredom.

Both the traditions of the Early Church and the Middle Ages agreed that the phenomenon in question was the result of a spiritual defect, that is, a weakness of the mind. Thus to combat this "accidia" it was necessary to strengthen the mind in order to make it resistant to this creeping dullness. It was held that this bad influence on the soul could derive from the body which, if allowed to vegetate (otiositas), may develop many strange desires capable of affecting the soul. The remedy against this was work. As is well known, the munks' general slogan was "ora et labora", that is, "pray and work!" In this fashion it was thought possible to strengthen both spirit and soul and thus to prevent both elements from succumbing to accidia.

Of course, even today we are familiar with the thought underlying the proverb which states that "idleness is the root of all evil". Moreover, we are familiar with this idea from the practices of our society, and not just from proverbs. We also regard it as both dangerous and unfortunate if people are allowed to go for very long without work. So much leisure time leads to psychological trouble, spiritual decline, and social unrest.

As was already suggested back in ch. 2, the notion behind this idea was the concept we designated the "tripartite man", that is, man understood as composed of will, intellect, and spiritual contents. This individual becomes dull when he is no longer in possession of his spiritual powers. In Christian terms this en-

tails that the individual breaks down and becomes dull.
Sin and evil are not really self-sufficient concepts
or realities; rather, they are understood as the degeneration or dissolution of existing qualities. This is
the necessary result, when man is regarded as an existant, that is, as something which possesses his own contents and capacities, such as freedom of the will or
responsibility.

Now, the Middle Ages also fathered the notion of a
variety of tristitia which was fruitful and useful. The
idea is that sorrow and anxiety must necessarily precede joy in order, in a manner of speaking, to make
room for it. In fact, Bernard of Clairvaux was even
able to depict sorrow and anxiety as the pathway to
true humility.[3] In this way, tristitia could be considered a teacher or disciplinary aid to faith. Similarly, it was a common idea in the Middle Ages that the
Devil or Tempter in reality acted on God's orders,
since by being exposed to temptation man had the possibility to develop strength of character. Indeed, seen
in this light it is possible to regard temptation as
a strengthening agent, and thus as an indication of the
love of God. The parable of the Prodigal Son who ultimately repented, as well as the account of the conversion of St. Paul on his way to Damascus were both alle-
gorically explained as examples of a sort of beneficent
temptation, that is, a felix culpa: a thing which in
and of itself is evil, but the effects of which may be
good.

Of course, this view presupposes that one says no
to the temptation in question at the appropriate moment.
If one says yes, then all is lost. Moreover, if the individual succumbs to the temptation, then he will not
be happy. This was regarded as a particularly acute

problem as death approached, since there would then be
no time to undo one's error. For this reason the Middle
Ages saw the flourishing of a considerable literature
on the art of dying (ars moriendi), the whole point of
which was to strengthen the afflicted party so that his
weakness would not lead him so sin. It is against this
background that the last unction, that is, the sacrament of the Catholic Church accorded to the dying, is
to be understood, for it was precisely in this situation that the individual was thought to require strengthening.

On the other hand, it was also held that just as
temptation can become too great, so, too, can one's remorse over a sin be so great that it destroys the soul.
Judas Iscariot was the usual example of this phenomenon.
He could easily have turned to Christ and received forgiveness, but his remorse overpowered him instead and
so drove him to suicide.[4]

Thus as far as both temptation and remorse were concerned it was a matter of a bitter medicin, one which
could cleanse and heal the soul, if taken in small dos-
es, but of which an excessive dosage could either kill
the soul or make it dull. Those capacities and powers
with which either nature or grace have endowed us become corrupted if pushed past the breaking point.

Now if, as I have suggested, the view of man as tripartite with its attendant implications, as illustrated
above, was replaced during the Renaissance by a different view of man, then we should expect that also the
mortal sin known as accidia would do so. If it is the
case that man is nothing in himself, that is, is only
a vacuum who is filled from without, then it is impossible to retain such a concept as dullness. The very
concept presupposes that the soul contains a variety

of contents, such as ability, strength of will, and so
forth, all of which may be dulled because the soul is
located somewhere on a scale ranging from the intense
and energetic to the dull or passive. But if the soul itself is a vacuum, then there is nothing which can be
dulled. Nevertheless, the Renaissance, too, had a concept of spiritual heaviness, but it was awarded the
name of melancholia instead of accidia. Even more important, however, is the fact that it also had a new
content, which we shall attempt to illustrate by examining two distinctive Renaissance works, namely the
Secretum of Petrarch and Dürer's famous painting, Mel-
ancolia I.

At some point in the 1340's Petrarch composed the
dialogue referred to above as "On the hidden inward
conflict between my strivings" (Secretum).[5] As the title
suggests, the theme of the dialogue is the fact that
Petrarch finds that he is at war with himself, that is,
is filled with thoughts and desires which oppose one
another. There are three figures in the piece, the
Truth (Veritas), St. Augustine, and Petrarch himself.
The Truth, however, says nothing except for the pro-
logue, where it asks St. Augustine (whom it calls "dear-
est to me of all men") to help Petrarch in his trials.
The Truth also promises to assist St. Augustine in the
course of the dialogue.

There are two things to be said about St. Augustine's
participation in the dialogue. In the first place, as
was suggested previously, it is hardly accidental that
it is he whom the Truth charges to lead Petrarch to
greater clarity. Augustine was an important transitional figure between the Middle Ages and the Renaissance,
since during the Renaissance people turned to Augustine
for help in formulating their new understanding of man.

There can be no doubt that St. Augustine's emphasis on
the concept of amor enabled him to serve as a catalyst
for the Renaissance breakthrough. In fact, Augustine's
understanding of man in general was of importance for
the Renaissance from Petrarch to Luther. One of the
reasons for this was, of course, Augustine's style of
exegesis which, in adhering very closely to the text,
was much more humanistic than was that of the Middle
Ages.

However, it is also important to recognize that during the Renaissance it was only possible to follow St.
Augustine to a certain extent. In reality, the Augustinian tradition of the 14th-16th centuries was only
"Augustinian" to a limited extent. The reason for this
was that scholars read Augustine as if he represented
the understanding of man as a unity, whereas in fact
his theology was only a modification of the tripartite
view of man (see above, pp.25ff). This fact sometimes
created some odd misunderstandings, as it occasionally
did to Luther, who tended to find his own opinion in
Augustine's text and therefore thought he was much more
in agreement than was in fact the case.[6]

Petrarch lived in the same ambiguous situation, as
his "Secretum" indicates. He, too, finds Augustine to
be the second best source of truth after the Bible, but
he saw more readily than Luther did the points at which
their paths diverged, as we shall see in the "Secretum".

The Augustine of the dialogue proclaims a sort of
stoical philosophy: virtue is related to happiness as
cause is to effect. Conversely, the vices produce un-
happiness. This was not only a stoic position; it was
shared by virtually every philosopher of antiquity, and
probably also by the historical St. Augustine himself.
To this Petrarch replies, "I think I have seen very many

people, and I am one of them, to whom nothing is more distressful than the inability to break the yoke of their faults, though all their life long they make the greatest efforts so to do. Wherefore, even allowing that the maxim of the Stoics holds good, one may yet admit that many people are very unhappy in spite of themselves, yes, and although they lament it and wish they were not, with their whole heart." (Eng. trans. of W.H. Draper: Petrarch's Secret, or The Soul's Conflict With Passion, London, 1911, repr. 1975, pp. 13-14, Dialogue One).[7]

Augustine, however, is dismissive of this; he maintains that where Petrarch had said "unable" he ought to have said "unwilling".[8] (ibid., p. 19) Petrarch nevertheless remains stubborn; he claims to have suffered much. He also claims that no one wishes more fervently than he to escape from his powerlessness.

It should be noted that the will is the main topic of discussion. As was mentioned previously, during the Middle Ages and the Renaissance scholars were much engaged by the problem of the will, and their main point of departure was the work of St. Augustine. The presupposition of this discussion was that man was not held to be identical with his mere reason, but that the will, with its attendant affective states, was the superior part of man. An indication of this is revealed by a list of the key terms of the humanists' self-characterization: philosophia Christi(ana), that is, the philosophy of Christ or, Christian philosophy; studia humanitatis, the study of the human/human studies; sapientia (wisdom); prudentia (prudence), and so forth. All of these terms either signify moral philosophy or else regard such philosophy as an important goal. Thus both Augustine and Petrarch are agreed that the will is central to the discussion.

Where they disagree, however, is whether the will is divided or a unity. Petrarch insists that it is divided, for which reason his is a divided personality. This leads Augustine to recall that he, too, was once in a similar situation, when he tore his hair, struck himself on the forehead, sighed, and wept because he felt that he was being torn apart. The reference, naturally, is to St. Augustine's own description of his conversion, as recorded in his Confessions.[9] Petrarch remarks that when he reads Augustine's account of being caught between two contrary feelings (inter duos contrarios affectus)[10] he does not experience it as someone else's, but as his own story.

Of course, this prompts the question as to what sort of division is actually under discussion, as well as the question as to how to overcome it. Is it a contest between the soul and the body, or perhaps between the reason and the physical appetites? Or is it an inner psychological struggle between love and hate, hope and fear, in which it would be meaningless to term one sort of feeling "spiritual" and the other "carnal", since both of these affects, that is, feelings, make their demands upon the entire man? It would probably be impossible to answer these questions unambiguously as far as either Augustine or Petrarch is concerned.

Nevertheless, it seems to be the case that the historical St. Augustine chose the first solution. This emerges from, for example, De trinitate, Book XII, in which he distinguishes between that which we have in common with the animals, and that which is proper to man. The latter consists of man's reason, the "eternal bases" of which allow us to assign all things to their proper place. Like so much in the Augustinian worldview, the Neoplatonic contrast between the highest form

of being (God/the One) and the material world forms the
background. In Book XII we also find an interpretation
of the narrative of the Fall which has become quite no-
torious, thanks to the modern discussion of women's liberation. Augustine rules that the account in which the
woman lures her husband into eating the forbidden fruit
of the Garden of Eden is in reality an allegory, the
point of which is to show how the body and temporal
reason captivate the spirit. On the other hand, against
the Platonists and the Manicheans Augustine also claims
that sin not only abides in the body, but also in the
soul.

Petrarch's position is much more ambivalent than is
Augustine's. He attempts a number of times in the Secretum to convince himself that the right way out of the
morass lies in meditation, which will permit the soul
to gather its thoughts and so to free itself of the
burden of the body and its earthbound tendencies. At
the same time, Petrarch's dilemma is also depicted as
a battle within the soul, as one in which the soul is
assaulted by fantasies and various self-contradictory
longings, so that it no longer knows just what it is
to reject and what to support. A sort of paralysis sets
in, as "when many plants are sown in a little bed: they
hinder each other's growth".[11] The soul is possessed by
anger and confusion with itself. In Book II of the Secretum, St. Augustine offers a diagnosis of accidia or
melancholy. The psychological consequence of the inner
struggle of the soul, in which one's internal contradictions counterbalance one another, is dullness, accidia. None of the plants of the soul (that is, the feelings) is able to grow. One loses interest in everything.
This self-destructive equilibrium is compared with the
golden mean of Horace, but neither Augustine nor Pet-

rarch can see anything golden about it. In his treatise entitled "On the Solitary Life" (De vita solitaria), Petrarch allows this criticism to apply especially to city dwellers, whose lives contain many different influences and interruptions.

How, then, does one combat this weakness of accidia? If it is man's spirit which is attacked and weakened by temporal concerns, then it is necessary to strengthen the spirit, which is a natural result of meditation. In this fashion it is possible to put some distance between one's self and the temporal world by directing one's attention to life's vanity and the approach of death. This allows one freely to meditate on the noncorporeal and eternal truths; it is that state in which man's will, love, and affects are erased during the mystical union or communion with the divine. In his Confessions, the historical Augustine provides a description of such an experience which he underwent together with his mother.[12]

This view also recurs in Petrarch's work, but he also advocates another approach, namely, the rhetorical one. As an Augustinian, Petrarch advocates the silence of meditation, but as a rhetorician he is an advocate of speech. A goodly part of Petrarch's authorship insists that the difficulties of the soul can be combated with the aid of rhetoric, that is, language, since on his view language is capable of penetrating into the soul and of bringing order to the chaos which reigns there. In the technical terminology of the rhetorician, this effect of the word on man is called faith. And, as Petrarch maintains, it is only the word about God's love and omnipotence which is able to create that faith which is capable of expelling the divisions caused by doubt and anxiety.[13] Now, faith and virtue are matters pertaining to the orator rather than the philosopher. This view is especially prominent in the Petrarchan treatises, De studie eloquentiae (On the Study of Eloquence) and De remediis utriusque (Remedies Against One Thing and Another). The whole of Petrarch's authorship reveals a deep division between the vita solitaria or contemplativa (the solitary or meditative existence) and the vita activa (the active life, that is, a social existence), which is brought about through speech and language, and which reaches its zenith with the aid of eloquence.[14]

On the latter issue Petrarch and St. Augustine went their separate ways, as Augustine, a sometime teacher of rhetoric, would not accord such significance to eloquence.[15]

Thus the concept of accidia had two meanings for Petrarch. In one sense it was a sort of dullness caused by the weakening of the spirit by worldly desire. The other variety was a kind of tension which may superficially resemble dullness, but which in reality is the earmark of an individual who is on the verge of an explosion. The appearance of dullness is the result of the equal balance of opposing forces. In psychological terms Petrarch has two completely different explanations of the problem of boredom and dullness. These arise contingent upon whether one embraces the tripartite view of man or the unitary view which predominated during the Renaissance.[16]

The emergence of the phenomenon of melancholia during the Renaissance also indicates a second feature of this period. Scholars revived the ancient teaching about the four humors, that is, about man as determined by the relationships obtaining among four fluids (called humores). Ideally, these quantities should be bal-

anced in relation to one another, which explains the
term humor, a derivative of the word for liquid (humor),
which was extended so as to apply to the balance among
the humors.[17] To possess "humor" is in fact to be in
equilibrium, and thus to be able to see things in their
proper proportions. As a rule, however, the humors were
not thought to be in balance; one or another of them
is usually dominant. If the one in question is choler,
or yellow bile, the result is irritable and excitable
temperament (choleric). Choler is related to fire and
the dryness of summer. On the other hand, if phlegm(a)
(mucous) is the dominant humor, then one is characterized by what is cold, moist, and dull, to which old age
and winter correspond. Then again, blood stands for
moist warmth and is connected with spring, fresh air,
and youth. Finally, the black humor (melancholer) is
associated with autumn and middle age. It is the last-
named of these which is interesting for our purposes.

It is clear that these concepts relate psychology
(in the form of the teaching about the four humors) to
physics, which included the theory of the four elements
and the seasons of the year (and accordingly also astronomy and astrology). Moreover, these concepts also had
room for man's biological development through the various stages of his life. It was the passionate concern
of the Renaissance to attempt to combine the different
sciences into a unity. Thus, while astrology was on the
one hand a description of the organization of the stars,
it was also held to have psychological and ethical consequences. Numerology, the development of which was
frequently prompted by the newly achieved knowledge of
Jewish Kabbalism, sometimes figured as a connective el-
ement among the sciences, that is, as a common language
capable of combining many different insights into an

organic unity. As such, it was the forerunner of the
use of mathematics in the modern natural sciences. Alchemy is yet another example of this confluence of material, psychological, and spiritual approaches to reality. On the periphery of these phenomena were magic and
witchcraft. The common goal of these efforts was to
break down the distinction between the physical and the
spiritual worlds. As a result, man and his will were
transformed into a function of the influences of a variety of foreign factors and powers which had dominion
over him.

This is especially clear in the very fact that the
concept of melancholia came to replace that of accidia,
as is well illustrated in Petrarch's psychological re-
flections. By nature, melancholia is an intermediate
state. Just as the autumn is the transition between
summer and winter, the black humor is situated between
the volatile yellow bile and the motionless phlegma.
It is precisely in transitional situations that it becomes most painfully clear that man is subject to foreign influences. Painful, beacuse we have to do with
the division, or indeed with the rending apart of the
individual, who is the prey of numerous competing powers. Recognized as a universal phenomenon, during the
Renaissance this was held to be especially characteristic of the artist. The old theory according to which
the poet was a sort of vessal (lat. vas, which made
possible the pun on lat. vates, poet or fortuneteller)
was revived; according to this theory the poet had first
to be filled with inspiration in order to be able to
create.[18] Since melancholy both clearly and painfully
reveals that the individual is the victum of powers and
influences over which he has no control, it is not remarkable that on Renaissance theory melancholy was de-

signated as the earmark of the artist. It was a specifically artistic temperament. During the late Middle
Ages melancholia was associated with the planet Saturn,
which was then thought to be cold, bitter, and black;
its purported influence was to "freeze" things in opposition to each other. Thus the soul is both dull and
stupid, while at the same time possessing the ability
to gain knowledge and to contemplate. Both the anxious
and frightening paralysis (Petrarch: perplexitas) and
the liberating divine inspiration were thought to derive from Saturn. Particularly Marsiglio Ficino and the
Platonic Academy in Florence thoroughly explored this
ambivalence in their studies of "melancholia genero-
sa".[19] The dimensions of the concept may be illustrated
by an examination of Albrecht Dürer's engraving, Melen-
colia I (1514), which adorns the dust jacket of this
book. In terms of iconographical history, Dürer's engraving is part of a lengthy tradition of the Middle
Ages which was concerned with the illustration of accidia, dullness. The usual motif is that of a dull or
sleeping woman at her spinning wheel, while the background usually contains a man sleeping at a bench. Dürer, however, has replaced the latter by a putto, that
is, a little boy, who is sitting and writing energetically on a tablet. Nor is the woman dull or bored, as
can be seen from her eyes. In fact, as personified by
the woman, Dürer's Melencholia is wide awake; her pierc-
ing glare reveals an intense, incisive, but nevertheless vain searching. She is not inactive because she is
lazy, but because her work has become meaningless to
her. Her energies have not become paralyzed by sleep,
but by her imagination.[20] In the foreground a variety
of tools and instruments are strewn around which have
to do with geometrical tasks, or with practical artisan-

ship. However, there is no order among them, and the
woman is unable to use them for anything. The little
hyperactive child in the background exemplifies the absurdity of sitting and scribbling without having anything to communicate. On Panovsky's view, the implication is that theoretical knowledge, as represented by
the woman, and practical ability, symbolized by the
child, have no contact with one another. Note that the
woman also possesses both keys and a purse, that is,
the traditional symbols of power and wealth, respectively; but she has no pleasure in them, since the keys
are disordered and the purse drags on the ground.

For reasons of space, it will not be possible to
study Dürer's illustration in greater depth, so it must
suffice to refer to Panofsky's detailed study. Panofsky
investigates the picture in terms of its historical
context, the basis of which was the Florentine Platonism whose chief exponent was Marsiglio Ficino, and which
had undertaken the new analysis of the nature of melancholy in the decades prior to the composition of the
picture.

Here we have a combination of the Aristotelian idea
according to which all exceptional men are melancholics
with the Platonic notion of divine madness, mania. Fur-
or melancholicus is held to be equal to furor divinus.
Thus the notion of the poet as an inspired seer, which
had emerged early in the Renaissance,[21] receives yet
another nuance, and in the process becomes accomodated
to the new times. As it was said, "Melancholia signi-
fica ingegno", that is, melancholy signifies creative
genius.[22] As Robert Burton, the greatest Renaissance
student of melancholy, noted in his book The Anatomy
of Melancholy (1621),[23] melancholy is not just a temperament alongside of the other three. It is also a con-

dition to which every man may temporarily succumb. At
the same time, it is a phenomenon which one most frequently experiences when confronted with divine inspiration. The Saturnian melancholy or theology has two
sides to its concept of the divine: Saturn is both the
evil and the good planet. It is both that which drives
man to despare, and that which saves him from it. Therefore real insight is both heavy and painful, but also
joyful and exalting:

> A thousand pleasures do me bless
> And crown my soul with happiness
> All my joys besides are folly
> Non so sweet as Melancholy.
>
> Doleful outcries, and fearly sights,
> My sad and dismal soul affrights.
> All my griefs to this are jolly,
> None so damn'd as Melancholy.[24]

In other words, the acquisition of knowledge is no easy
matter. To say that the process was "dialectical" would
probably be inadequate, for the Renaissance concept entails that one is so filled with contradictions that
one risks being exploded by them. Both anxiety and confusion accompany the sweet pleasure.

We may conclude that completely different psychologies underlie accidia and melancholia. The former is
a sort of dull-ness which seizes the individual who
is understood to be in possession of both powers and
will, while the latter attacks the individual who is
more like a mirror. A mirror is only able to reflect
whatever presents itself to it; thus, if several things
present themselves at the same time, the resulting image

becomes self-contradictory - or melancholic.

Now, if melancholy was a central concept of the psychology of the period in question, the question is what sort of theology of the relationship between God and man could emerge against this background? I think the answer to this may be summarized in three points. First, such a theology had to regard man as dependent on external forces. Thus Milton can say, "Thy rapt soul sitting in your eyes",[25] where "rapt" signifies captured. Man as seen from the vantagepoint of rhetoric and melancholy was in a hazardous situation. For this reason, faith, confidence, and trust (gradations of _fides_) stand for a central concept. Second, the individual who has encountered the divine must be divided, torn apart. Third, man was the field upon which mutually hostile powers waged their combats - after all, it is just such combats that were held to be the nature of melancholy. In the subsequent chapters, we shall try to determine whether these features also characterize Luther's theology.

By way of conclusion, it would be appropriate to ask as to whether the psychology of melancholy of the period could provide a general theory for theological reflection. If this psychology really was typical of the time, should we not expect that it would be determinative for the actions and mental states of the people of the period? For example, should we not expect that Luther would personally behave in a characteristically melancholy fashion?

Well, actually yes, so he should, and in fact, so he does: "I hate life, as being something evil. I fear death, and lack all faith; but I have many other gifts which, as Christ only knows, I care only very little about, if I am not able to serve him ..."[26] This remark

dates from 1519, that is, long after he is supposed to
have experienced his reformatory breakthrough in the
years 1511-1516. Nevertheless, this is a mental state
and a way of life which Luther retained throughout his
life, as a wealth of evidence assures us. Thus the basic structure of Christian existence is apparently melancholic. In spite of this the actual crises in Luther's
biography are nevertheless quite striking, when we note
the connection with melancholy. Both Luther and the men
of his times emphasized that the decisive breakthroughs
originated in deep crises. In Luther's career there were
two such transitional periods. The first occurred when
Luther was caught by a violent thunderstorm and fright-
ened by lightening, as a result of which he promised
the holy St. Anne that he would enter a monastery. However, this lightningbolt did not break from an open sky,
since Luther had suffered for some time of tentatio
tristitiae, "the temptation of sadness", which was by
no means unusual among the leading spirits of his day.
Unfortunately, the cloistered life did not avail much,
as it was in the monastery that he experienced confusion (turba, turbatio), anxiety (angustia), and a sadness (tristitia) which paralyzed him. Indeed, he was
so stunned that he was unable even to cry out, "Help,
O Lord!"[27] In his commentary on the Letter to the Romans
(specifically on 9,33) Luther discusses that confusion
which seizes the soul after the encounter with the Word
of God. Presumably some personal experience underlay
Luther's remarks. All this was brought about by the encounter with the Word of Christ, and, as he says, only
it could release him from his anxiety again.[28] Luther's
struggle in the monastery consisted in, on the one hand,
the necessity to accept the justice of genuine repentance, and on the other hand, his inability to live up

to this demand. This is precisely the situation of the typical melancholic of the Renaissance.

5. Luther's Understanding of Faith

Up to this point we have examined in various ways how an anthropology which divides human nature up into reason, feeling, and sensuality is replaced by a view which regards human nature as indivisible. I have mentioned a number of reasons for this fact, among which I emphasized rhetoric as being important. We further noted that Luther shared the interest of his comtemporaries for rhetoric, and that this interest came to expression in his own work.

Thus in what follows we shall take a decisive step and investigate the extent to which this rhetorical-anthropological horizon determines Luther's very theology; in this connexion it would be appropriate to begin with his understanding of faith.

As mentioned above, Klaus Dockhorn has pointed to a number of correspondences between Luther's description of the speech of the Holy Spirit and Quintillian's account of the task of rhetoric. These resemblances are so striking that Dockhorn characterizes them as "fast bestürzend".[1] Accordingly, it is our intention here to examine the extent to which Luther's theological breakthrough can be traced back to this rhetorical framework.

In contemporary communications research it is a commonplace to employ a metaphor presumably deriving from the jargon of radio to explain what happens in the course of human communication. Thus one refers to a transmitter, a text, and a receiver.[2] Among the presuppositions of successful communication one would expect to find that the transmitter and receiver are on the same "wavelength", and that there is no disturbing "static" which could prevent the message from being received. The receiver may not have built-in "filters" in it, for example in the form of lack of ability, prejudice, antipathy, dullness, interest in other subjects, or the like; in short, things which would prevent him from being a good "receiver". The radiophonic model is reasonably applicable to rhetoric, in that there is both a transmitter and a receiver between which a message is communicated. But the analogy is to some extent also inexact, since it emphasizes all the difficulties standing in the way of successful communication. In rhetoric one does not concentrate primarily on removing impediments in the various phases of communication; rather, one attempts to make the message so powerful that it defies all resistance and makes itself heard by the listener. This is not because the listener's presuppositions or interests, i.e. his "filters", are without significance; both the speech and the speaker must on the contrary make allowances for these factors. Nevertheless, rhetoric enjoys such confidence in its facility and its power that it presumes it is also able to change or remove obstructive "filters". In what follows we shall attempt to transfer the rhetorical method of communication to the relationship between God and man.

The Transmitter - God

Let us begin at the beginning, with the transmitter. Already at this point it appears that rhetoric modifies the contemporary "radio" model of communication. On one hand, people tend to emphasize the importance of the transmitter. On the middle style level, that of ethos, it is important to make the listeners comfortable and well disposed, so that they conceive sympathy for the goals of the speaker. This sympathy, however, can not

be detached from sympathy for the person of the speaker.
If one dislikes the speaker or author, one also dislikes what he has to say. Thus sympathy for the subject
must also apply to the person. Something similar is also true of the highest level of style, pathos. Here,
too, the speaker is also a part of the picture. How can
I make someone weep, says Quintillian, if I myself am
unable to do so? One is only able to mediate the understanding and feelings one possesses oneself.

Nevertheless, one could also claim that the author/
speaker is not present, since in some sense he is not
an independent reality who exists outside of or parallel to his account. The audience conceives sympathy
for the speaker, not as he is in himself, but as he appears in his message. It may well be that they are moved or swayed by him, but this takes place through the
medium of his words. Thus in some sense the speaker does not exist outside of his speech. One could perhaps
to this object that the audience may have heard of the
speaker previously; they will perhaps have heard about
him or even have heard him on a previous occasion. However, it is the speaker's task to presuppose this earlier familiarity, and to work it into his current effort, if he is familiar with it, in such a way that it
becomes either implicitly or explicitly a part of what
he is trying to say. A politician who advocates a particular case must be prepared for the fact that people
evaluate him independently of the matter in hand, or,
in short, on the basis of what he otherwise has said
or represented. If he does not take account of this
factor in his communication, people will be suspicious
of him, that is, if they are able to recall his views
in other cases.

These considerations are also applicable to the new

Testamental account of God. Believers were familiar
with him from the Old Testament, so that when he decided to reveal new aspects of himself in the New Testament by begetting his son Jesus, he was forced to include the old presuppositions in his declaration of the
new era: "You have heard that it was said to the men
of old ... but I say to you (Mt 5:21-22, 33-34) ..."
From now on, he is a different God than the one they had
previously known. In this way the New Testament is included in the Old. In this fashion the transmitter is
identified as "transmitter" both formally and in terms
of content by his message. Thus even though we know the
speaker because of earlier experience, in the last analysis it is through his words we know and understand
him.

This is the rhetorical insight employed by Luther
when he identifies God to an extraordinary degree with
his Word. The Word is thus "ein ewiger Gott und nicht
ein Creatur" ("an eternal God and not a created creature").[3] Luther attempts by a variety of expressions to
make explicit the fact that though both words and
speeches are different quantities, yet in a sense they
are the same, since it is through the Word that we know
God. This is a typically rhetorical way of understanding the matter; God's "Word" is not understood as some
cryptic speech or phenomenon different from human
"words"; rather, it is the same "word" which we encounter in ordinary life. Without this, the Holy Spirit would
not be the greatest Rhetor;[4] to be a great speaker is
in fact to speak in such a way that one's words do not
go over the heads of one's audience.

The Word as the Source of Understanding
The word is thus ordinary human speech, and it is in
the latter that meaning is to be found. During the Re

naissance it was a widely held opinion that one could
not convey understanding or awareness to others unless
one's message was phrased in words. Meaning and words
belong together as a matter of course in rhetorical activity, which in fact uses words precisely to attain
understanding and new insight. Thus words are not trivialities which one must cast off in order to arrive
at more profitable pathways to awareness and communication. The word is not an "empty wind or shell; it
brings its entire divine nature along with it."[5] In
other words, Luther does not distinguish between the
subject itself and the word as a derived designation
for it, so that the word merely "signifies" that which
is spoken about. The fact that subject and language belong together is an obvious presupposition of rhetorical activity,[6] just as it is through the word one arrives at understanding and linguistic insight.[7]

    This point of departure, is by no means obvious if
one examines the theological and philosophical currents
of antiquity and the Middle Ages. In these epochs, language was not without more ado accorded this ability
to create awareness; on the contrary, scholars held
that actual understanding was not achieved by means of
language, which is limited by time and space, because,
among other things it is an auditory phenomenon. Thomas
Aquinas (died in 1274) and most of the scholars of the
Middle Ages did not feel that we achieve knowledge by
means of our words, but by means of our concepts, which
are timeless and universal. Scholars agreed with Plato
that it was a struggle for man to arrive at universal
knowledge, and that, moreover, language was not only
useless to this end, it was also to a great extent an
obstacle to this achievement because of its temporality
and imperfection. Thomas asserted that man's use of

writing was an important step in his attempts to detach
himself from language.[8] It would be yet another step
to create a sort of "mathematical language" (mathesis
logos), which could avoid all of language's imprecision
because of its clear depth structure. A purified language such as that of logic was thought to be suitable
to formulate and make explicit, while natural language
was destined to be handicapped by ambiguity. Occam (d.
in 1347) mentions as an example the fact that "fire"
is able to designate the pain of a sick patient and the
inner warmth of happiness. Behind all of the meanings
of "fire" lies the actual concept of fire; but we understand this concept directly without the use of language.[9]
Thus, according to Occam, understanding is a presupposition for the use of language, and not the reverse.

Thus intuition, i.e. direct awareness, was thought
to be the most important by most of the scholars of the
Middle Ages. The same idea can be more explicitly the-
ologically formulated with the aid of the Holy Spirit.
St. Augustine (d. in 431) inquires as to what happens
when the Word of God is proclaimed to us; the fact that
we hear the words is clearly not the same as understanding what they are about. If the Holy Spirit fails at
the same time to illuminate our hearts, then we understand nothing. Thus the Christian message is only mediated linguistically in a secondary sense. Augustine argues for this idea in his De magistro, in which he describes language as the process of finding designations
for something with which we are familiar in advance.
We cannot speak of what we do not know; for this reason
it is impossible to know the Christian message as it
is proclaimed in human words if we do not somehow previously already know what it is about. This foreknowledge must come from the Holy Spirit. Here Augustine

is indebted to a line of thought that goes all the way
back to Plato, though with the decisive difference that
for Plato knowledge was something one achieved through
"recollection", where for Augustine this function is
assigned to the Holy Spirit.

This notion of reduplicated communication is also
to be found in Thomas, who held that the Holy Spirit
accompanies human speech to make it intelligible. One
understands language via audition, but meaning arises
with the aid of the Spirit. Naturally, Thomas regarded
this "inner" type of communication as the more important.

Some scholars went even further and not only held
the spiritual communication to be the more important
of the two, but also to be the only type. This consequence was frequently drawn by the mystics, who in fact
operated with a concept of entirely wordless communication: the inner unity of the spirit with God, which
made superfluous any external linguistic/auditory communication alongside of it. The mystics often asserted
the idea of direct spiritual communication outside of
the realm of language. In this discussion, the "Word"
of God is to be taken as a sort of metaphor: it was not
the audible word, but something quite different, namely, the supernatural, supersensual, and superlinguistic
reality, which could only be apprehended directly with
the help of the spirit.

We shall return later on to this type of distrust
of external language, when we examine various views on
the understanding of Scripture. For our present purposes, it will suffice to conclude that whether one af-
firmed the radical mysterical concept of the form of
communication or chose the more common view of the philosophy and theology of the Middle ages, according to

which there are two different types of communication, in either case one was prone to distinguish between hearing and understanding. The latter was thought to be inexpressible in language; it could only be apprehended internally.

On this last point a completely different point of view came to expression in Renaissance humanism. According to this view, there is no legitimate distinction between hearing and understanding, or, in other words, language comprehends meaning, which thus has no other channel than the word as its medium. It was a recurrent theme from Petrarch (d. in 1374) to Erasmus (d. in 1536) to attack the Scholastic-theological use of language. The humanists seemingly never tired of ridiculing the philosophical language developed by the Scholastics during the Middle Ages, and which still enjoyed prominence in the universities and other institutions of higher learning. It would be a mistake to suppose, or so the humanists argued, that one could eliminate the alleged imperfections of ordinary language with words like quidditas ("whatness") or haeceitas ("thisness" - unique individuality); rather, one merely wrapped oneself in darkness with such homemade designations. They further held that words always lead back to the things themselves, while abstractions lead away from them. This is one of the fundamental insights of rethoric. Abstraction was allowed, but they held that is must take place in full awareness of the fact that its foundation was always the thing (res), which we know through our natural language.[10] Thus Erasmus writes in his In Praise of Folly,

> There are countless varieties of this sort of sophistry (among the theologians), some of which are even more subtle, concerning instances, concepts, relations, formalities, essences and na-

tures, none of which can be seen with the naked
eye, not even Lynkeus, who is supposed to be able
to see something in the darkest darkness that is
not there."[11]

This ridicule constitutes a rejection of the notion that
reality is structured in a way that does not come to
expression in natural languages, or, in other words,
the idea that there is a difference between language
and knowledge.

"Oralness"

This congruence between language and knowledge is a
consequence of the presupposition that to hear is the
same as to understand. The latter insight is concealed
in the fact that speech is an oral operation which in-
volves both the speaker and his listener in a fellowship out of which understanding arises. Rhetoric in
fact insists on the characteristic aspects of language
as that which is heard and spoken. The use of writing
is only to fix that which is oral: "In the nature of
things, written language merely corresponds to musical
notation, and has only the designative value of notes."
(Vilhelm Grønbech).[12] Or, as it was formulated in antiquity, written language is "sermo absentis ad absentum"
- the speech of an absent speaker to an equally absent
listener.

It would exceed our purposes here to demonstrate the
extent to which all of the fundamental concepts of rhetoric presuppose oral communication, so I shall instead
merely call attention to some specific points. The dispositio concept is primarily a concept of rhythm. The
contents of a speech have to be correctly proportioned,
i.e. so that the individual sections succeed each other
in such a way that the contents are correctly understood. Understanding is accordingly contingent on time.

The rhetorical term for "style" is elocutio (from
eloquor, to speak), which also takes its point of departure in the oral and audible. Following elocutio,
one makes use of a number of figures which are princip-
ally aural, such as alliteration, assonation, and so
forth; the same word may be repeated (anaphora), or one
may change the usual sequence of words. Rhyme proper
is usually reserved for poetry. An important part of
a well-constructed lecture is that the sentences conclude correctly; in fact, use of the right clausulae
(conclusions) is a science in itself. It is not merely
a question of whether the last syllable is to have mas-
culine or feminine closure, but also whether the last
syllables are to be accomodated to a particular metre
(anapaest, trochee, etc.). Moreover, such features as
stress, resonance, gesture and so on are also to be
considered. In short, understanding is held to be contingent on acoustical features. Finally, we should also
consider the concept of memoria, according to which a
speech is not to be read aloud, but recited by heart.
The underlying assumption is that the speech is to be
a part of the speaker (or author, with reference to our
previous discussions of the idea that the author is
"included" in his message). In our society we are most
familiar with the phenomenon from theatrical actors
who, in order to be able to interpret a text, have to
know it by heart. Thus the listener's understanding is
predicated on the assumption that the message is contingent on the speaker by reason of its oral character.

We must stop at this point, although there is naturally a great deal more to be said on this subject. The
oral character of communication is a pronounced feature
of the humanistic endeavour, a notion which encompasses
written materials which were written from their incept-

ion and were never intended to be communicated in other
form. Even here theorists insisted on keeping to the
strictures of oral rhetoric; moreover, and more important for our purposes, the humanists maintained that
whatever we write is ultimately aimed at a particular
audience. Accordingly, they often termed their various
treatises "oratio" ("speech": some of them were in
fact publically delivered at one point or another), and
practically all of their works are formally addressed
to a particular individual, or are conceived as contributions to a particular discussion. It is not always
possible in literature to maintain the fiction of an
audience, so in this event the humanists usually inter-
jected a fictive audience to whom the poet speaks.[13]
In short, orality requires that an expression is always
said by someone to someone.Thus the implication is that
the message, including the written exemplar of the
spoken/heard word, itself contains both message and
meaning; one may not seek "behind" the text or seek re-
course to a "languageless" understanding, perhaps communicated by the Holy Spirit. No distinction was made
between hearing and understanding.

   This discovery had profound consequences for the understanding of Scripture. It became a recurrent theme
of Renaissance humanism from Boccaccio to Erasmus[14]
that the Bible itself is an oratio, a sermo, which is
delivered by the greatest orator of all, namely God
himself. Thus scholars began to pay attention to the
Biblical narrative styles, which were regarded as the
highest form of rhetoric: the perfect historical narratives, the poetic language (the prophets, too, were
characterized as poets), the lovely poetical use of metaphor, of which Jesus' parables were naturally held
to be the finest examples. The Lord was thought to be

able to express himself so clearly by means of his sublime facility of expression and his unswerving sense
of style that his message could not fail to affect the
human heart.[15] Meaning was found in the words themselves
and not behind the text, from which one previously had
had to salvage meaning by symbolic interpretation. The
external expression was thought to be sufficient and
clear; God said what there was to be said.[16] This point
of view brought about a theological revolution, since
Thomas and Duns Scotus, the masters of Scholasticism,
and their spiritual father, Aristotle, no longer provided hermeneutical assistance. Instead one was obliged
to learn from poets like Vergil, or writers like Quintillian, who understood poetry and rhetoric.

We shall return to the explicit consequences of this
revolution in connection with Luther's understanding of
Scripture in subsequent chapters. We shall here be concerned with another matter, namely the fact that in his
theology he so strongly emphasizes the meaning of the
word. Luther goes on from a new understanding of the
nature of language to a new theology, and one wonders
why this fact has not previously been seen, within the
framework to which it is appropriate, that of rhetorical humanism.

According to Luther, "the Church is a mouth-well,
not an inkwell".[17] The expression contains two aspects:
first, that there is no preaching that is not mediated
by language. As we have noted, we shall return to this
shortly. Secondly, man is characterized as receptive;
to Luther this means that we understand that we are sin-
ners through the word of God, and that we understand
who He is (the forgiving and saving God) via the same
medium. These types of understanding are presupposed
by Luther as something given, a notion of central im-

portance to him. In an analysis of Luther's concept of
audire (to hear), Wilfried Joest has shown how Luther
opposes hearing to iudicare (to judge and evaluate):
man is not able to arrive at the truth via his own powers of evaluation and judgement (iudicare), but only
by hearing the word of God. Man himself is namely a li-
ar and sinner. As Joest also demonstrates, there is also an opposition between audire and videre (to see);
Luther understands vision as if man is more readily
able to pretend to himself that he is lord over what
he wills himself to see.[18] To Luther, "sight" implies
an active contribution from man's side; for this reason
he is able to compare sight with "comprehension". The
same idea recurs in his writing on the two "regiments",
in which he terms the spiritual regiment a "kingdom
of hearing", as being the situation in which one receives the grace of God through the proclamation of the
Gospel, whereas he calls the wordly regiment a "kingdom
of vision", both because in it one encounters visual,
material things, and because man has an active role in
it. However, according to Luther, the latter is only
partly true, since also the wordly kingdom imposes certain external restrictions on man ("regulations").

The oral and aural character of all speech that man
is able to understand is powerfully expressed in Luther's view of the Incarnation: the Word is made flesh,
the Son of God has become man. Or, to put it in our
terms: the Word has become sound. This idea distinguishes Luther in comparison with, for example, the mystics, who, however much Luther was opposed to them (and
especially the German variety), did not take the Incarnation seriously. Thus Luther warns severely against
the idea of the "naked God" (Deus nudus), i.e. a God
who is directly knowable by the spirit, rather than by

his incarnate and crucified Son, Christ. This for Luther was as if all communication between God and man took place with the aid of a "verbum increatum" (the un-created word), the direct, intuitive speech of the Spirit to man. God only communicates himself to man via the incarnate word, which, again, to Luther was an auditory phenomenon. Thus one arrives at the truth "by hearing and believing the audible word (verbum vocale) and by desiring to know nothing except Christ, and him crucified."[19]

Another aspect of this emphasis on hearing and the spoken word is to be found in the nature of the communication itself (which in an extended sense is dependant on the understanding of man presupposed by rhetorical communication). The relationship between God and man is like that which obtains between speaker and listener (Tu esto auditor et ego ero predicator): "You shall be the listener, and I will be the proclaimer,"[20] which is how Luther paraphrases and makes explicit the thought underlying Ps. 81,9: "Hear, O my people, and I will witness for you." Here, as Luther puts it, the word of God,

> "is only understood by hearing and is believed in faith, since it can not be apprehended in any other way, neither through the senses, nor through reason; In the same way the Gospel can not be understood by any other faculty than that of hearing."[21]

Reception of the Word is thus no Socratic situation in which language and conversation play midwife to some knowledge already deeply buried in man. The listener is the object of an announcement; he receives something he did not previously possess. Luther is not encumbered

by any sort of "idealistic" anthropology, and the notion
that every man possesses a fundamentally ethical or divine awareness is extremely remote in his works.[22] Modern Luther scholarship, which has been inspired by dialectical theology, has generally been aware of this, but
it is unfortunate that scholars have tended to emphasize the command as the place where God encounters man.
In Denmark the Tidehvervs-movement has been especially
preoccupied with the "command" concept, also in connexion with Luther; the important thing is to "stand at
attention for the Gospel" (N.O. Jensen in "Luther's Guds-
tro"). This model of military discipline has something
to it, at least to the extent that it stresses the importance of God's word as the source of understanding.
Moreover, linguistically considered it is no accident
that one "hears" a command.

Nevertheless, this view is too confining, since
language has more ways of influencing man and capturing
him than by commands alone, which are indeed one of the
least subtle of the forms of language. This view implicitly underrates the power of language, which is
able to convince, persuade, threaten, cajole, comfort,
disquiet, and so forth, in addition to merely giving
commands. The reason dialectical theology has been so
reluctant to use other modes of speech than that of
command is that scholars have erected a very sharp distinction between theology and psychology. As far as
Luther is concerned, scholars have followed in the foot-
steps of Emil Brunner by asserting that it is "the clear
witness of the Reformation" that God is only apprehended by faith "against all experience which, as our experience, is always and at every point riddled with
worthlessness and Godlessness."[23] Similarly, as Gogart-
en says, "To believe in God is the opposite of experi-

encing God."24 The idea that faith has no "Anknüpfungs-
punkt" to human existence and accordingly can not be
described in psychological categories - if these have
any reality at all - is a commonplace of dialectical
theology. This is easier to maintain if one limits the
word to the category of command, for then it is a simple
matter to concentrate on what happens on God's side,
and to ignore what occurs on the human side. This last
is not perhaps completely true, in the sense that the
meaning of a command is presumably that it is to be ob-
eyed. However, this does not occur in the forum of the
God-man relationship, since man is disobedient and thus
as a sinner is totally subject to the judgement of God;
however, when God reveals himself to be both loving and
forgiving, the result is ultimately fortunate.

Within this framework of thought, it is not possible
to discuss how man experiences this situation, or indeed, to discuss such concepts as "experience" at all.
In a strict sense, the concept of "faith" also becomes
meaningless in this context. Can one require someone
to believe? Not, at least, according to ordinary language. Thus, in the scheme of dialectical theology the
concept of faith is on the verge of absurdity and mean-
inglessness, a fact dialectical theologians often acknowledge with satisfaction. For Luther, however, the
concept of faith was quite meaningful, and to achieve
an understanding of his thought in this respect we shall
move on to the last stage in our communications model:
we have dealt with the transmitter and the message; it
is now time to examine the receiver.

What it means to believe
"Faith in God's work in us, which transforms us and
gives birth to us anew (Joh. 1) and kills the old Adam

and makes us new men in our hearts, minds, thoughts,
and powers and bestows the Holy Spirit upon us. Indeed,
faith is so living, creating, effective, and powerful
a thing that it is impossible that it should not achieve
something good for ever."[25]

This quotation from Luther's introduction to the
Epistle to the Romans expresses one of his most central
ideas: that faith is not something achieved by man; it
is dependent upon God. This is often difficult for contemporary man to understand. Is faith, then, not something man accomplishes, i.e. is it not his response to
God's address? Priests and Christian laymen are often
confronted with the statement that "I am unable to believe" or "that ability has nt been given me". Similarly, many regret that they have lost the faith of their
childhood and are unable to regain it. Several years
ago a danish commission concluded that the teaching of
religion in Danish schools should seek to strengthen
the "religous tendencies" of children. In short, children seem to have, or are supposed to have a religious
capacity (perhaps in varying degrees) which can be
trained and learned like other abilities. The scholastic theology of the Middle Ages followed   similar
pathways; for example, Thomas Aquinas called faith a
habitus, i.e. a capacity of man which is made possible
after the individual has received divine grace. But even
prior to this the individual is not wholly unprepared,
since he possesses a fides informis ("unformed faith")
which makes up man's predisposition to receive faith.
Both sorts of faith are a habitus, by which Thomas
means something inherent to human structure (psychology). Thus faith develops as an ability of both the
will and the intellect.[26]

Luther objected strenuously against this idea, since

he felt that the scholastic theologians had reduced
faith to a habitus, even though the whole of Scripture
gives no other name to faith than that of a work of
God.[27] In fact, it is important to Luther to demonstrate
that man has no presuppositions for faith other than
those he receives from God, and Luther's motive for so
arguing is his desire to set God and man in their proper
relation to each other. The question is, how did Luther
arrive at this position? It is normally assumed that
he did so as a result of theological considerations.
This is entirely possible, but not particularly likely,
since Luther's concept of "faith" resembles that of
"faith" considered as a rhetorical concept. Here, too,
faith, conviction, and feeling are received quantities.
There is nothing peculiar about this, if we recall our
previously-delineated communications model: just as
there is a transmitter, so there is also a receiver.
The receiver is namely the recipient of the knowledge,
experience, or feeling which the transmitter shares
with him. In short, it is an aspect of the structure
of the communication that it does not belong to the receiver, but to the transmitter. In the same sense, faith
is not man's capability, but God's.

In reality we are speaking of something quite simple,
and with which we are familiar, even though our understanding is often obscured by a wrong way of regarding
communication and the human subject. When we use such
words as "believable", "credible", or "charming", we
are not referring to our own ability to believe, or to
have confidence in something, or to care for some thing.
If I say that I find a politician credible, he is the
subject I am talking about, i.e. his comprehensive pro-
gramme or his solid political fieldwork. Whether I am
to believe in anyone, be he a politician or God himself,

it is not my affair, but that of the politician or
God.[28] It is their job to make themselves believable.
For this reason there is "no other name for faith than
that of a work of God"; it could not be otherwise.

The fact that Luther's viewpoint is not founded on
a particularly theological position, but has to do with
ordinary conditions which are based in the human "receiver"'s situation is confirmed by his language concerning faith. Luther speaks of faith as "to experience" (erfahren), "to feel" (fühlen, empfinden),[29] and
"to understand" (intelligere). This can be illustrated
by reference to the most common Latin word for "understanding", sentire. The word is interesting in that it
essentially means to feel, sense, but already in antiquity its semantic field was expanded to include both
"to comprehend", "to acknowledge as a feeling", "evaluation", and "intuition". Thus this word is helpful in
showing how all understanding can be traced back to the
senses, as well as the fact that there is no sharp distinction between understanding and feeling, which is
precisely the most important philosophical and psychological conclusion of the rhetoricians (see above, p.
52). At the same time it is also evident that all of
the things comprehended by the word "sentire" are things
characterizing man as receptive. Man receives his knowledge and his evalutaions from outside, just as he receives a message. In the scholastic way of thinking,
in which the trifurcated active man is emphasized as
depicted in chapter 2, this must - like everything else
in man - be reversed. Sensus becomes something inherent
in man, a potentia, i.e. a power or ability which is
capable of development. Against this notion Luther has
sentire and its derivative, sensus, apply to that "knowledge" according to which one feels above the reception

of God's word. "Sensus proprius": this is that form of
intellectual self-sufficiency which prevents people
from hearing the word of the Gospel. Luther prefers the
term intelligere (to understand) to designate the knowledge one opens oneself to.[30]

To summarize for the moment: faith is something which
is communicated, or rather, it is the result of a communication and not the property of the believer, in the
same sense that everything else he knows is something
he has managed to "hear". But it is possible to say
more than this.

Faith is a sentiment

If we are to follow our communications-theoretical model, one of its logical consequences, however surprising it may sound, is that faith is a feeling. We recall
that there are a number of stylistic modes, among these
being a low one in which we speak of trivial things,
a high one in which we discuss important matters, plus
a medium mode. Natural considerations suggest that the
address of the Gospel to man must take place on the
"pathetic" plane. It would be difficult to imagine a
more significant message. The "understanding" of a pathetic address entails that one is seized by a feeling
appropriate to the message. Thus the mesage of the Gospel that God is infinitely good and loving towards sin-
ners can only be "comprehended" with the aid of love,
confidence, and faith. If the message fails to awaken
these sentiments, it has not been understood, and its
recipient is not aware of the significance and implications of what has been said.[31]

In one sense this must appear to be a natural and
easily grasped way of thinking, and yet at the same time
it conflicts with the distinction between understanding

and feeling that is predominant in Western culture. On
one side we have reason, whose expressions have to do
with reality. Reason is measured by its ability to describe and comprehend an object correctly. On the other
side of the ledger we have the sentiments; these do not
say anything about that reality they apparently describe. An expression such as "this prospect is lovely"
at least in theory says nothing about the view, but a-
bout the person who makes the statement. Thus emotive
statements are not communicative about their contents,
but about their author, who gives information about
himself in his communications.

In rhetoricl psychology, as in Luther's, the situation is reversed, for here the object determines what
the sentiments are all about. Perhaps some sense of this
understanding of feelings can be attained by reference
to the Latin word _affectus_, affect,[32] which of course
also has this nuance in English, Danish, and German.
It is derived from the verb afficere, which actually
means to set something in relation to something else,
to function as a contributory (but not sole) cause.
Therefore when the word is applied to people it is clear
at once that we have to do with a reaction to something
external to man himself. In other words, "this prospect
is lovely" is an expression which pretends to say something about the view and the impression this view - with
some reason - has made on me; it is not just a report
about my private and internal feelings.

Thus sentiments arise from contact, which is also
implied by our words about emotional experience. We
speak of being "moved" or of having our "hearts wrung".
If we take these expressions at face value we can see
that in reality they convey the idea that a sentiment
is a movement which has been brought about by other

movement.[33] "Cor ex motu Spiritus sancti intelligit"
("the heart understands via the motion of the Holy
Spirit").[34] God loves the poor, wretched, and despised,
and "when one recognizes this, one is filled by love
for Him, and then the heart wells over with joy and
beats with delight at his goodness."[35] Or, "Should it
not give us a strong and insuperable confidence that
Christ died for our sakes ...."[36] Luther means here
that it is a simple and natural situation that feelings
are awakened in us by our experiences. Therefore faith
is a psychological reality like any other feeling; indeed, man is in some sense only to be understood as affect, sentiment.

In his commentary to the Epistle to the Romans (to
8:7), his notable work "On Christian Freedom", and in
several other writings, Luther argues powerfully against
the notion that "flesh" and "spirit" designate respectively body and soul. Consider the statement of St. Paul
that "To set the mind on the flesh is death, but to set
the mind on the Spirit is life and peace" (Rom 8,6).
In the early Church and during the Middle Ages this was
most often understood in such a way that the attraction
of the flesh was the same as carnal desire, that is,
the sexual drive, or other physical attractions, while
the spiritual attraction was understood as the soul's
pious worship of God. Luther does not feel this to be
correct. "Flesh" does not for him designate the corporeal, but revolt against God, whether it occurs on the
physical or the spiritual plane, though he considered
the last to be by far the worst. Spirituality meant to
Luther to live one's life in accordance with the Word
of God and to adhere to it. "By 'flesh' is meant the
entire man and by 'spirit' again the entire man; both
the external and the internal man or the old and the

new are not to be separated from each other by means
of a distinction between soul and body, but by means
of the sentiments (sex iuxta affectus)".[37] If one is
directed by belief and confidence in God, one acts in
only one way, namely out of love; if one is steered by
"one's own", then one acts selfishly. Man is thus identical with his feelings. This concept is reminiscent
of St. Augustine's statement that "a man is his love",
with the difference that for Luther affectus is a re-
ceiver-concept, which is to say that affectus is not
characterized as a drive or desire (contra Augustine)
but as an experience that comes to one from Augustine.

However, one might object that all this may very
well be true of feelings for another, but does it also
apply to the selfish feelings - where one's own person
is central? Luther answers in the affirmative, and employs the famous metaphor for the selfish person as one
who is "bent into himself" (incurvatus in se ipsum).[38]
This image may be compared with the Narcissus of Greek
mythology, who fell in love with his own reflection.
In this way sentiment remains determined by its object.

The theological consequence of Luther's psychology
of affect may also be demonstrated in other ways. For
example, in the ancient Church it was regarded as problematical as to which motives provided acceptable
justification for obeying the law. Was love of justice
(amor iustitiae) the only acceptable motive, or could
one also recognize compliance with the law that was motivated by fear of punishment (timor poena)? Augustine
maintained that the latter was also acceptable, and his
view became the dominant attitude during the Middle
Ages. The question recurs in Catholic penetential practice, which presupposes remorse prior to absolution,
the forgiveness of committed sins. In both cases it is

evident that the central ideas are the desire to obey the law and the requirement of repentance, no matter what motivates these actions. It is not the object of the sentiment that is important, but the sentiment itself. What prompts the sentiment is unimportant; the main thing is that one has it.

Luther finds this way of thinking unacceptable. To him the decisive thing is what the cause of one's sentiment is, since to him it is not man's spiritual life that creates the effective state, but its object. Accordingly, Luther sees a significant difference between performing the works of the law out of love of justice or because of fear or the desire to earn one's wages. Rightly considered, according to him, the last-named does not even constitute keeping the law. Thus Luther radicalizes the idea so that true compliance with the law can only occur because of faith. God's love for us is the only relevant and possible basis for our love, and thus of our compliance with the law:

> For if he finds in his heart the assurance that his work is pleasing to God, it is good, even if it is so insignificant as to pick up a straw; on the other hand, if he lacks such assurance or has doubts about it, then the work is not good, even if it consists in awakening the dead and burning himself to death"[39]

Thus whether a feeling is true or false can only be measured on the basis of its cause, and nothing else. The wish to fulfil the law is not good in itself; it can only be accepted if it has the right cause, namely a particular feeling, faith.

The same point can be illustrated if one compares

Luther's point of view with the prescriptions for awakening the sentiments which are to be found in a good deal of mystical literature.[40] According to the mystics, it was possible to learn by means of various meditative practices how to awaken the right sort of feelings. The same notion underlies the so-called "mirrors of confession" which even today are to be found in Catholic catechisms; a long series of sins are listed with the intention of prompting the penitent to recall his own sins and thereby to achieve the appropriate feelings of guilt. If this should prove insufficient, it is "advisable to include one of the major sins of one's earlier life."[41] This thought is foreign to Luther, since to him the individual's relationship to God is not determined by the presence or absence of the right feelings; rather, the feelings are the result of one's relationship to God.

Another example is the theological understanding of humility. According to Catholic theology, humility is a good and noble sentiment which always suggests piety and a spirit dedicated to God. To Luther, on the contrary, humility as such is worthless - quite the rereverse, since he holds that feelings of inferiority have their own cause, namely - inferiority! Humility is therefore really the opposite of faith, since, if one takes God's love of man seriously, there is no reason for it. The love of God brings namely both wealth and superiority with it.[42] It is a different matter entirely that humility may serve as a weapon with which to beat down such selfish feelings as overconfidence and pride; in this sense it can have a negative but justifiable function.

The description of faith as feeling, affect, or experience will doubtless be displeasing to the many con-

temporary Luther scholars who have adopted the contempt
of dialectical theology for everything that has to do
with psychology.   In the wake of
Karl Barth's (died in 1968) work scholars have rejected
the idea that faith has anything at all to do with
sentiment or inner experience. The concept of "experience" is especially important in this connection, since
scholars associate with it the contents assigned to it
in the 19th century, according to which experience occurs on one's own terms. This corresponds to the concept of feelings mentioned above: feelings tell us nothing about the external world, but only about the
person who entertains them. From this one might further
conclude that, like the aesthetic and the ethical, faith
and religion are private matters, that subjectivity is
truth. If I believe in God, then God exists for me, and
thus in a certain sense it is my ability to believe and
experience which enables me to believe in God. Against
this humanized concept of God Karl Barth opposed a proclamation intended to emphasize to man that he was nothing and could be nothing in and of himself; he was
merely a "vacuum". Man's only hope in this context was
that God would condescend to meet with him, which Barth
saw as occurring through the proclamation of the Gospel.
Man himself could not contribute to this in any way at
all. Thus Barth found it necessary to reject psychology, since it was, among other things, the study of
man's "experiences".[43] Apart from this very primitive
understanding of psychology, Barth's view is at least
correct to the extent that most of our psychology is
based on what we in ch. 2 designated the "active man".
Psychologists still speak of feelings as determined by
needs or drives (Freud, for example, builds an immense
structure on the sexual drive); they thus allow man to

serve as the point of departure for everything that has
to do with evaluation, experience, and faith.

If one transfers the dialectical-theological apparatus to Luther's theology, the question is whether these
scholars are not fundamentally altering Luther's thought.
When Luther employs a number of "psychological" terms,
such as "affect", "fühlen", "empfinden", and so forth,
or speaks of particular feelings, such as anxiety, love,
fear, or happiness, he does so on the basis of a different psychology! It is meaningful to speak of a "vacuum" or of a "vacuum psychology", to the extent that
all psychological phenomena, and especially affective
states, are inflicted on man by causes in which man has
no share. Thus Barthian theologians and Luther students
have, by taking their starting point in a psychology
that was not Luther's, rejected all psychology as such.
This, I submit, is throwing the baby out with the bath-
water. It is important to stress in this connexion that
Luther's "vacuum thinking" is not solely theological,
but also anthropological and thus ultimately psychological. It applies not only to the relationship between
God and man, but to man's situation as a whole. And a
good thing, too, since if theology's discussion of the
Christian faith were unable to make use of ordinary
conventional experiences and modes of expression, we
should shortly approach the incomprehensibility of glossalalia.

Faith as experience
Luther often asserts that faith is an experientia or
an experimentia, that is, an experience. Here too, we
encounter a different anthropology than the one we usually acknowledge. If we may be permitted to set a fine
point on it, Luther's "psychology of perception" is

different.   nce is ineluctably subjective;
experiences   he individual, although perhaps
not to the   : as his feelings do. We speak of
"his" or of   ciences, and we say that he or I
has them. Ou   uggests, then, that experience requires activ   :ipation. Luther sees things quite
differently,   t in his view experience comes to
one or happens to one.

It is in this sense that Luther uses the terms experientia, cognitio, and Erfahrung.[44] Tauler and Gerson
use the concept in the same way; like them, Luther connects experience with sentiment. For example, he distinguishes between merely regarding something to be
true and cognitio experimentalis or experientia.[45] The
latter is the real experience or feeling of God's love.

Luther uses the concept of experience of both important and prosaic matters. In the latter category,
Luther notes that when one is full of food and drink,
the mouth is full of words and the ear is pleased to
listen, and so forth,[46] all of which are prosaic experiences accessible to everyone, and which are often expressed in proverbs and maxims. I think it is important
if one wishes to understand Luther to recognize that
to him faith experiences and mundane experiences are
not radically different; rather, they differ only in
degree. The former are naturally far more important
than the latter, and more comprehensive. Luther was accordingly unable to accept the mystics' concept of a
special experience of the divine distinct from every
other kind of experience, among other things because
it was directly mediated.[47] This is so for Luther because to him experience is largely synonymous with
feeling and must accordingly be located within the
spectrum adumbrated by the rhetorical modes of style:

some are important, others meaningless, some are merely
registered (docere), while still others are crucial,
i.e. pathetic, communications. After experiencing God's
love one is happy, thankful, trustful towards Him; In
short, one believes. Faith is therefore an expression
of the fact that one has experienced something.

Justification of faith

In pedagogical tradition, one usually represents the
conflict between Luther and the Catholic Church in the
following manner: according to Roman Catholicism one
must do good works in order to be saved, while according to Luther faith is sufficient. If one merely believes, works are of no importance. If one inquires of
a schoolboy as to what faith is, one often receives the
answer that faith is trust or love, and that only if
one has this trust and love can one be saved. It would
be difficult to construct a more wrong-headed understanding of Luther's thought, yet on the other hand
this view is quite logical, if one presupposes that
faith and feeling are something built into the fabric
of man as part of his spiritual armament.

Luther himself once entertained a similar view to
that propounded above by our hypothetical schoolboy;
in fact, it was this very theology that nearly drove
him mad. He had learned that one could only obtain forgiveness if one repented correctly, which is to say,
if one regretted his sinful acts and felt remorse about
them.[48] Luther, however, found this to be impossible;
he discovered that he repented because he feared punishment, or because he wished to obtain forgiveness,
which entailed insincerity. Thus he had to repent once
again of the sin of not having repented sincerely, and
so on ad infinitum. According to his own account, this

drove him to despair, which is hardly surprising. Luther had constructed for himself a sort of king who decided to chop off the heads of all those of his subjects who did not love him sincerely. In so doing, he demanded the impossible of them, unless they were able to dissimulate love, which is obviously impossible if one presupposes that one's king is able to try both hearts and minds.

In this fashion the idea of justification is far more merciless than a concept which awards wages for works; in fact, it corresonds to the way Jesus radicalizes the law in the Sermon on the Mount by extending the command not to kill to encompass being angry with one's neighbour. Nor is this the Biblical intention. The Christian is in the same situation as Abraham, who "believed in the Lord, and he reckoned it to him as righteousness", as we read in Gen 15,6. This account is, of course, St. Paul's point of departure for his analysis of the Christian nature in the Epistle to the Romans, ch. 4 ff. When we are told among other things that "he who believes in him will not be put to shame" (Rom 9,33), it is unsurprising that Renaissance scholars understood this (presumably in complete agreement with St. Paul's own intentions) as a divine promise and nothing more. They held this view for the simple reason that they regarded faith as God's affair and that it could not be otherwise. If one presupposes the rhetorical anthropology of the Renaissance, "faith" can not be a phenomenon which is rooted in the subject, and faith is therefore never man's own, as I have suggested above. The cause of faith was thought to reside in the one who commanded such trust or imparted such confidence. Justification by faith thus did not mean that man was understood to receive payment, or to be saved

because of some new, personally initiated activity (i.
e., faith), whereas it had previously been understood
as the result of works. Faith is never man's own, and
therefore righteousness and justification are "foreign"
to man, in the sense that man does not owe it to himself, which does not entail that man should not be able
to have faith, or to enjoy its benefits.

This understanding of faith has, as I have suggested, little actuality today. It was already dead back
in Grundtvig's days, and he was accordingly forced to
reformulate the Lutheran teaching about "justification
by faith" because this concept had become incomprehens-
ible. By Grundtvig's time "faith" had again become a
sort of habitus, because the thrust of Romanticism had
been to elevate all spiritual expressions as human property in the form of "longings" or "intimations" or
"fundamental feelings" (Schleiermacher). To avoid the
(modern) misunderstanding of "justification by faith",
Grundtvig suggested that it be reinterpreted as "justification by the Word of God", which retained the aspect
of dependence on God's will.[49]

Faith and works

Indeed, faith is so living, creating, affective,
and powerful a thing that it is impossible that
it should not achieve something good for ever. It
does not ask whether there are good works to a-
chieve, nay, because it has already carried them
out before the question comes and is always efficacious ... thus it is just as impossible to separate works from faith, as it is to separate heat
and light from fire.[50]

To contemporary man this must appear naive. Faith and

works are not necessarily inseparable. We are accustom-
ed to the idea that feelings are internal concepts (as
is the will, for that matter), which do not necessarily
have to express themselves outwardly. One can easily
have an opinion about something without automatically
realizing it in practice. For example, even though we
do not do anything significant for underdeveloped
countries, we can (and do) continue to feel compassion
towards them. Luther sees things differently, largely
because of two ways in which his thought differs from
that of contemporary man.

1) The feelings are interrelated. As early as 1513
Luther had discovered that the theological cardinal
virtues, faith, hope, and charity, are not separate;
rather, he saw that they produced each other, or at
least he saw that both hope and charity resulted from
faith.[51] If we return to the pathetic understanding,
there is nothing remarkable about this view, since the
pathetic understanding is characterized by the notion
that the same feeling permeates the entire human psyche. Thus there is nothing strange in the idea that the
feelings are practically synonymous, or that on this
plane there is an internal connection between the sentiments.

2) We recall that rhetoric assumed that knowledge,
feeling, and action comprise a unity. In a certain
sense it is impossible to "understand" something without this "understanding" expressing itself in action
(i.e. if that is what the understanding is about). Thus
a judge has not "understood" what the lawyer has been
saying, unless he judges in favour of the latter's client. The political speaker has not made a satisfactory

account of his subject if people fail to vote for him. A businessman who does not succeed in selling something cannot console himself with the fact that people approve of his wares. In the same sense one does not feel or believe in something if one does not realize it in action. If one regards man as a unity in which there is no substantial difference between the parts of the being in which feeling and activity are located (namely soul and body, respectively), then it is necessarily true that faith and works are interrelated. "A good man does good and pious works".[52] This is how Luther understands the relationship between faith and works; works are not something that "ought to" arise from faith, or something that can be summoned up upon request. Rather, they occur quite automatically.

> Thus faith is the source of love and desire for God, and love is the source of a free, compliant, and cheerful life in which one serves one's neighbour without thought to reward.[53]

This central Lutheran position is in no way naive; on the contrary, it has the authority of a several thousand year old and well-tried theory behind it.

6. The Enslaved Will

Of all Luther's works, the one he was personally most satisfied with was entitled De servo arbitrio, the enfettered choice, or, perhaps better, the enslaved will. In this work the author maintained that everything man does is determined by forces external to him, which in the last analysis implies God, who determines everything. In particular it was the latter aspect that Luther regarded as important, since it was Luther's intention to demonstrate that man had no part in achieving his own salvation. To the contrary, he felt that salvation was awarded by God alone. It was from this viewpoint that Luther attempted to counter De libero arbitrio diatribe (A Discussion of Free Will), which was published by Erasmus of Rotterdam, the leading humanist of the time. In his work, Erasmus had attacked some of Luther's earlier writings. Erasmus admits that the will is not able to achieve very much, but he also claims that it is at least able to "will or not to will" the salvation of the individual. Erasmus freely admits that the will is weak and as such unable to attain its goal, but he denies that the will is without significance or non-existant. Erasmus felt that in one way or another it was necessary to insist that God and man collaborate on the matter of man's salvation, even though it is clear that by far the greater honor in this respect must be accorded to God.

Erasmus' view sounds attractive, and Luther's contrary claim that man has no will and that he is both ruled by God and receives everything from Him without reference to his own merits has led many scholars to feel that in this respect Luther virtually reduces man to a will-less robot. Scholars have referred to the optimistic understanding of the humanist Erasmus of man's potential in contradistinction to the dark and pessimistic view of Christianity entertained by Luther; a view which denies to man any sort of power of self-determination or ability to do good.

Before we proceed to examine Luther's view more closely, it would be appropriate first to determine which factors apparently necessitate a concept of free will, and how scholars have attempted to reconcile this freedom with God's omnipotence.

The Freedom of the Will

What sort of ordinary, quotidien experiences could be held to give rise to the notion that our will is free? At first consideration, one might be tempted to point to the differences between man and other forms of life. Plants and animals behave as they do because their behavior is, as it were, built into their constitutions. A tree develops in a particular way, and it is only capable of changing the pattern of its growth and develop to a limited extent. This is also true of the animals; they, too, are programmed for a particular type of behavior. As we put it, they are confined by their respective natures; they are compelled to react to the impulses supplied them by their environment in particular ways. In other words, they have no freedom of choice, no alternatives.

By way of contrast, man's situation seems to be quite different. It seldom occurs that we are confronted only by a single possibility for action. In general, we are confronted by numerous possibilities, so that man is usually in a position to make choices. As a rule, those arguing for the existence of freedom of the will are not content to stop at this distinction between man

and the animals, which consists of the difference between the few alternatives open to the animals and the
many open to man. Most would also claim that the difference between the behavior of man and the animals is
not merely a matter of degree, but also of kind, a point
which our daily experience seems to confirm. It is impossible to predict human behavior in the same way we
can predict that of the animals. Non-predictability is
actually the earmark of freedom of choice or free will.
To put it another way: man is not determined by his environment; rather, he is at some remove from it. Thus
man is not identical with his potential, since he relates to it in freedom. The human subject, that is, the
"self", is able to form reservations about its relation
to its environmental and the impulses or demands issu-
ing from it.

Yet another elementary observation appears to necessitate a concept of free will. Concepts such as responsibility and accountability seem necessarily to presuppose that man is free and able to choose between alternatives. Having previously mentioned that non-predictability seems to be the earmark of the freedom of the
will, I should perhaps also mention that is is precisely this feature which makes it possible to assign guilt
or responsibility to an individual. By way of contrast,
the fox who breaks into the henhouse and runs off with
the farmer's hen cannot be held accountable for his
actions. It is merely following its instincts, and
therefore acts out of necessity. Admittedly, the fox
is "guilty" of breaking-and-entering, but this is not
guilt in an ethical sense, as this would presuppose
that the fox could have avoided following its instinct-
ual desire to devour hens.

Human responsibility may be similarly abridged, as,

for example, in the case of some spiritual disturbance which may render the individual unaccountable at the moment the crime is committed, a possibility which plays a significant role in Western juridical praxis. If the defense attourney is able to demonstrate in court that his client is either permanently or temporarily unaccountable, this is a decisive argument for not demanding that he be brought to account for the crime in question. However, as mentioned previously, it is only occasionally that man's responsibility is in abeyance. Thus, unless there is definite evidence to the contrary, the individual is held to be responsible for his actions, unlike the animals.

These considerations allow us to conclude that our concept of free will is based on at least two elementary experiences, namely the awareness of potential alternative courses of action and the consciousness of responsibility and accountability. Now, these very considerations return us to paths upon which we have already wandered. The description of the situation of choice presupposes that man is a subject or a self who encounters a number of objects which it is possible for him to choose between. Moreover, these alternatives are in fact alternatives precisely because the subject is able to initiate action or make a choice. In short, we have returned to the tripartite view of man which was delineated in ch. 2. According to this view, man experiences himself as an outwardly-directed force which has the potential to initiate action. Furthermore, it is to be recalled that on this view it is precisely the will which is the center of the human structure. The will is the center of the personality and the symbol of its outwardly-directed movement.

Already at this point it is possible to see why Luther felt himself compelled to arrive at a completely different view. In ch. 3 we dealt with the undivided self, a concept which is, among other things, a consequence of rhetorical theory: man is receptive in nature, and accordingly receives his convictions, faith, actions, and, naturally, his will, from outside himself. If Luther's thought was influenced by the rhetorical ideas of Renaissance humanism, he would be forced to reject the concept of free will. However, before we proceed to this subject, we shall briefly examine the non-Lutheran Christian understanding of free will.

Free Will and Theology

The personal experience of the freedom of the will seems to collide with yet another fact of our experience, namely that all behavior is caused behavior, that is, that everything is determined both with respect to being and nature by something else. This is the problem of determinism, which seems to rule out the possibility of real freedom. In earlier times people did not usually think in terms of a chain of causes, but in terms of the omnipotence of God. If the divine omnipotence is a fact, then it is obvious that God must be able to determine everything, including the most intimate decisions of the will. As Jesus says, that is, as reported in Matt. 10,29, not even a sparrow falls to earth unless God so wills, and this maxim must necessarily apply to all other events. A single exception would suffice to obliterate God's omnipotence. Accordingly, what is generally true must also apply to the specific case, that is, to salvation: grace is accorded to man by God's own decision, and not by man's. To God alone is the honor for man's being forgiven, accepted, and saved. Thus the concept of omnipotence assigns all responsibility to God.

However, responsibility also entails guilt. If God really is omnipotent, then is He not also accountable for evil, including the evils of which men are guilty? Also, we might ask, what about those whose souls are lost; was it God who determined their perdition? Neither in the time of the Early Church nor during the Middle Ages was it felt acceptable to answer these questions in the affirmative. As a result, scholars continued to insist on the existence of free will in spite of the concept of divine omnipotence. St. Augustine was probably the first to grasp the full dimensions of the problem, and he proposed a variety of solutions to it. The reason for setting "solutions" here in inverted commas it that Augustine does not actually manage to solve the difficulties, but only to reduce the paradox somewhat, which is probably all that can be achieved in this direction.

Augustine harks back to the Platonic philosophy of being, and thus claims that only the good can truly be said to exist. As a result, evil is merely a negation of the good; thus it is not-good, or, to put in another way, not-being. It does not exist at all. In consequence of this, God cannot be said to have created evil, for which reason He cannot be said to be responsible for it. Evil consists of holes in reality, just as the cheesemaker cannot be said to have created the holes in his cheeses, since these make no difference to the weight of the cheese (which is the appropriate unit of measurement).

On the other hand, it is obvious that both God and the cheesemaker are fully aware that there are holes in reality and in cheese. This forces St. Augustine to propose his famous distinction between God's foreknowledge (praescientia) and his ability to predetermine

(<u>praedestinatio</u>). God was, for example, well aware that
Judas would betray Jesus, but he did not determine that
this would occur. In this fashion Augustine attempts
to maintain that Judas was actually guilty of his crime.

Most people would probably claim that Augustine's
is only a superficial solution, and that God is also
the cause of whatever He happens to foreknow. Luther
points out that man is able to predict a solar eclipse,
but this fact does not oblige it to occur. On the other
hand, if God has foreknowledge of an eclipse, then it
would be meaningless to say that it could not take
place, since it is He who decides.[1] St. Augustine has,
as mentioned, other attempts at a solution to our problem, although they all seem to suffer from the same
deficiency. Thus, for example, he maintains that God
has decreed the distinction between good and evil, but
He did not create evil. Alternatively, he employs the
art of painting as a metaphor: it is impossible to represent light without including shadows.

As a sometime teacher of rhetoric, Augustine also
refers to the necessity of contrast in order to represent anything. A speaker cannot solely utilize the elevated style, since it is precisely the well calculated
use of the low style which lends conviction to the
final result. In an analogous way, the components of
reality exhibit a sort of eloquence (<u>eloquentia rerum</u>),
that is, they are mutually balanced in their context,
so that good and evil have their respective parts in
the whole.[2]

However, there is also a specifically theological
reason for not making do with the concept of predestination alone. The notion of human responsibility, that
is, the notion that we receive our just deserts (merit-
um), is impossible for Augustine to abandon. Therefore

he holds that man must do something in order to deserve his salvation. Grace (gratia) lends its aid in this process, in that it liberates the will and endows it with the ability to act. In this way, Augustine thinks to have assigned actual responsibility to God, since it is, after all, His power which - in the form of grace - achieves everything. At the same time, man's salvation can be said to be the result of his own actions, an assertion which is only possible if man has a will of his own.

In this connection it is important to note that the will is unaffected; on this view, man will always possess free will (liberum arbitrium), but it may be so overburdened by sin that the individual is unable to exercise his capacity to choose. In this event, the will is free, but not liberated (arbitrium, inquam, liberum, sed non liberatum).[3]

It was previously observed that Augustine does not sharply distinguish between the various stages in what was described as the tripartite individual, since according to him feeling (amor) was the central part of man. Thus the decisive question is, what is the nature of his love? in respect to this feature, the sharp divides between reason, feeling, and impulse are relatively unimportant. Of course, this does not prevent Augustine from insisting on the understanding of man presupposed by the tripartite anthropology, that is, as a being who undertakes actions and is responsible for them. Therefore Augustine is forced to attempt to reconcile this with the notion of God's omnipotence. As we have seen, this cannot be accomplished without ending in contradiction or paradox.

The Augustinian solution became the basis for the way the problem was treated during the Middle Ages, which does not mean that scholars were invariably in accord with him. The Catholic Church eventually concluded that Augustine attached too little importance to man's role in attaining salvation. However, this was essentially merely a question of emphasis, since nothing was fundamentally changed in this view, which simultaneously insists on man's free will and God's predestination.

Thomas Aquinas was the greatest theologian of the Middle Ages. His treatment of the problem of free will took its point of departure in the Augustinian understanding of the concept, which led him to produce a model which is in some ways more clear than Augustine's, but which accordingly cannot be held to have avoided internal contradictions. Among things, Thomas points out that man was created in the image of God. Thus, since God possesses free will, man must also do so,[4] although Thomas understands this as freedom of choice: no matter what situation confronts him, man always possesses the ability and power to make his own decisions.

This power (vis) cannot be taken away from man in any circumstances; nor was it lost when Adam fell. Accordingly, regardless of man's circumstances, he continues to retain both his free will and his accountability. However, alongside of the ability to choose (electio) which the will possesses, it also contains a desire (appetitus voluntatis) which compels it to seek the good, that is, ultimately, blessedness (beatitudo). Seen in this light, the fall of man constitutes an obstacle to the real striving of the will. The grace (gratia) of God is the antidote to the inhibitory activity of sin. Thus grace assists man in seeking the realization of his true nature, which is designed to attain blessedness, salvation, and happiness. "Grace

does not annihilate nature; rather, it completes it".
Grace leads the individual to his destination.

But if the reborn and sinless will only desires the
good, and not evil, it is then still meaningful to speak
of free choice? Thomas would reply in the affirmative,
since he holds that the ability to choose evil does
not correspond to freedom. This is so, he holds, because evil is not an independent existant. It is instead simply the destruction or perversion of the good.
Such "freedom" he terms a "libertas perversa". In this
fashion, Thomas attempts to reconcile the possibility
of choice with the necessary striving of the will towards the good. However, not even Thomas himself claims
that this solution is without its contradictions.

There still remains the problem of reconciling free
will and God's predestination. Thomas attempts to avoid
this dilemma by proposing a concept of the accidental
or contingent. He defines a contingency as something
which both could be the case, and which could not be
so (quod potest esse et non esse). For exemple, if I
announce that I have met an acquaintance, then it necessarily follows that I have encountered a living person.
On the other hand, in relation to this assertion it is
merely accidental whether or not the person in question
was wearing an overcoat, or was in good humor, or whatever.

Thomas proceeds to utilize this distinction to illustrate the relationship between God's will and His
omnipotence. He maintains that it is obvious that God
both knows and determines everything that happens. It
is accordingly also he who determines that I should
meet my friend, with all the contingencies which accompany that event (overcoat, humor, etc.). However,
God has precisely determined these things as contingen-

cies; thus there is no necessity involved in the encounter; God has created it as an accident. Accordingly, seen from man's point of view, God is able to determine things differently, unless they are matters
which are ruled by logic (eg., if I have met a friend,
then I have met a living person). One could perhaps say
that there is a difference between the ontological necessity which is reserved to God and the logical necessity which is appropriate to man. As far as man is concerned, everything else is accidental. For this reason,
or so Thomas maintains, the human will has real possibilities for choice. On the plane at which the will
functions, necessity is not a factor.

It would be possible to sketch more thoroughly the
scholastic discussion of the Middle Ages concerning the
will and its freedom (or the reverse) than we have done
in our brief survey of St. Thomas' position. Scholasticism is especially interesting for our purposes since,
as mentioned, it places special emphasis on the will
(as above, pp. 37). In connection with Luther's views,
it would be particularly appropriate to mention Gabriel
Biel (died in 1495), in part because he stressed the
will's potential for initiating the work of salvation,
and in part because Luther expressly attacked his
ideas.[5] However, I think what has been said so far is
sufficient. In theological terms, which in this connection means soteriological ones, it is a question of
collaboration between God and man. This collaboration
is not caused by Revelation, nor is it required by purely theological considerations; rather, its motivation
lies already in the anthropological interests of the
time. Pelagius, St. Augustine, and the theologians of
the Middle Ages remained within the parameters of that
theological anthropology which we have called the tri-

partite view of man. The inevitable result was a paradoxical contradiction between the wills of God and man,
since this framework required both to have their own
free will. Moreover, as far as salvation was concern-
ned, it also required a collaboration between God and
man. In other words, a particular anthropology dictated
a particular theology, rather than the opposite. The
same applies in the case of Luther, whose new anthropology also led to a new theology.

The difference between these two ways of conceiving
of the will is illustrated by the respective signifi-
cances they assign to the self: "Is the choosing self
merely the battleground for various motives, or do the
various competing motives constitute the horizon of the
choosing self? does the strongest motive determine my
choice, or do I determine through the exercise of choice
which motive seems to me to be the strongest?"[6]

The Conflict between Erasmus and Luther

It is actually rather difficult to make out just what
Erasmus' intention was when he attacked Luther in 1524
in "A Discussion of the Freedom of the Will". The historical situation was extremely complex. There is much
which suggests that Erasmus felt himself obliged to attack Luther because of pressure from within Catholicism
itself. If this was the case, then it might be correct
to assume that he approached the task with some reluctance, which perhaps explains why Erasmus writes that
he does not think the matter to be actually all that
important.[7] On the other hand, it is important to recall that Erasmus was the greatest humanist of his day;
he was the master of the art of communication as well
as the author of what was probably the first thoroughly non-serious literary work in the history of the

world, namely In Praise of Folly. Thus it is uncertain
whether we are to take his words in this connection at
face value, as it is possible that his real intention
is to be read between the lines, as it were.

Generally speaking, it would probably be advisable
to take the efforts of these two battlecocks with a
pinch of salt. In reality, the reader finds himself in
a sort of imaginary court of law, in which two contend-
ing attourneys are attempting to win, cost what it may.
Every rhetorical device is unleashed in a manner reminiscent of the choicest juridical rhetoric. Above all,
each attempts to gain ground by unmasking the other's
"rhetorical" style in order by way of contrast to reveal himself as the plain, unreflective, and non-rheto-
rical John Smith who merely wishes to discover the
truth in all its simplicity. It would take us too far
afield in these pages to illustrate the numerous devices, including the conscious suppression of some details
and the equally intentional misrepresentation of others,
to which both figures resort. Thus when Erasmus claims
that his topic is only of peripheral interest, his opponent is naturally forced to assert that it is the
most important conceivable subject, and that it is indeed a shame that his honorable opponent does not realize the fact! Similarly, where Erasmus recommends that
we wave the requirements of strict logic in favor of
a common-sensical approach, Luther adheres stringently
to the logical implications of his opponent's words. If
Erasmus asserts that Luther commits the logical error
of reasoning in a circle, he is promptly scorned by
Luther for following the dictates of human reason.

Even the very time when Erasmus' treatise appeared
may have been determined by tactical considerations.
As we have seen, Erasmus may have had private reasons

for choosing the date in question: It is probably not
unimportant that at this time the Lutheran movement was
experiencing its hour of truth, threatened as it was
by both external Catholic enemies and by internal ecclesiastical, political, and extremist movements of an
"enthusiastic" (Schwärmerisch) character. It was this
internal disunity on which Erasmus capitalized without
hesitation. Conversely, can it have been accidental
that Luther waited a whole year to reply to Erasmus'
treatise, with the result that his work appeared unac-
companied at the autumn bookfair at Leipzig? Erasmus
had no doubt that this was a deliberate strategem on
Luther's part, but by a supreme effort which entailed
working round the clock in the printshop he nevertheless managed to work out the first part of his own reply (called Hyperaspistes) to Luther's attack.

Naturally, there is room for discussion as to the
extent such external factors influenced the course and
contents of the debate between these two figures. But
in any event, knowledge of these aspects of the situation may help us to relativize to some degree the
pathetic seriousness and literalness with which adherents of both Erasmus, and (not least), Luther have
treated the golden phrases of these two "attorneys".
These observations may also encourage us to be cautious
about taking Erasmus strictly literally, a procedure
which could easily lead one to misleadingly conjecture
the existence of a gap between the Reformation and humanism.

What, then, was Erasmus' intention in writing his
treatise? If we keep to the work itself and momentari-
ly ignore the by no means improbable theory that it may
only be understood in terms of the ecclesiastico-polit-

ical situation then obtaining - nor should we ignore
Erasmus' own situation - then there appear to be two
reasons for attacking Luther. In the first place, Erasmus is irritated about the onesidedness of Luther's position. He regards Luther as a logician gone amok, that
is, as a man who seeks a univocal solution to a problem
which can really only be solved in terms of a "both/and"
answer, that is, a paradox. Erasmus acknowledges that
we cannot do without the idea of free will, since moral injunctions would be meaningless without it. Similarly, the divine recompense after death would be meaningless without free will, just as the punishment meted
out at that time wold be gruesome and unjust. On the
other hand, Erasmus concedes that it is obvious that
the will is in God's power. Nevertheless, he feels that
it is able to express a desire for one thing or another
(to will and not to will: velle et nolle). In relation
to medieval tradition, this is by no means a radical
affirmation of the freedom of the will.

The second goal of Erasmus' attack is presumably to
show that Luther is an upstart, a theologian whose
scriptural exegesis is arbitrary and whose knowledge
of theological thought and of the great theological
figures in particular is sadly wanting. The purpose of
this attack is not merely to prove that Luther is un-
cultivated, but to assert that a balanced and well-con-
sidered judgement is only possible when one has a wide
variety of views and arguments to choose from. One can
only develop a discriminating sensibility when one's
field of view includes many subtleties of meaning. And
on this point, Erasmus maintains, Luther is deficient;
he sees only one side of things. Thus Erasmus notes
that Luther used the term assertio (i.e., assertion or
confirmation) in the title of an earlier work in which

he had dealt with the freedom of the will.[8] This lea
Erasmus to remark that when ever he sees the word a?
sertio he feels compelled to oppose, since such finish-
ed views require contradiction.[9]

Yet another matter is important in this connection.
It was one of the most important claims of the humanists that the truth is not terribly important in its
own right, as its importance depends on what one intends to use it for. In short, how is it useful? (quid
utile). Thus they attacked the scholastics for not con-
sidering this principle, and for instead discussing a
topic without reference to its significance. Accordingly, Erasmus holds that the question of the freedom of
the will is germane to the work of theologians, but
that it can have no great relevance for laymen. It would
be quite inappropriate to lead laymen out into depths
which even professional theologians cannot fathom.

One view which Erasmus apparently did not hold, in
spite of Luther's accusation to the contrary, was a
humanistic (in the modern sense of the word) confidence
in the potential and innate goodness of man. Erasmus
never claims that man is able to develop himself of his
own accord, in contradistinction to a more theological
view of man as weak and unable to manage without the
assistance of God. To the contrary, Erasmus, too, believes that the Bible is the sole guideline and sole
path leading to man's salvation. Luther has been allowed to shape our understanding of Erasmus entirely too
much on his own terms.

Luther on the Enslavement of the Will
Luther himself reckoned the issue to possess vast significance. To him it was simply decisive that man has
no part in achieving his own salvation. I instance the
following statement:

"I must admit in all honesty that even if it were
possible I would be most reluctant to have free will
given me, or that anything should be given to me by
means of which I would be able to work for my own salvation ... since, even if I lived forever, my conscience
would never be certain and convinced as to how much
it ought to do in order to satisfy God."[10] Thus Luther's
work on the enslaved will has a theological purpose,
namely, to reassure people that they are not to be concerned about their salvation, since it is entirely in
God's hands. The question is, however, how does Luther
achieve this goal? What is his concept of the will? K.E.
Løgstrup has called attention to the fact that Luther
offers a phenomenological description of the will
which, although it differs from the traditional description, is not for that reason the less realistic.[11]
Luther inquires as to what it means to say that one
wills something. To him it means to say that one intends something, desires to carry out some action or
achieve a goal one has selected in advance. On this
basis, as Løgstrup concludes, to will something and to
choose something are not identical, since to will something presupposes that one has chosen! Choice is no
longer important; one has gone beyond it in order to
attempt to realize the object of one's choice.

If one encounters obstacles to one's project, then
one engages one's entire will and all one's resources
in order to overcome such resistance. Indeed, the greater the resistance, the greater the need for will. Accordingly, will is identical with personal commitment,
that is, with involvement. Accordingly, Erasmus' attempt to assert the existence of a "disengaged will",
understood as the mere ability to choose without willing something, is self-contradictory. The medieval

scholastic monk, Johannes Buridanus, once proposed a paradox in which a donkey was confronted by two equally large haystacks. Having in effect nothing to choose from, the poor creature in Buridanus' parable starves to death. Analogously, if one could conceive of a true situation of choice in which the possibilities were equally attractive, the result would necessarily be that one would be unable to make a choice. In a word, one would find the alternatives offered quite uninteresting. As Løgstrup puts the matter,

"The determinate nature of the will signifies that we are actually unable to determine what we desire and strive for, that is, what we will. The object of our willing is determined before we will it, because man himself is bound and thus our will is as well."

Unfortunately, Løgstrup does not delve further into the fact that this is a purely phenomenological description of the will which requires to be tested as to its adequacy, that is, it must be shown whether or not the description is sufficient to illustrate the usual use of the concept of the will. Instead he concludes that Luther held this understanding of the will not as "a general truth, but as God's truth." But apart from this deficiency, Løgstrup has very accurately described how the will may be determined without in fact being forced. Even though he does not express the concept clearly, Løgstrup is on the verge of acknowledging that the will is governed by its object, that is, by what it wills. Since this object is something the will really does desire this means that it is by the same token quite voluntary.[12]

At first glance it might appear strange that Luther's most striking characterization of free will is that of "a captive beast of burden which belongs to Satan, and

which it is impossible to rscue unless Satan would be
expelled by the finger of God."[13] Thus the will is not
its own master, but a pack anmal which is obliged to
obey its master, that is, either God or Satan. "Accordingly, the human will is in the middle, like a beast
of burden. When God mounts up on it, it does what God
intends, and goes were He wishes, just as the Psalm
says: I am as the cattle, and always together with you.
But when Satan rides on it, then it does as Satan wishes, and goes where he desires. Moreover, it does not
lie in its power freely to choose to address itself to
one or the other of its (prospective) riders; rather,
they vie with one another to catch it and secure it in
their possession."[14]

In short, there is no refuge where the riders' power
does not apply, not even in man's innards. There is no
place where the will can develop freely, in contradistinction to one's external activities, which are governed by necessity: "It is an error to suppose that
the free will is able to do good works internally. As
we have already said in connection with faith, to will
something is to hope, rejoice, be moved, or wholly borne
away by the word of God ..."[15]

In the last-mentioned passage, Luther is in reality
touching on the fundamental question of the self: the
"self" is apparently not the same, dependent upon whether one is in the power of God or the Devil. Of course,
it is characteristic of pack anmals that they have no
independent will of their own, but that they must do
as the coachman or rider orders: thus the "self" varies
in proportion to what it is that controls it.

In other words, these considerations lead us to the
problem of identity. I shall not attempt in these pages
to solve the problem as to whether or how the individu-

al can be said to be identical with himself. Here it
will suffice to call attention to the fact that in a
certain sense we can be said to change our identities,
just as the chameleon changes color to match its surroundings. This is perhaps most easily illustrated by
referring to our experience of literature or film. We
tend to identify ourselves with what we hear or read.
When we were children we shudderingly accompanied the
fortunes of the tin soldier in H.C. Andersen's story
about the brave tin soldier. We were with him when he
sailed through the gutter in a paper boat, and we suffered with him when, at last, he was tossed into the
stove. A few years later, some of us fenced our way
through 17th century France as members of Alexandre Dumas' corps of musketeers. And so on. Among other reasons, all important literature has become so thanks to
the fact that we are able to identify with it. The ways
in which we conceive of this process of identification
are illustrated by the expressions we use in connection
with our experience of art: we are "gripped" by great
literature, just as we sympa(and empa)thize with the
individuals whose fortunes we follow. In an extended
sense, one might be tempted to ask as to whether the
answer to the question "who am I?" is, in a manner of
speaking, a story. If I reply that I am a Dane, I have
thereby said that the history of Denmark is also my
history. If I acknowledge that I am a Christian, it may
be supposed that my basic narrative is the Biblical
account of Christ.[16]

Of course, one could also suggest that every experience is a sort of identification. Take, by way of example, the American television serial on the "Holocaust", that is, the destruction of European Jewry by
the Nazi's during the Second World War. Although the

serial itself was of a somewhat dubious quality, re-
viewers stressed as one of its values the fact that it
was possible to identify with the main characters in
the narrative. In this fashion, one comes closer to the
horrors involved than by seeing some of the many docu-
mentary films deriving from the historical concentra-
tion camps, and which we have seen on television and
in the movies. The serial made this subject vivid for
us.

Perhaps it would be more correct to say that the television serial allowed us to empathize with the ter-
rible tragedy, or that it was more the case that the
main characters identified themselves with us than we
did with them. This is because this is mainly the direction in which such identification proceeds. The primary fact is not that we recognize something of ourselves in the characters, but that they take up resi-
dence in us. Every properly told story possesses its
audience and takes them captive, so that they become
members of a new universe. Thus we begin to play along
according to the terms stipulated by the narrative in
question, rather than on our own terms. This phenomenon
is entirely parallel to the conditions applying to rhetorical communication: if the hearer has not in some
way received a new identity via the communication or
possession or proclamation or narrative to which he has
been exposed, then the words in question have been
wasted on him. Furthermore, this can only occur when
we are ourselves identical with those whose case we are
pleading, just as actors become identical with their
roles, as is indicated by the expression "to live one's
way into a part". Similarly, Quintilian remarks that
"We must identify ourselves with the persons of whom
we complain that they have suffered grievous, unmerited

and bitter misfortune ... our words must be such as we should use if we stood in their shoes." (Quintilian: Inst. Orat. VI.2.34 trans. H.E. Butler, Loeb Classical Library, Cambridge, Mass., and London, 1966).

Naturally, the same applies to the Word about Christ. A true understanding of this fact signifies that the content of the Word takes possession of the individual, as St. Paul suggests in Gal 2,20: "I have been crucified with Christ; it is no longer I who live, but Christ who lives in me." To this Luther comments that, "thus this faith connects me more closely to Christ than any husband could be connected to his wife."[18] In this connection he even takes the occasion to attack, as elsewhere, the notion of "fides formata caritate" (faith shaped by love), that is, the scholastic idea which maintains that faith was already present, and that all that remained was for it to be given form by love.[19] We have shed the old self, so that Christ can live as a new self in us. To this all individual wills must succumb, as is necessarily the case when "everyone's will is captured (rapi) so as to will or to act, whether this be for good or evil."[20]

Thus we return to the concept of affect, that is, feeling or touch. Christ has touched us, so that we have been transformed. Actually, "touch" is insufficiently strong to express the notion of identification or flowing-together. Perhaps we could clarify matters slightly by pointing to the Greek and Latin terms, respectively, for moving and touching: rhythm (rytmizein) and beat (tangere). As these roots indicate, we do not have to do with any superficial contact; rather, the entire person is set in motion - one swings along. Rhythm is transferred to one's person, so that one may be defined by it.

Every vivid story forces its audience into its rhythm and lays them under its sway. Of course, this takes place to an especial degree when we have to do with the story of stories, the narrative of narratives, that is, the Passion of Christ. As Luther puts it in a remark on Ps 68[21], "everyone dies by virtue of this identity (actually: feeling, *ita affectus*) and descends with Him into Hell, just as they rise again with Him and ascend to Heaven." Thus to believe is not the same as to be Christian, but to be Christ himself. In this vein Luther finds it possible to wish "that the presently weak Christ may become strong within me."[22]

However, one might object that it is not one's self or something pertaining to one's self that indwells in one, but something foreign. Against this, Luther argues that it is possible to use such words as "our" of something which does not originate from within the self: "Are we not to call Christ 'ours' because, instead of having created Him, we have only received Him?"[23] He also maintains that "Christ and faith are to be reconciled. And we must be in Heaven, and Christ in our hearts. He lives and acts in us. He does not live and act in a theoretical sense, but truly, as one present, and extremely efficaciously (*sed realiter, praesentissime et efficacissime*).[24]

Luther illustrates the identity between Christ and the believer with the aid of a variety of metaphors. Thus, for example, he employs such "sticky" expressions as *adhaesio* (adhesion) or *conglutinatio* (cementing) to emphasize the indissolubility of the bond in question.[25] Similarly, in extension of St. Paul's ideas he utilizes marriage as a metaphor to characterize the relationship between Christ and man: "Not only does faith give so much that the soul becomes identical to the divine word,

that is, full of grace, free and blessed; but it also
conjoins the soul to Christ like a bride to her bride-
groom. The consequence of this marriage is, as Paul
says, that Christ and the soul become a single body
(cf. Ephesians 5,30). Accordingly, the things peculiar
to both, such as property, fortune and misfortune, and
all things, are held in common, so that all that Christ
possesses also becomes the property of the believing
soul; and what the soul possesses becomes Christ's
property. Thus, Christ possesses all goods and all
blessedness, and they become the property of the soul,
so the soul possesses all vices and sins, and it becomes the property of Christ. Through this arises the
joyful exchange (fröhliche Wechsel) ...[26] Note that
Luther uses the marriage metaphor to reverse the process of identity! It is not only the case that Christ
becomes my "self", but also the reverse is true: I become Christ. This is necessarily the case when the confluence of the two quantities in question is conceived
of as actual and not merely metaphorical.

But, then, one is tempted to ask, how could it possibly be actual? Is one part of a television program
while one at the same time sits and drinks coffee in
front of it? Can one simultaneously sit in a chair and
read a book, while also being a character in the book?
Luther points to this conceptual difficulty in connection with the Pauline statement, that "it is no longer
I who live, but Christ who lives in me" (Gal 2,20).
Luther asks, "but what are you saying, Paul, that you
do not live your own natural life, in the flesh, but
in Christ? Whereas I, however, see your flesh, but not
Christ ... and yet you presumably have your five senses and do all that natural man usually does in his cor-
poral life?" To which Luther has St. Paul reply: "he

says that   this life is not his, and that he does not
live for the sake of those things whereby life is maintained. Although he does in fact use them, he does not
live by them, or for them ..."[27]

In other words, St. Paul is a dual person, possessing more than one identity. There is no other possibility, nor is there anything strange in this. It is an
experience with which we are all familiar, and which
Luther therefore utilizes, just as St. Paul employs ordinary human experience to explain the relationship between that with which man is preoccupied, namely the
love of Christ, and the   self, which is inhabited or
enthralled, that is, conquered or possessed by a foreign power. Thus it is hardly strange that there is no
room for free will. "Everyman's will, whether good or
evil, is captivated (rapitur) so that it both wills and
acts."[28] And this must be the case, since "the Word is
pure and good, and makes the one who adheres to it pure
and good."[29]

The Exemplum

A keyword in rhetorical communication is the concept
of the exemplum.[30] This does not merely mean that one
illuminates his representation of something with a number of examples, but rather that the representation itself is intended to provide examples for imitation. A
well known example of this phenomenon was the genre
cultivated in antiquity under the title De viris illus-
tribus (of exceptional or illustrious men). This genre
was revived during the Renaissance by Petrarch, and it
became the primary model for humanistic historiography.[31] Behind this concept lies the notion that any account whatsoever, whether historical or otherwise, has
an intention, that is, it proposes a model for thought

or action which the speaker desires his audience to accept. These examples are most often of a moral nature; indeed, it would probably not be an exaggeration to claim that the origin of the historiography of antiquity lay in this desire to provide moral explanation and incitement for good actions.[32] In other spheres, however, the concept of the exemplum is not restricted to apply only to moral acts. It simply signifies that the audience is offered a model into which they may be absorbed and thus find their identity.[33]

To Martin Luther, the idea of Christus præsens, that is, of the present and living Christ, was the same as the Christus exemplum.[34] In other words, he understood Christ to be my lord, as well as the creator of identity for my life.

Guilt and Responsibility

As mentioned previously, one of Erasmus' more important reasons for writing his treatise was that he regarded it as important that man could be assigned guilt and responsibility for his actions. Otherwise it would be impossible to get men to act ethically; it would be likewise unjust if God punished men now and again if they were not really guilty of their own faults.

Free will seems to be the ineluctable presupposition for meaningful talk about guilt and accountability. If the fox breaks into the henhouse and steals a few hens, it is obviously guilty of their deaths, and of the loss suffered by the farmer. Nevertheless, we do not feel that it is guilty in the same sense that a man would be who committed the same crimes. The reason for this is that the fox is governed by its instincts which, in a manner of speaking, compel it to chase hens whenever the opportunity presents itself. It has no possibility to make conscious choices. It acts spontaneously and of necessity. Thus it would also be meaningless to punish the fox, since it cannot learn not to act in this fashion (although this is probably a limited truth, according to modern behavioral psychology). Accordingly, the reason for shooting foxes is not because they are evil, but because they cause damage in one way or another. In contradistinction to this, we find it meaningful to regard man as responsible in some sense. By assigning man the possibility of choice, decision, the selection of alternatives, and so forth, we also signify that we find the punishment to be reasonable. If self-determination and freedom of choice are not present, it becomes impossible to mete out punishment, as is indicated by our legal system, according to which "temporary insanity" is held to be an extenuating circumstance.

This apparently rather obvious concept of freedom and responsibility is followed closely by Erasmus, who also thinks to find support for it in the Bible. For example, he cites the following passage in Sirach 15,14-17: "It was he who created man in the beginning, and he left him in the power of his own inclination. If you will, you can keep the commandments, and act faithfully as a matter of your own choice... Before a man are life and death, and whichever he chooses will be given to him."[35] Erasmus holds that this sort of emphasis on choice would be meaningless unless man in fact possessed free will so as to be able to choose between competing alternatives. He interprets the Commandments in a similar fashion, on the theory that it is impossible to demand that someone do anything if he does not possess free will. Thus Erasmus holds that injunctions as well as summonses to repentance and to improve one's way of life would be meaningless without freedom. In-

deed, as he points out, such summonses frequently presuppose the notion of willing something, as in "If you
would be perfect, go, sell what you possess ..."[36], or
perhaps better, "If any man would come after me, let
him.[37]

Erasmus' thoroughness is undeniable. Not only does
he offer an analysis of the Gospels, but a study in
depth of the Old Testament as well, in which he finds
many examples of human fates which are only intelligible if one presupposes that man possesses free will.
He further assumes that the commandments of the Penta-
teuch and the injunctions of the prophets also presuppose free will. Finally, Erasmus includes a study of
the Pauline epistles in which he finds indirect evidence of the concept of free will. St. Paul utilizes
metaphors of combat or similes borrowed from the race-
track, such as "Do you not know that in a race all the
runners compete, but only one receives the prize?"[38]
As Erasmus suggests, it is hard to imagine that these
allusions to battle, competition, and reward could be
meaningful, if everything is determined in advance.

Like Erasmus' work, Luther's, too, is in reality a
lengthy exegetical study of various Biblical passages,
since he also attempts to illustrate and demonstrate
his views on the basis of the Bible. Luther's approach,
however, is radical. He does not merely question parts
of Erasmus' argumentation, but the lot. Nothing whatever is left. Luther's actual argumentation is based
on a single fundamental observation, one with which
Erasmus, who was not only a humanist, but one who was
quite conversant with language, was familiar. This was
the principle that words cannot be understood in isolation from one another, but only from context. In a
word, one must pay attention to the mode in which verbs

express their meanings. The sentence, "if a donkey fli-
es, then it has wings" by no means states that flying
donkeys actually exist. This is immediately obvious in
the Latin version of this expression, since the verb
in question would be in the subjunctive. Thus "if you
would be perfect" says nothing about the will of the
person addressed. As Luther even goes on to point out,
the insight implied by the expression may in fact be
the exact opposite, namely, to point up the fact that
the addressee does not so intend. Luther also mentions
that parents frequently urge their children to attempt
one thing or another of which they are not capable without their parents' help, so that they may learn from
their failure.[39] Offering a somewhat theoretical example, Luther compares man's situation with that of a man
who has been bound to a chair. Having forgotten the
fact, the man can be induced to recall it merely by
asking him to stretch out his arms, so that he will
discover his incapacity.[40] In the same sense, by com-
manding man to keep God's law it is possible to force
the audience to discover the impossibility of doing so.
In other words, Christ is the sole avenue of escape,
and the intention underlying the proclamation of the
law is not to bring about its fulfilment, but the consciousness of sin. Language does not assign to words
any constant meaning. To the contrary, their meaning
arises from the context and the situation in which they
are used. Thus, according to Luther, Erasmus' examples
are in reality merely examples of the general rule on
which commandments and orders do not presuppose the
free will of their recipient. Quite the opposite, in
fact, as the idea it to make the recipient's decisions
for him! There is no question of proposing a choice to
the audience so that they may choose in peaceful seclu-

sion. Instead, the goal is to influence the hearer so as to make him act in accordance with one's wishes.

Luther's example is based on everyday experience. Such expressions as "would you please pass the salt" or "would you please be quiet" are only questions in point of form; hence, it is only superficially that they offer their listener a choice. It is precisely this insight that Luther exploits in dismissing Erasmus' previously-mentioned passage in Sirach: "If you will, you can keep the commandments" is not a neutral expression, but rather a strong injunction, as is in fact implied by the previous sentence ("He added his commandments and statutes").[41]

In so constructing his position, Luther is utilizing insights deriving from the revival of rhetoric, and in particular the observation that language not only alludes and refers to things, but that it also in its way acts and creates. The purpose of communicating one's views it not merely to describe a state of affairs, but also to start something in one's hearer, that is, to produce a movement (motus) in him, a movement which may in effect consist in understanding, feeling, or action. Interestingly enough, this perlocutionary function has been discovered yet again by the modern study of the philosophy of language. From a rhetorical point of view, it is against the nature of language to allow one's audience any measure of freedom. Indeed, it would be a misunderstanding to believe that language attempts to appeal to a subject possessing free will. Quite the contrary; the speaker knows his own will, and by expressing it in language he attempts to get his audience to accede to his views. Admittedly, it is conceivable that the hearer may in the first instance have some objections to what is said. He may exhibit reluctance.

The speaker attempts to subdue this resistance by means of his refutation (refutatio), in hopes of getting his way in the end.

But then, what role does guilt play in all this? Well, in a certain sense the listener has no more guilt than we earlier assigned to our paradigmatic fox. Of course, the fox was guilty of making the hens disappear, for which reason it was liable to be shot by the farmer. Similarly, the sinner runs the risk of being punished by God. Every cause has some effect; hence a bad ax may lead one to chop badly, just as pollution may eventually cause the disintegration of our society. Likewise, a man may be guilty of another man's misfortune. The point of all this is that the same meaning of the term "guilt" applies equally well to the cases of men, axes, societies, or foxes. All of these run the risk of paying the price for the guilt they have acquired. On the other hand, as far as man is concerned, there is no question of any particular ethical guilt.

In this vein, Luther offers a number of examples of guilty parties who are not guilty because they have done something of their own free will, that is, by free choice, but simply because they have in actual fact trespassed against a particular statute. He adds that some men are good, while others are not, for which reason their careers are good and bad, respectively. In this connection Luther refers to St. Paul's Second Letter to Timothy (2,20); as he says, in a similar fashion, some axes are good, while others are bad.[42]

This unquestionably raises the problem as to why this is necessarily the case. If God is omnipotent, then there can only be one explanation for this state of affairs; nor does Luther hesitate to make God responsible for all facets of existence, including the existence of evil. It was God who created both good and ignoble vessels, just as it was He who hardened Pharaoh's heart, as we read in Exodus.[43] God does everything in everyone, according to Luther, who thus makes no attempt, as St. Thomas did,[44] to argue for a kind of double necessity, or, as Augustine attempted, to utilize a hole-in-the-Swiss-cheese model, that is, of evil as non-existant. To Luther, God is responsible for evil, even if we cannot determine how. In short, Luther does not merely reject the concept of free will in connection with the immediate facts of man's life. He also rejects the notion on the universal plane, so that he accepts without more ado the idea of God's predestination as denying to the will any room for maneuver or freedom at all. St. Thomas had maintained that if God has free will, then man must also do so. Luther draws the opposite conclusion, namely, that if God has free will, then man cannot do so, since man is eternally subject to God's omnipotence.[45]

Both Justified and a Sinner

In this and the preceeding chapter we have been concerned with an ideal, namely, to be completely Christian. We have spoken of faith as a feeling approaching a state of possession. It demands absolute mastery over the soul, so that the latter becomes led by the Gospel of Christ alone. According to this view, man is either flesh or spirit. In the same sense, we spoke of the will, which was either dominated by God or by Satan (note, however, that in the ultimate sense, everything, Satan included, is subject to God).

In the course of our discussion of the problem of identity we did, however, briefly mention the possibility that man may be more than one thing at a time,

even though this may be limited to the acknowledgement
that he may be one thing in his imagination or soul,
and another corporeally. Thus, even if I identify myself with Christ (or, rather, the reverse takes place),
in a certain trivial (physical) sense I remain myself.
It is important to note that this polyvalent identity
also extends to senses in which it is not trivial, since
even the real self may be two or more things at one and
the same time. Consider, for example, Dürer's engraving
of Melancholy, in which the psychological state in
question is depicted as a sort of stalemate between two
mutually competing internal tendencies or drives. This
situation had nothing to do with dullness, even though
this might superficially appear to be the case. To the
contrary, it was a situation of considerable tension
brought about by the opposition of two powers. Luther
seems to express the same notion in his famous slogan,
simul justus et peccator, that is, both justified and
a sinner. In the scholarly literature on Luther it is,
however, more common to understand this in another way.
It is held that the term justus, that is, justified,
does not apply to any individual in his own right.
Rather, God "pretends" that this is the case. On the
other hand, "peccator", that is, sinner, is the correct
description of man in his natural state. Luther's understanding of justification is generally held to be
forensic, that is, legalistic. The idea is illustrated
by a procedure in a court of law in which a judge finds
the accused not guilty. In this example it is essentially irrelevant as to whether the accused really is in-
nocent or guilty, because it is not his actions, but
the decision of the court that is important and juridically valid. Accordingly, God is compared to a judge

who, by reason of his great love for the accused, just-
ifies him no matter what sort of criminal he may in
fact be. In external things the individual has become
justified, while as far as the inner man is concerned
he is still the old Adam, that is, a sinner. This perspective leads to the claim that man is both a complete
sinner and completely justified; these are integral
quantities whose mutual relations are dialectical or
even paradoxical.[46]

There is no doubt that this interpretation says
something important about Luther's thought, but if my
presentation of Luther's conception of the process of
identification is correct, then it should be possible
to get even further along. Seen from this viewpoint,
we should no longer maintain that sin and justification
take place on two different planes, that is, in man's
life and in the judgement of God, respectively. Instead,
it would be possible to speak of a direct confrontation
taking place within man himself, since he has managed
to identify himself with both God and Satan at once.
Within this framework, grace and sin are not integral,
but partial entities. Furthermore, this view indicates
that we do not have to do with any dialectical relationship, but with a battle taking place within man. It
is waged by two competing forces, and its goal is the
dominion over the individual in question. It would
therefore be incorrect to describe man as consisting
of either flesh or spirit (concerning this distinction,
see p. 107). Rather, he consists of both quantities,
and is thus in a certain sense schizophrenic. Moreover,
this is not the sort of harmonic and humoristic plural-
ity and sophistication which is expressed in the middle
(ethical) level of rhetorical discourse. Instead, we
have to do with two affects or identities or wills

of a pathetic nature, each of which seeks the total do-
mination of the individual. This discrepancy causes the
conflict.

Luther employs numerous metaphors to illustrate this
situation, including some which touch on the forensic
aspect as well as that of internal struggle. In his
commentary on Romans he speaks of the sick body and the
half-completed house. The body is regarded as sick with
respect to the actual illness which may be disturbing
it, and as healthy, to the extent that it seeks to be
healthy. Thus one and the same body may be seen from
two viewpoints (sub idem corpus sub utroque).[47] Admittedly, this relationship could be called dialectical,
although there is nothing contradictory about it on the
level of understanding. On the other hand, sickness and
health contradict each other to a high degree, in the
sense that they compete with one another for mastery.
The same is true of the half-completed house, which is
a not-house, in the sense that, for example, one cannot
live in it, while in terms of the purpose of its construction it is nevertheless a house. In this picture
the conflict in question is to be found within the process of construction itself.

In other words, simul justus et peccator refers not
only to some aspects or viewpoints from which it is
possible to regard man, it also says something about
the conflict which takes place within man. Thus in connection with Rom 7,19 ("For I do not do the good I want,
but the evil I do not want is what I do"), Luther remarks that it is both correct to say that man (as such)
acts, and that "it would be correct to say that only
a part and not all of man acts".[48] In other words, an
internal, psychological, struggle takes place within
man, since the inner and the external or the old and

the new man are separated, not by virtue of the difference between soul and body, but by virtue of the feelings (sed iuxta affectus).[49] In short, man is possessed by contradictory feelings.

It is only possible to grasp the deeper significance
of simul justus et peccator if one takes seriously the
idea that man or his feelings or his will are determined by a foreign power or by the object towards which
attention is directed. If one adheres to an anthropology according to which man is or possesses a self which
is constant in some fashion or another, no matter what
happens, or if one maintains that he possesses a will
which in some sense is always able to will itself and
thus retain its freedom of choice, regardless of the
influences operating on it, then it is only possible
to regard justification (and perhaps also sin) as something to which man is a mere observer. God is logically
the only active agent.

Of course, this is not wrong, but this insight fails
to illustrate the fact that simil justus et peccator is
also a description of Christian psychology. W. Joest
has arrived at the conclusion that justification is
merely a forensic act of judgement which, in a manner
of speaking, takes place in outer space. Instead, he
maintains that a transformation occurs within man in
which God is the subject. Joest regards this as a paradox.[50] This does not become less paradoxical when we
consider that at the same time (simul) yet another subject is present within the individual, a subject not
identical with God, namely Satan. However, from the
point of view of a rhetorical-humanist anthropology,
there is nothing paradoxical about this. There will inevitably be an aspect of the identificatory about understanding, faith, feeling, and the will. And if it is

the case that there are a number of forces which levy
demands on territory within the human soul, then this
state of affairs can naturally only be expressed by a
"simul".

7. Use of the Bible

Having by now examined the basic lines of Luther's theology in the light of his understanding of man, it would
be appropriate to turn at this time to his view of the
Bible. Actually, it would perhaps have been more correct to begin with this topic, since Luther may be particularly characterized as a Biblical theologian because it was through intensive studies of central Biblical texts that he in fact developed his new theology.
The greater part of Luther's production consists of
commentaries on the Biblical texts, as well as of sermons about it or discussions of it. To Luther, to be
a theologian or a preacher was the same as to be an interpreter of the Bible. He immortalized this conviction
in two well known and striking phrases, sola scriptura
(only through the Scriptures) and scriptura sui interpres (The Scriptures are their own interpreter). It
might therefore have been fitting to have introduced
this work with an account of Luther's Biblical interpretation rather than a study of his ideas. Indeed,
many scholars have already done this. In my opinion,
however, this is a risky approach, since Luther's presuppositions and understanding of man are quite different from those dominant in our time. Thus it is all too
easy to misunderstand Luther and his interpretational
approach if one is not extremely cautious.

The fact that Luther attached such vast importance
to the Bible has to do with the considerations mentioned in the previous section. If it is correct that Luther
was, in company with the rest of his contemporaries,
influenced by the rhetorical way of thinking, then his
interest in the Biblical text is readily intelligible.
If the truth comes from what is heard and communicated,

then it must be transcendantly important to investigate
the source of such communication. It is more important
to do this than to clarify one's understanding of, for
example, man's own presuppositions, by means of which
he employs his reason and rationality to comprehend the
contents of what is said. It is namely impossible to
separate the truth from its source. In rhetorical terms,
there is never any question of contents alone, but always of contents which have been formulated in one way
or another. In connection with every message whatsoever
there are the further questions as to how it is expressed and to whom it is addressed. For this reason,
the humanists were never concerned with the mere contents of a message, but always with the text itself.
Thus for them Scripture was the locus of truth, and its
interpretation was of the utmost importance.

Of course, it was no innovation to maintain that the
Bible was the basis and handbook of the Church; no figure during the period of the Early Church or the Middle Ages would have questioned this. Nor were the sentiments expressed in Luther's two phrases cited above unknown during the Middle Ages.[1] But there is nevertheless a significant difference between the Catholic
Church's and Luther's views as to who was entitled to
interpret the Bible. For its part, the Church insisted
on three factors which would insure that the Bible was
understood correctly. In the first place, there was the
sacred office of the Papacy. Of course, Jesus had an-
nounced to the first Bishop of Rome, that is, the
apostle Peter, that, "I tell you, you are Peter, and
on this rock I will build my Church, and the powers of
death shall not prevail against it. I will give you the
keys of the kingdom of heaven, and whatever you bind
on earth shall be bound in heaven, and whatever you

loose on earth shall be loosed in heaven" (Matt 16,18-
19). Catholic tradition holds that St. Peter's authority to bind and loose has passed on to his successors,
the Popes, and that his authority extends to the right
to interpret the Bible authoritatively. Only the Church,
which in the last instance means the Pope, has the
right to say what the correct interpretation is. Laymen
have no such authority.

Therefore, during the Middle Ages it was regarded
as either superfluous or dangerous to translate the
Bible into the vernacular. Admittedly, the New Testament itself was composed in a demotic language, the so-
called _koine_ form of Greek, and it was later translated
into yet another demotic language, namely Latin, by St.
Jerome around 400. After the great European migrations,
however, Latin was no longer the language of the people,
but the Church nevertheless largely refrained from
translating the Bible into the newly emerged vernacu-
lars. Of course, these developments correspond quite
closely to the evolution of the Church into a central-
ized and hierarchically structured institution. It was
only possible to obtain correct advice as to the reading of the Bible from the right instance, namely the
sacred office.

The second aid to interpretation within the Church
was the so-called tradition, just as a judge has legal
commentaries and the assistance of earlier decisions
to aid him in interpreting the law. The tradition consisted of a sizeable and not very well defined corpus
of the writings of the Church fathers. The more prominent of these were such figures as Tertullian, Cyprian,
St. Jerome, St. Augustine, and so on; the major figures
of the Middle Ages included Albertus Magnus, St. Bonaventure, and St. Thomas Aquinas. The writings of all

these and other great scholars were to provide assistance in reading the Bible.

The third aid to interpreting the Bible was a very highly developed interpretative art called the allegorical method. The goal of this approach was to enable the exegete to penetrate to the remotest secrets of the text. It was not only felt possible to uncover the literal meaning of the text, but also to reveal the various figurative meanings which attached to it.

These three approaches characterize the approach to the Bible which was dominant during the Catholic Middle Ages. It is therefore against this background that scholars have attempted to depict Luther as the figure who 1) made the Bible accessible to the people by translating it and disencumbering it of Papal authority 2) removed the tradition, understood as the interpretative skeleton key; as signified by the expression sola fide 3) did away with all allegorical interpretation and replaced it instead with the literal meaning, as is expressed in the notion that "Scripture is its own interpreter" (scriptura sui interpres). This traditional description of Luther's contribution arose in the course of the 19th century, but it has persisted, with various subtleties, until the present. Even though it contains some truth, it is far from being an adequate description of Luther's radicality, as we shall proceed to show.

The Translation of the Bible into German

After the Diet of Worms, Luther was "kidnaped" by his protector, Frederick the Wise, who ensconced him in the castle of Wartburg. It was during this sojourn in 1521 that Luther translated most of the New Testament into German. In the history of the German language, this was

a decisive event, and nationalistically minded lingu-
ists have not hesitated to describe this event as the
foundation of the German nation. (It should be noted
that the government of East Germany, which is not otherwise especially interested in the inheritance from the
Lutheran Reformation, makes a special exception in this
case. Thus the castle at Wartburg is honored as a five-
star attraction and is kept in exemplary condition,
with airconditioning and so forth. The same is certainly not the case with Wittenberg).

In this sense, the government of East Germany has
taken over the national mythos of the Germany of the
kaisers; Luther is regarded as an exemple of true Ger-
manness: he has no style whatsoever, he obeys no rules
and is entirely free of foreign influence. Being a true
German genius, Luther derived the forcefulness of his
language from his own profound depths: "Die innere Er-
regtheit Luthers enfaltet sich ... als stilbildende
Kraft". Indeed, this is held to be a special characteristic of "das deutsche Sprachtum" (Petsch).[2]

Naturally, none of this bears closer examination.
As mentioned previously, the Swedish student of German-
ic languages, Birgit Stolt has shown how Luther's linguistic innovations are dependent even in the smallest
details on the basic rules of Latin rhetoric. In his
famous "Epistle on Translation", Luther tells us something about the principles underlying his translations.[3]
He claims not to aim at an elevated or ceremonious Biblical language; to the contrary, he has addressed himself to women, children and plain people in order to
find out how they actually speak, since it is in this
language that he intends his German translation to be
formulated. He has been attacked by the Papists for lack
of precision, and for adding his own words here and

there. Thus, for example, in connection with his translation of Rom 3,28 Luther has added the word "alone"
after "faith". Luther admits that the word is not in
the text, but adds that the sense of the verse becomes
clearer by its addition.

Now, it was a typical view of rhetorical humanism that
an easily intelligible and free translation was in certain
circumstances preferable to a literal, but not striking
or unclear one. Thus the Florentine Chancellor of State,
Coluccio Salutati (d. in 1406), had reworked a translation
of Plutarch into a free and expressive Latin, "for my own
and others' improvement, and for Plutarch's own honor."[4]

However, in his own German translation Luther was more
radical than were most of the Renaissance humanists,
especially those in Germany. Humanism was at this time
still a predominantly Latinist movement, even though some
figures, particularly in Italy, were also interested in the
vernacular, that is, the language of the people. This interest began to gain ground especially after the middle
of the 15th century.[5] Nevertheless, whether translation
was undertaken into one language or another, or whether it
was merely undertaken in the interests of achieving a
better and more understandable language, the very interest in translation itself was a humanistic characteristic
of profound significance, since it signified a new understanding of language. I have already dealt with this
phenomenon at some length, and I shall return to it presently. At this point, only a single aspect of the matter concerns us.

Modern people may wonder at the fact that the Catholic church has been able right up to our times to make
do with Latin Bible texts and with a Latin liturgy.
The reason is the conviction that the very pronounce-
ment of the words themselves is important, irregardless

of whether or not they are understood. This is virtually a magical view, and the sacred texts approach the
significance of conjuring formulas, sometimes quite literally. Take, for example, the words of institution
of Holy Communion: "this is my body, given for you".
It is held that the moment these words are uttered, the
bread becomes transformed into the body of Jesus, while
the wine becomes his blood. In this way, the priest is
a sort of magician who conjures by enunciating the sacred Latin formula, "hoc est corpus meum ..." It is not
remarkable that laymen thought these words to be something quite extraordinary, so that they were perceived
as hocus pocus. No doubt some were tempted to conjure
with them in other contexts.

Seen in this light, the sacred language of the Church
resembles magical incantations, and signs such as hier-
oglyphics or sacred numbers, amulets, and so forth.
None of these contains a message; they do not create
a community of understanding, since they possess magical efficacity. Popular traditions offer numerous ac-
counts of the use of Biblical passages or the Apostles'
Creed, the Cross, and similar other signs to subdue evil
powers or drive them out.[6]

The humanistic approach to language is quite different from this. According to this approach, language
speaks about and deals with something, so that it has
not achieved its goal before its audience has arrived
at the understanding or the experience intended. Language is a medium of a sort different from magic. As we
have discussed previously, the aim is to see or hear
what a particular subject is about, that is, to find
out what a particular case stands for, or, to coin a
phrase, to under-stand it.

In magic one has to do with foreign powers which act

on and through man without his understanding the process. In rhetorical and humanistic terms, language also
affects man, but without blockading his intellect, since
it is precisely by winning the intellectual acceptance
of the   listener that language is able to influence
him. The fundamental theological perception of the Renaissance was that the Bible relates such an important
and gripping story that one should spare no effort to
make people realize its deepest significance, so that
they may enjoy its benefits. "For this reason," as E-
rasmus says, "the theological profession is dependent
on ... the affects" (feelings),[7] since it is only the
feelings which are able to bring about this sort of understanding.

It is in this context that Luther's activities as
a translator are to be understood. It is only if people
understand the Bible that they have the possibility to
realize that they have received salvation. Man is not
to be manipulated about like a piece in some enchanted
game of chess. Instead, he is to understand what he
hears to his very depths, that is, in his heart.

Only through the Scriptures

Luther is often praised for having broken with the
Catholic doctrine of tradition and office as essential
for the correct understanding of Christianity. Against
these teachings, it is claimed, Luther posed only the
Bible itself, sola scriptura. This principle is generally termed the formal principle, that is, that the
truth is only to be found in the Scriptures. This view
has often been understood to suggest that the individual believer has direct and unmediated access to the
Bible. Thus understanding is conceived of as a matter
pertaining to the reader and the text; no other factors

should be allowed admission to the process or influence on it. Thus it should be theoretically possible to ignore all historical and dogmatic mediatory instances; in a manner of speaking, everyone has the possibility to be his own witness to whatever the Bible relates.

It is far from clear that this is what Luther intended, even though this was a prominent understanding of the matter within Pietism and much of the Christianity of the 19th century. As a faint expression of roots extending back to the extremist movements of the Reformation, that is, the so-called "Enthusiasts", people tended to emphasize the enlightenment of the heart brought about by the Holy Spirit. A related view was the so-called fundamentalist understanding of the Bible which manifested itself already during the period of Lutheran Orthodoxy in the 17th century. On this view, the Bible is always true; every single word has been pneumatically inspired by the Holy Spirit. For this reason, the Biblical word is absolutely reliable; it is also directly accessible to the reader. Thus it appears that if one rejects the authority of tradition or office and refuses to acknowledge other sources of revelation than the Scriptures, the general result is a tendency to supplement the hermeneutical process with the aid of the Holy Spirit, whether this be conceived as affecting the reader or the text itself. If the Holy Spirit is left out of the equation, this viewpoint means that everyone has the right to read the Bible as best he can - a not-uncommon view in our day.

A derivative of this tradition for reading the Bible is the so-called historical-critical approach to Biblical studies. This approach made itself powerfully felt during the 19th century. It attempted to employ the methods of historical science in order to find the Jesus

of history, so that we might discover what he was like
in reality. Here, too, it was thought possible to avoid
all tradition and dogmatism and so to be able to perceive Jesus and his times without prejudice or colored
spectacles. Unfortunately, this type of research encountered serious problems caused by the fact that the
sources, that is, the Gospels, turned out to be quite
unhistorical and unobjective. Nevertheless, it remains
one of the primary goals of exegetical studies at the
universities and other institutions of higher learning
to attempt to rediscover, if not Jesus himself, then
at least the conditions obtaining in his day, the life
of the early congregations, and so forth. Scholars still
adhere to the dream of becoming some sort of eyewit-
ness; getting so close to the events that it is possible to conceive how they actually took place remains the
goal of the true historical search for understanding.
Here tradition and office and even the Holy Spirit have
been replaced by the historical-critical method, which
also seeks to arrive at a correct reading of the Bible.[8]
Luther's principle of sola scriptura has figured as the
basis for all of the ways of reading the Bible which
are opposed to reading deriving from an authoritative
tradition (i.e., the readings based on personal experience, on fundamentalist presuppositions, or on historical-critical ones). Adherents of each approach have
tended to regard Luther as the originator of their way
of reading the Bible; they have read their views into
his.

Can We Do Without the Tradition?

In recent times it has become increasingly apparent
that it is extremely difficult completely to do away
with the aid of the tradition. Perhaps this acknowledge-

ment will enable us to distinguish some features of
Luther's own views which up to the present have been
relegated to the background of the discussion. It will
additionally enable us to understand Luther in the context of his own times.

Modern hermeneutical studies have demonstrated that
we do not have any direct access to the past. We do not
understand things "as they are", but on the basis of
our own presuppositions. This is to say that in knowing
something, we come first with our pre-judices (i.e.,
prejudgements), which is not to be taken pejoratively.
The fact of the matter is that our knowledge of the
past is not merely influenced by our expectations, interests, attitudes, knowledge, and so forth; it is determined by them. Indeed, it is thanks to these very
factors that we are able to establish some sort of relationship to the past and so to examine it. If we did
not possess pre-judices (i.e., expectations and so on),
then we would have no tool with which to approach the
past.

Yet another perspective enters into the discussion.
This is the fact that the past has a grip on us before
we even begin to inquire into it. In a certain sense,
the past itself formulates the very questions we pose
it. H.G. Gadamer has termed this phenomenon "effect-
history" (Ger: Wirkungsgeschichte).[9] Thus, for example,
the Christian command to love one's neighbor has exer-
cized a complicated influence on European thought
through the last 2,000 years. This entails that when
we today inquire as to the implications of the Biblical
command, then both our question - and, to a certain degree, our answer to it - are determined by our participation in European thought, and hence by the command
itself! To put it simply, it would be naive to imagine

that we can simply enter into the past in order to ask how things really were back then. Tradition always intervenes between us and our past, and, for that matter, between us and our present and future as well. It is accordingly impossible for us to inquire or to obtain and understand an answer without in some fashion being situated in that context from which the answer itself arises. Therefore it would appear to be reasonable to assert the validity of the concept of tradition, since this factor is apparently both real and efficacious, whether we will this to be the case or no.

Instead of attempting to repress the tradition by pretending that one has no presuppositions or is entirely objective, it would seem best to take cognizance of it, or of some parts of it. The Church, for example, has always been extremely conscious of the traditions she has accumulated; there has been no tendency merely to sit idly by and allow developments to dictate the nature of the ecclesiastical tradition. The Church has instead understood her tradition to consist of the conclusions of numerous concilia, the teachings of the fathers of the Church, Papal decrees, and so forth. One of the first and most important elements in this tradition was the formulation of a creed, a procedure which made it possible to arrive at a particular understanding of Christianity, and thus also a particular way of reading the Bible.

However, this was not merely true of the Catholic confession. The Lutheran Church, too, was forced to seek a normative tradition which could be said to characterize the Evangelical Lutheran faith. Indeed, this term is used by the Danish People's Church to describe itself. It is namely the case that one does not become Lutheran by merely reading the Bible, but by doing so

through rather special glasses, the "prescription" for
which is described by the Augsburg Confession of 1530
and the Lesser Catechism of Luther. Does this mean that
already in Luther's day people had broken with the principle of sola scriptura? The answer is that it does,
at least in the sense attributed to it in modern times.
In this connection it is worth noting that neither
Luther nor his church ever abandoned the creeds formulated by the Early Church; in fact, the Lutheran Church
in part found its identity through the use of these ancient texts as its basis.

Moreover, the cultivation of a particular tradition
in order to strengthen a sense of identity is by no
means confined to the Church, since virtually all religious, political, and other movements do the same. Just
as the Church has her "fathers", Marxism has Lenin;
where the Church has her creeds, Mainland China has
Mao's Little Red Book. Similarly, where the Church has
an annual cycle of festival and memorial days, other
movements have such important events as the 1st of May
or the 17th of October. In short, no one desires to do
away with tradition, since it helps to constitute its
adherents. Of course, this is also true of the Lutheran
Church, just as it was true of its founder. Nor is this
fact as paradoxical as might at first appear, since
Luther is not responsible for the interpretation of the
principle of "sola scriptura" which has been dominant
since the Reformation. Luther did not think of scripture and tradition as mutually exclusive quantities. Instead, he operated with a view which emphasized the
question of ·quality, that is, he held that the Scriptures are a more important source than the one which the
Church describes comprehensively as "tradition". In
fact, Luther felt that most of the mass of tradition

was directly harmful, and that the contents of the Bible were simply more true and correct than the fathers of the Church and others had held to be the case.[10]

If we take Luther's own day, that is, the Renaissance, into consideration, any other viewpoint would have been quite surprising. The designation for this period means rebirth, and it is important to recall, as we have seen, that this does not refer to a rebirth of antiquity. The reason the people of this period employed the concept of rebirth and other, similar, metaphors of their epoch (see above, pp.   3), was that they were referring to themselves and not to antiquity.[11] The Renaissance was not an antiquarian period; throughout this era a debate raged as to the relationship between ancient and modern, and in this debate it was repeatedly concluded that the goal was not to become like Cicero, but to use Cicero in one's efforts to arrive at clarity and linguistic expressiveness. Thus no one suffered from the naive belief that it was desirable to resuscitate antiquity in some way. Nor were people generally concerned with the antique in and of itself, that is, in its objective or actual condition. To the contrary, they expressed a living, existential interest in a particular age and the writings that age once produced, since they saw in that era a golden age, the products of which could conceivably enable progress in their own present.

This was not a matter of a historical interest or historical study along the lines of the modern discipline of history, in which one attempts cooly and objectively to find out what were the actual conditions of a given time. As far as this issue is concerned, the humanistic battlecry, "ad fontes" has often been misunderstood, since its real implication was to find the best and truest sources, those capable of endowing us with the best and truest life. Thus it was not the age of the sources, but their quality, which was held to be important. This was a criterium of content and not a formal criterium.

The same views applied to what was regarded as the greatest of ancient texts, the Bible. Luther's own interests in this respect are a natural extension of the general humanistic interest and enthusiasm for the Bible. The humanists attempted to read literature as they did the Bible, and the Bible as literature. This was the program for the humanistic way of reading the Bible which began with the so-called "Biblical poetics",[12] which in turn was replaced by the more neutral exegesis of modern humanism.

Thus, if Luther is to be understood in conjunction with the humanism of the Renaissance, we must recognize the qualitative basis of his principle of "sola scriptura". Of course, it is hard to imagine Luther undertaking extensive comparative studies, only to conclude that the Bible was in fact the best book available. No such objective freedom existed at the time with respect to the Book of Books. Accordingly, the principle of "sola scriptura" was a polemical one; It was not directed against all tradition, but against a particular one, that is, the bad tradition. And in what did this consist? In the tradition of the Middle Ages. In other words, Luther's mission was similar to the humanists' break with Scholastic philosophy; it was characterized by a loathing for a philosophical debate which in part was over-subtle and in part was based on a misunderstanding of language and thus of the Word of God. We shall go into this more closely below. In other words, the idea of "sola scriptura" as a "formal principle",

that is, as the notion was subsequently interpreted,
was foreign to Luther. This is not to say that there
was no difference between Luther's new understanding
of justification and, for example, the humanists' understanding of philosophia Christiana, which had to do
with moral philosophy in contradistinction to sophistry. But there are nevertheless structural similarities
in the sense that the enemy was the same theology of
the Middle Ages. Furthermore, just as Luther and the
humanists were agreed in their evaluation of the bad
tradition, they were also able to agree as to the good
one, which included both ancient authors and the fathers
of the Early Church. The favorite father of the Church
during the Renaissance was St. Augustine, so it is hardly surprising that he was also Luther's favorite.[13]

Scripture is its own Interpreter

To use the Latin phrase: scriptura sui interpres; the
very phrase implies an opposition to the allegorical
method of interpretation which was developed during the
Middle Ages. Moreover, it was also an attempt to ensure
that the Word of God would be retained pure and uncon-
taminated by human additions. Thus it was held important that interpretative methods not take their point of departure outside of the text, that is, outside of Scripture
itself. The text must be allowed to communicate its own
criteria to the reader. Only in this way can one be
certain that it actually is God's Word one is hearing,
and not a human, so-called "reasonable" voice (Luther
frequently and loudly declared his mistrust of human
reason, or "Frau Hulda", as he contemptuously called
it). Finally, it was extremely important to Luther to
read the Bible as an integral whole, so that details
not be abstracted from their context. This was called

"scopus-reading", the goal of which was to read a text
with a view to determining its intention, or scopus.

These three efforts are quite closely related, for
which reason it is appropriate to describe them as part
of the same approach.[14] Furthermore, it appears that
what is true of Luther's anthropology and understanding
of the will is also true of his textual interpretation.
We do not have to do with a specifically theological
problem or approach; in his way of understanding the
Bible Luther is simply transferring ordinary methods
and insights which were derived from the textual interpretative praxis of Renaissance humanism. Nor ought
this to surprise us, when we consider that the Renaissance was characterized by a new, that is, rhetorical,
way of reading texts and understanding language.[15]

Luther's Relationship to Allegorical Interpretation
In the opinion of most scholars, a central factor in
the understanding of Luther's way of reading the Bible
is his rejection of the allegorical method. It is un-
deniably the case that there are many passages in his
authorship in which Luther is severely critical of the
allegorical interpretation which the Biblical exegetes
of the Middle Ages had produced. After having examined
the four "meanings" which the earlier exegetes had
thought to find in the Epistle to the Galatians, Luther
remarks, "With such foolish, unreasonable, and shrewish
chatter by means of which they have pulled the Scriptures apart into so many different understandings and
meanings they have caused that great misery that it has
been impossible to teach and to instruct the conscienc-
es (of believers) certainly and thoroughly about anything at all."[16] On the other hand, there is nevertheless some reason to believe that we should be cautious

about saying that Luther rejected the allegorical approach as such, since, among other reasons, it is likely
that Luther meant by "allegorical" something different
from the modern meaning of the word.

During the Middle Ages, scholars utilized a fourfold
interpretative approach (quadriga) which had been adumbrated by Origen as early as the 3rd century, and
which in large measure was part of the inheritance of
Platonism.[17] These four approaches, when taken together,
were intended to ensure that the Biblical word would
be correctly understood.

The first method was termed the literal or "historical" approach (sensus literalis/historicus). In contemporary textual exegesis we speak instead of the
"outside" and "inside" of a text. The literal interpretation explores the outside of the text, in the sense
that one examines just what the text is about, that is,
what actually "happens" in the text. It might perhaps
be confusing to a modern reader that this approach is
called "historical" or "literal" even in conjunction
with texts which may very well contain reports of events
which must be regarded as quite unhistorical. Also, the
"historical" understanding of the text may take account
of such factors as the will of God or the religious
significance of the events depicted. To us, these are
not "historical" categories; we assign them instead to
the realm of interpretation, and indeed to a particular
sphere of interpretation which has become suspect in
our day, namely to the sphere of faith, religion, or
whatever else we should choose to call it. However,
from the Middle Ages and virtually up to the present
the specifically religious also characterized historical events, for which reason God, too, was held to be
a cause, and not merely the product of an interpret-

ation of Moses as the prototype of Jesus could easily be seen to cohere with the historical character of a narrative, exactly as was the case with St. Paul.

The next three methods "go behind" the texts, and they do so both intentionally and with a clear conscience, since they distinguish between the letter and the spirit. They did not do so as St. Paul, and later, Augustine, did, that is, in the words of the Second Epistle to the Corinthians: "for the written code kills, but the Spirit gives life." By this St. Paul meant that the "code" was the old Law or Covenant, while the "Spirit" referred to the Gospel. During the Middle Ages the external letter was regarded as the literal aspect of a narrative, that is, its sensus literalis, and scholars held that it was incorrect to stop at this level, since it was important to arrive at the spiritual contents of the account, which lay at a deeper level. Indeed, in certain cases this was held to be of paramount importance, since the text in question simply could not be taken at face value. For example, Jesus was not sent merely to save sheep, even though he speaks much of "lost" members of the species. Yet another example, and one which was frequently employed during the Middle Ages, was the second creation narrative and the account of the Fall. in which God behaves in entirely too human a fashion. Thus he appears as the gardner who "speaks", "becomes angry", and so forth. It was held that this sort of thing could in fact only be understood figuratively, and that not to do so would be to destroy the narrative.

After the literal method was the moral or tropological one (sensus tropologicus). On this approach it was important to decide just what moral could be derived from the narrative; one inquired as to what the text recommended that we should do. Thus, for example, a Danish preacher interpreted the account in which the twelve year-old Jesus found that he had to remain in the Temple, so that his parents were forced to go home without being able to find him, as an injunction to humility. We should no doubt find this a somewhat precious interpretation, but on the one hand it should be noted that the very fact that God became man is an indication of humility, while on the other he held that the narrative showed how much God loved the world, since one does not remain for a long time in a place one does not care for.[18]

The third interpretive method is the allegorical method per se (sensus allegoricus). This represented an attempt to find the actual meaning of a given text. For example, in a particular narrative Jesus feeds a whole multitude in spite of the fact that he only has at his disposal seven loaves of bread and a few fish. What could be more natural than to attempt to find the significance underlying the seven loaves? In this connection some scholars interpreted the loaves as "The seven gifts of the Holy Spirit or the Word of God, prayer, repentance, recollection of Christ's Passion, the sacrament of Communion, and the comfort provided by the Holy Spirit. But the loaves were also understood as the seven virtues with which Christ refreshes his servants, namely repentance, work undertaken in the fear of God, patience, mercy, Christian instruction, comfort in adversity, and the joys of Heaven. The seven loaves were also taken to be the acknowledgement of a bad way of life, fear of relapsing into sin, the self-accusation of the Confessional, sorrow over one's sins, the wish to reform oneself and others. Alternatively, they were taken to be one's daily bread, the Scriptures, the grace of God, the sacrament of Communion, spiritual consolation (number 7 is missing), while the few fish were symbolic of the saints." These examples have been extracted from Anne Riising's work on Danish sermons of the Middle Ages;[19] they illustrate, very well in my opinion, the way exegetes abstracted a single detail and then attempted to endow it with deeper significance. In the example in question the various preachers arrived at quite different results, but this does not necessarily entail that they felt themselves to be in disagreement, since they no doubt felt that the same words can easily have a variety of meanings, so that the best results are achieved by finding as many of them as possible. Thus the expression "the seven loaves" could be held to be a sort of window onto a rich and varied prospect.

Finally, there was the mystical or anagogical method (sensus mysticus/anagogicus). This was actually regarded as the most important of all, but at the same time it is the most difficult to describe. The idea was to concentrate on the text in question as a point of departure for one's meditations. Thus with the aid of the text one was lifted up (anagein) to a complete or partial mystical union with God. Accordingly, it was possible already in this earthly existence to anticipate the future heavenly coexistence with God.

The "fourfold method of Scripture" implies that the Biblical texts are not immediately clear or intelligible, except at the literal level. In other words, there is something between the lines, as it were, which is first able to affect the reader when it has been made accessible by an interpretation. There is nothing especially unusual about this view, since even in our day we conduct textual interpretation and also employ the assistance of professional exegetes when a given text is not immediately intelligible to us. This is above all when we have to do with ancient texts which the great gap of time has rendered difficult of access. The Bible offers a good example of this, which is why theological faculties and seminaries have numerous corps of exegetical teachers whose job it is to attempt to build bridges between students and the Biblical text. Indeed, some would probably claim that this is the very purpose of the theological endeavor.

However, the fourfold approach of the Middle Ages went considerably farther with respect to textual exegesis than we would attempt today. In particular, the anagogical and allegorical approaches imply that we have to do with a special kind of text, a sort of riddle or parody. The outside of the text was seen as being only loosely related to its inside, as the examples mentioned previously show. Thus in a certain sense, one was not to take the text as it is seriously, but to seek a different and higher meaning behind the literal level. Of course, it was understood that God was the author of the Bible. Accordingly, since God's divinity could not be contained by the written word, he was in some way obliged to restrict himself as to what he should say; language would not be able to contain it. On the other hand, in some manner God had nevertheless managed to express himself completely in his Word. Understood in this fashion, there was infinitely more present in a given Biblical text than the literal level was capable of representing.

This viewpoint entailed that it was unnecessary to study the texts in their given sequence. Not only every one of the individual writings of the Bible, but even every verse or individual word in it, was capable of pointing to a vastly greater world behind the written level. For this reason it was thought legitimate to interpret such details as, for example, the 30, 60, and 100-fold yields returned by the good earth in the parable of the sower (Mk 4,1ff.). Read at the literal level, these were only elements in a story, but they could attain independent significance in an allegorical interpretation, as signifying, for example, laymen, priests, and munks, respectively. This was a common approach during the Middle Ages; by means of it the Scriptures became a sort of puzzle or rebus containing other figures than those immediately apparent, the elucidation of which was the task of the exegete.

Symbol Instead of Allegory

In contemporary language we would probably not call this sort of interpretation allegorical, but symbolical. But what, then, is a symbol? It is something by means of which one identifies oneself. One can tear in half a card or dollar bill and give one half to the person who is to identify himself, which he can do simply by showing the half in his possession. The idea is that the half in his possession must fit together (symballein) with the other half. If it does so, then the possessor has successfully identified himself (for example, as a member of a group of conspirators, or the like). It may be said that in a way this half bill stands for the whole thing; alternatively, one could say that it symbolizes the whole bill. If one has the fractional part, then one can conclude the existence of the whole, or at least infer it. In other words, the half bill is nothing in and of itself, as it is only so long as one comprehends the whole that it has value. If we transfer this notion to the study of texts it indicates that it is not their face value, or the action recounted in them that makes up the text as such; rather, these aspects must be seen as signposts pointing beyond themselves to something else. For example, the Cross is not merely the wooden cross upon which Jesus was hung. Instead, it opens up a whole world of symbolic associations whose perspectives are endless, far beyond the borders of what can be said in human language. This does not mean that we can do without the external word or the text in front of us, just as in the example above we could not dispense with the half bill, but it does mean that we are not to be content with the external aspect. The task of the wooden cross is to point beyond itself and so to serve as a sign or symbol. Moreover, not only the Cross, but the entire Bible is a sign which points onwards to divine truth. This sign theory was perhaps most thoroughly explored and unfolded by St. Augustine, according to whom all created things are symbols which in the last analysis point to God.[20]

On the basis of this understanding of the word "symbol" it could be asserted that the entire textual theory of the Middle Ages presupposes symbolic interpretation, for the reason that the text itself was regarded as a symbol.[21] Thus we may find it confusing that scholars during the Middle Ages termed their way of understanding texts "allegorical". Unfortunately, modern Luther scholarship has taken this term at face value and assumed that there really was a question of allegorical textual interpretation. Therefore some serious mistakes have also been made as to the nature of Luther's break with the Biblical exegesis of the Middle Ages, since Luther was not concerned to do away with the allegorical, but with the symbolic interpretation of Scripture.

What is Allegory?

In the beginning of the 1950's there was a scandal involving political corruption in Denmark. Some of the
Danish police actually collaborated with a number of
smugglers and figures from the black market. The worst
of the latter figures, known as the "Spider", was im-
prisoned, but he continued to direct his smuggling empire thanks to his good relationship to the authorities. This situation was exploited by the Danish author
Hans Scherfig in a book entitled The Scorpion, which
was an allegory whose basis was the real story of the
"Spider". At the same time, Scherfig's work was also
a sort of model of reality, although it contained the
sorts of forshortenings and accentuations that are inevitably present in models.[22] The author's goal was to
enable his reader to understand the case better than
he could do by just reading the newspapers, so that he
would be able to realize that "spiders" or "scorpions"
do not arise by accident in a capitalistic society;
rather, they are created by the system itself.

Thus, to a certain extent Scherfig's book is to be
read as if it dealt with something quite different than
what it seems to recount. There is an appearance of
similarity to the previously mentioned symbolic text
theory. However, there is a decisive difference. The
symbol only presents itself as the occasion by which
knowledge arises; thus one either understands it, or
fails to do so. For this reason symbolic thought is
frequently supplemented with the notion of a special sort
of spiritual understanding, such as that which is, for
example, held to come about through the aid of the Holy
Spirit. Alternatively, it may come about because one
is a genius who intuitively understands the power of
the symbol in question. The latter idea emerged during
the age of Romanticism.[23]

Allegory, however, is another matter. When Scherfig's
book appeared, its readers had the "Spider case" fresh
in their memories thanks to the newspaper coverage of
it. The interest aroused by the book and the insights
provoked by it were the results of this fact. Many people
felt that they were enriched by the book precisely because they compared the model contained in it with reality and were thereby able to understand both better.
Thus the ability of an allegory to create knowledge resides in the tension between two known factors rather
than in the pointing of a known thing to an unknown one.
A symbol can reveal itself to a talented observer who
possesses the special spiritual presuppositions necessary to the job, whereas an allegory is intelligible
to anyone.

The same applies to metaphor, which is why Aristotle
says that an allegory is an extended metaphor.[24] In
other words, a metaphor also juxtaposes two known quantities. When one speaks of the "lion Achilles", there
is nothing remarkable about the lion, which is an animal with well-known attributes. Nor is there anything
remarkable about Achilles, with whom we are familiar
from Homer's famous narrative. No, the remarkable aspect lies (or lay, for this metaphor is by now 2500
years old) in the juxtaposition or comparison of the
two quantities. In a surprisingly new, striking, and
intelligible way, something has been said about Achilles'
courage, power, and so forth.

However, people have frequently had a different view
of metaphor and allegory; indeed, this has been the
case from the age of Romanticism until the present. The
tendency has been to deny that such figures of speech
contained any ability to convey new knowledge. Instead,
they were usually simply regarded as banal and uninter-

esting examples of linguistic camouflage; one said
"scorpion" and meant "spider": a slightly strained joke.
Perhaps this sort of thing could be used in pedagogical
situations: one may wrap things up so as to give children the fun of unwrapping them again. The net result
would be to make the classroom somewhat less boring,
but the things to be learned would naturally remain the
same.

While the Romantics and later figures despised the
allegory, they evaluated the symbol rather more posi-
tively. The symbol was not merely camouflage of something well known; to the contrary, it was a pointer to
a larger reality than our own. The symbol was a corner
of life's own apron, so that if we cling to it we actually have a grasp on life itself. Thus we do not participate in an unreal maskerade consisting of our own
selfcreated metaphors and allegories. To the Romantics,
it was primarily in poetry that the vital symbols were
to be found. They were capable of mentioning, but not
of description or explanation, since the reality inherent in the symbol was held to extend beyond the possibilities of language,so that it could only be glimpsed.

Romanticism became a dead issue quite some time ago,
for which reason it is all the more strange that many
of its leading ideas have survived unchanged into an
era which otherwise seems to be quite unromantic. And
yet, it is observable that such things as the romantic
understanding of love have also survived surprisingly
well. Similarly, our understanding of symbol and metaphor have also been influenced by the romantic understanding of these phenomena. We persist in saluting
Goethe's idea of the symbol as a creating, mind-expanding
point of departure for knowledge. Contrariwise, we continue to believe that allegory and metaphor lock the

the individual within himself, since they are products
of man's own old and rational language.[25]

This understanding of symbol and allegory has been
of partidular importance in theological and religio-
philosophical thought. In recent times such concepts
as, for example, that of a specifically religious reality have become increasingly diaphanous and implaus-
ible. Nevertheless, in order to defend such notions,
theologians have attempted to make use of the above-de-
scribed symbol theory, according to which it is namely
acceptable that the divine reality is not immediately
present, since we think to possess symbols which can
point beyond our present reality to a higher one. Similarly, for example, the liberal theology of the 19th
century described such external forms of the Church
and Christianity as the services, doctrines, and so
forth as symbols of an inner reality which was held to
be located in the conscience. In this century, such
scholars as, among others, Paul Tillich, have attempted to reformulate Christianity with the aid of a symbolist procedure.

Probably of equal importance for the theological attempt to make fruitful use of symbolic thought is the
fact that up until modern times people have generally
thought in symbolic terms. Most ordinary people regard
such things as, for example, the graphic arts, to be
symbols indicative of the inner reality of the artist.
We have great difficulty accepting the idea that an ab-
stract picture might not have referential character.
The same is true of poetry. It is of no importance as
to whether the artists or poets in question agree with
this understanding; on the general view, a true artist,
like the founder of a religion, must be a symbolist.
Of course, this also applies to those historical per-

sons who have helped to shape Christianity; if they are
to be acceptable to the modern consciousness, they must
in some way be symbolists, not allegorizers or special-
ists in metaphor. In the same vein, both Jesus and
Luther have been dubbed symbolists by modern research,
which like modern man in general has inherited its spiritual orientation and attitude towards artistic and
religious phenomena from the age of Romanticism. We
shall briefly see how this came about, by taking a brief
glance at Jesus and then pressing on to Luther.

Adolf Jülicher's Understanding of Parables

Modern research on the parables of Jesus was initiated
by Adolf Jülicher through his work, Die Gleichnisreden
Jesu, which appeared in 1888/89.[26] Using the previously-
mentioned distinction between symbol and allegory, Jülicher worked out a system enabling him to determine
which parables Jesus had personally related, such as
the story of the Prodigal Son, and which (allegorical)
parables he had not told, such as the story of the unfaithful vineyard workers in Matt. 21,33ff. Jülicher
held it to be inconceivable that Jesus himself could
have recited allegories. Indeed, this view was so obvious for a post-Romantic that he did not even bother
to investigate it further. The same applies to most of
the exegetical research on the parables up to the present. Using this point of departure, if it should prove
possible to distinguish sharply between parables and
allegories, then we would possess a basis for determining just which of the "words" of Jesus are authentic,
and which are not, or so Jülicher maintained. The evangelists must have derived the latter category from other
sources.

    Now, it cannot be denied that, formally considered,

the parables of Jesus resemble those parables, fables, exemplary narratives and other pictorial narratives which were greatly enjoyed in antiquity, and which were held to "allegorizein", that is, to allegorize. In order to separate the parables of Jesus from the other allegorical narratives, Jülicher determined that the parable was a special form because it was usually introduced by "like", as, for example, when we read, "the kingdom of Heaven is like ...", followed by a narrative. Thus, instead of saying "Achilles is a lion" or "the lion Achilles", the parabolic mode would be to say that "Achilles is like a lion".[27]

Apart from the fact that the latter formulation is weaker than the first, since the identity of the quantities in question is not so forcefully asserted, it is not immediately clear that there is any significant semantic difference between the two types of expression. However, Jülicher energetically claimed that there in fact was such a distinction, and he utilized it in order to claim that the simile was not merely linguistic ornamentation like the metaphor or the allegory. To the contrary, the simile contains a proof of its truth, which means that it also says something about the nature of reality in that it clarifies for its hearer some aspect of the kingdom of God. The simile is namely real speech, since it allows Achilles to remain what he is (i.e., a man, a hero, or whatever). The comparison consists in the fact that, just as the lion is courageous, so, too, is Achilles. This is clear and immediately intelligible language, so that the simile is well suited for teaching purposes. Metaphor, on the other hand, represents a veil of mystification; one does not compare two quantities, but identifies them instead, so that they in fact can replace one another, as in, "the lion raged forth against the enemy".

In Jülicher's opinion, this sort of language is purely figurative, since something is said which is not actually meant (namely that Achilles went forth).[28] Such
language verges on the uncontrollable and ambiguous,
since the metaphor does not speak of what is, but instead replaces something that is (Achilles) with something else (the lion). The only limit to this sort of
"entbehrliche Zierrat" (expendable ornament), in Jülicher's phrase, is set by one's imagination. Perhaps
one could illustrate Jülicher's view by comparing it
with a crossword puzzle, in which the object of the exercise is invariably to find new words in place of the
ones listed. Therefore Jülicher feels that the metaphor
and its cousin, the allegory (which is, after all, only
an extended metaphor or several of them put together),
are primarily cultivated in times of poor literary cre-
ativity, that is, times lacking in true dramatic materials, in which one therefore attempts "to expell the
boredom by making difficult preciosities".[29] On the
other hand, if one - like Jesus - really has something
worth communicating, then one has no need of such gew-
gaws.

Jülicher's parable theory is not supported by the
classical understanding of the subject. Furthermore,
as mentioned above, it cannot bear closer investigation.
There is namely no significant semantic difference between "Achilles is like a lion" and "Achilles is a
lion", except that the former is slightly weaker than
the latter. It is to be seen that both types of language require imagination and fantasy of their audience.
It is not immediately easy to see the resemblance between Achilles and a lion if one has never considered
the matter before. However, the moment one recognizes
the appropriateness of the figure, it is solidly im-

printed in one's consciousness, thanks to the pedagogical clarity of the metaphor or simile in question.

Yet another objection to Jülicher's view is that he
makes use of a tertium comparationis which is the meeting
point between the pictural part and the factual part
of the matter in question. Admittedly, there is something in common between Achilles and the lion, such as
their courage. But it would be quite inaccurate to call
one aspect of this the pictural part, and the other the
factual one. Naturally, it would be inappropriate to
maintain that Achilles is real, while the lion is merely a picture, or figure. Both parts are equally "real",
or else we should not be able to compare them. In fact,
this entire distinction between picture and reality is
very problematical. "Achilles is a lion" is a pictural
or metaphorical expression which claims to say something about reality. In other words, the comparison
takes place in the picture or linguistic expression itself, which, if appropriate, also reproduces a comparison which applies to reality. Thus in actuality both
the metaphor and the simile make linguistic comparisons
with the aid of language, for which reason there is no
reason for distinguishing sharply between them.

Indeed, Jülicher himself ends in a self-contradiction
which shows that a picture or metaphor does not compare
a picture with a fact. He attempts to apply his theory
to Jesus' parables of the Kingdom, a number of which
begin with the phrase "the Kingdom of God is like ..."
This is followed by a narrative like the one dealing
with the unfaithful vineyard workers, or the prodigal
son, or whatever. On Jülicher's own view, such formulations concist of a pictural (or metaphorical) part =
the parable which has been recounted, and a factual
part = the Kingdom of God. In this context the job of

the listener is to find the point of similarity. The explanation is, of course, that one is not to compare the parable with the Kingdom of God in order to find common features. To the contrary, one must discover what other (well known) narrative the parable plays on. If one had not possessed the parable, one would have had no knowledge of the Kingdom of God.

How does one say something new? One does this by introducing something new, such as an unusual picture or metaphor, or else one relates a surprising narrative. In doing so, one is obliged to presuppose that one's audience has some expectations or previous knowledge. What is new is so only in relation to something old, and if one has no expectations, then nothing unexpected can occur. A large part of the proclamation of Jesus can be understood along these lines, and in particular his parables, which frequently play on the anticipatory understanding of his Jewish audience, in order to break with it. To be more precise, many parables take their point of departure in Jewish stories which Jesus retells, but with a different intention. The workers in the vineyard (Matt 20) is a telling example. The narrative describes the hiring of workers at various times throughout the day, for which they nevertheless receive the same pay, even though some of them were hired only an hour before quitting time. The point of the story must be that in the Kingdom of God, pay is not allotted according to one's merits. At all events, this point becomes fully clear when we compare the narrative with another well known, then-contemporary Jewish story in which the workers are also hired throughout the day, but the last of them three hours before quitting time. It is noteworthy that the last to be hired makes an extraordinary effort, and so accomplishes just as much as the others. Therefore he, too, deserves the reward for a whole day's work.

It is in this context that Jesus is so bold as to declare that his story says something about the Kingdom of God. But just what his point is can only be determined by the examination of the "normative" version of the story. It is only possible to compare two things which are known, never one which is with one which is not. Thus it is correct to conclude that both metaphors/ allegories and similes/parables achieve their communicative power thanks to the tension between two known quantities. Whether this tension resides in the similarity in spite of the difference or in the difference in spite of the similarity, it is nevertheless the new and creative aspect of the linguistic act in question. In other words, one does not exceed the limits of language and thus arrive at the matter itself by use of metaphors or other comparisons. We only possess reality, the matter itself, as we express it in our descriptions, metaphors, and so forth. Thus one cannot counterpoise or compare fact and description, but only one description with another.

Language and Reality

The intention underlying Jülicher's parable theory was to make the understanding of Jesus' proclamation so univocal and precise that it would be able to resist all types of misinterpretation. The means of achieving this was by doing away with the metaphorical and allegorical aspects of language in favor of a literal and figurative concept, according to which metaphorical language only takes place when a factual matter is compared with a pictural one. With the self-assurance that is made possible by a purely formal distinction, Jülicher thus attempted to purify the authentic words of Jesus (the parables) of the traditions made by the evangelists and early congregations (among other things consisting of metaphors and allegories).

My reason for devoting so much space to Jülicher's work is that his view of allegory was characteristic for the understanding of the phenomenon during most of the 19th and 20th centuries. It is this view which has also influenced our understanding of Luther's understanding of the Bible. This was in part the case because, narrowly considered, Jülicher himself exercised a considerable influence on Luther scholarship, since such leading students of Luther as Gerhard Ebeling derived their conceptual apparatus from him.[30]

The question as to whether one prefers to call Jülicher a nominalist or a symbolist actually depends on the viewpoint from which one studies him. He is a nominalist in the sense that he believes that we possess a reality which we know without reference to language. Thus in a strict sense we know the Kingdom of God already before we speak of it, which is why we understand parables about it. Accordingly, while language is indeed able to inform us about things, it can only tell us about things with which we are already in some way familiar. For this reason, Jülicher also compares the parable to a mathematical proof.[31] Mathematics and logic are not subject to the unreliability of language; rather, they speak directly to our reason, and so are able to show us how things really are.

But one can also term Jülicher a symbolist, and not merely because he evinces the Romantic contempt for allegories and metaphors. Nominalism and symbolism are in fact not so far apart as one might think. Symbolic interpretations, too, both medieval and modern ones, imply a deep-rooted distrust of language as a means of acquiring knowledge. They seem to presuppose that if we cannot penetrate behind language, then we will never attain to reality. On this view, the symbol is in all actuality not really a linguistic phenomenon, not even if the symbol itself is a word or takes the form of words which in turn are part of a text. A symbol cannot be translated into something else; language is permitted, but it is held to be at some remove from real life.

Now, Jülicher assigns to the parable something that is otherwise characteristic for the symbol, namely immediacy. Where the allegory is artificial and precious, the parable is in Jülicher's theory as directly accessible as the symbol was to the genius of the Romantics. Language veers off in favor of the things themselves in all their immediacy. Thus such concepts as "authenticity" and "validity" belong in this context. J.J. Rousseau gives expression to a similar thought when he says that to judge a writer on the basis of his works is like evaluating a man on the basis of his corpse. The authorial personality is something different from the authorship itself; a man is concealed behind the words. In this sense, both symbolism and nominalism are agreed that things, and above all people, are something both different from and more than we are able to say about them.[32]

Luther and the Scholars

The Danish scholar Thestrup Pedersen maintains, no doubt correctly, that "it is more or less unanimously claimed by scholars that Luther's main contribution and most significant merit resides in the fact that he broke with the allegorical method of interpretation, although, as they usually said, Luther was not always able in his

own exegesis to make serious use of his new theory."[33]
However, the problem with the modern study of Luther's
view of the Bible and his use of it is that both in
terms of contents and terminology such scholarship is
in reality located at a different spot than it thinks
itself to be. In the first place, Luther broke with an
"allegorical method" which in modern usage ought properly to be called the "symbolic method", as has been
suggested above. Second, it is usually on the basis of
false preconceptions that the modern reader of Luther,
be he layman or scholar, understands and agrees with
Luther's break with the allegorical method. In reality,
the modern reader is much closer to the symbolism and
nominalism of the Middle Ages than to the rhetorical
use of metaphor and allegory during the Renaissance.
Being symbolists ourselves, we make a symbolist of Luther, too (or else he would not be a reasonable man),
just as we also assume that he broke with the allegorical method (which he did not). We further assume that
Luther understood the understanding of language and
text enjoyed by modern scholars (which he certainly did
not).

As an illustration of the difficulties modern research sometimes creates for itself in this respect,
we may examine G. Ebeling's fundamental work, Evangelische Evangelienauslegung. Eine Untersuchung zu Luthers
Hermeneutik, München, 1942. Ebeling feels that Luther
underwent a development which led him away from the allegorical interpretation; thus his Ch. II deals with
Luther's use and abandonment of the allegorical method.[34] However, in this chapter we see that Luther has
by no means abandoned the search for allegories, typologies, and suggestive etymologies in the Biblical text;
this feature obviously bothers Ebeling, although he

cannot explain it away. Ultimately he is forced to acknowledge that Luther's surrender of allegory is mainly
"tacit". Quite so, quite so.

Twelve years after Ebeling's work appeared, Walter
von Loewenich spoke in his Luther als Ausleger der Synoptiker of his high regard for Ebeling's view of Luther's rejection of allegory - following which Loewenich himself treats the reader to an extensive selection
of Luther's allegorizing interpretations (p. 16ff). The
general view seems to be that from 1519-21 and later
Luther "rejects ... both in principal and totally the
fourfold exegetical method and prefers instead the literal meaning as the sole sense of Scripture. Nevertheless (!) Luther continues to struggle with the problem
of allegory."

Thus it is impossible that Luther should have been
an allegorist, and when he nevertheless appears to be
so the scholars in question acknowledge that there is
some sort of contradiction, but one with which it will
be necessary to bear over. This is an interesting situation, since it shows how a scholar can be so dominated by his prejudices that he is unable to free himself of them, even though he may be well aware that the
materials under consideration actually say something
different. A problem common to all three scholars is
that they confuse symbol and allegory. Luther rejected
the symbolic fourfold interpretation, but he never rejected allegory. Thus he was always able to find allegories, metaphors, and a good deal of other pictural
language, although he did so without resorting to the
fourfold interpretation.[35]

Luther's Understanding of Language
In order to approach this subject, it will be necessary

to examine Luther's understanding of text and language,
and in particular his understanding of metaphor and allegory. We shall also examine Luther's concept of
searching for the intention or "scopus" of a text.

Luther's tract entitled "On the communion of Christ"
informs us about his understanding of metaphor. The
problem in question has to do with the right understanding of the phrases "this is my body" and "this is my
blood", which of course are spoken as the priest gives
a piece of bread and some wine to the communicant. Does
this mean that the bread has become the body of Jesus,
and the wine his blood? This problem entailed an extended discussion during the Middle Ages, as a result
of which the Catholic Church opted for the doctrine of
"transubstantiation", according to which the bread and
wine became transformed as the words of institution
were pronounced.[36] In other words, the Church concluded
that the two substances relly were body and blood, although they retained the appearance of bread and wine.

Yet another interpretation, and by the same token
one which had been active throughout the history of the
Church, made itself particularly felt during the Reformation among the more extreme Christian congregations which emerged in the wake of the Lutheran reformation. These were the so-called "Enthusiasts" (Schwer-
mere). This interpretation has a number of forms, but
in its essence it does not maintain that the bread and
wine become the body and blood of Christ. Instead, it
is held that the elements of the sacrament refer to
or call to mind the blood and body of Jesus like a memorial or memorandum.[37] This "reminder" can be understood in a variety of ways. Some people tie a knot in
their handkerchiefs to ensure that they will remember

something in the course of the day. Every time they
touch the knot, they are reminded of its reason. Of
course, this simile presupposes that the practitioner
of this trick knows in advance what it is he is to remember. In this sense the bread and wine of the sacrament are merely external, accidental signs of some non-
visual and non-linguistic reality to which the "sign"
in question refers. It is essential that one know the
reality in advance, by, for example, an agency like
the influence of the Holy Spirit, which was a by no
means unusual view among the Enthusiasts of the Reformation. This concept is itself reminiscent of a thorough-
going nominalism, which, as we have seen, also asserts
that the connection between a sign and its significance
is accidental.

Of course, a more tangible connection is also conceivable; one might, for example, say that the bread
and the wine "represent" the body and blood. In this
event the sign would not be accidental, but expressive
and descriptive: the image itself gives some impression
of the reality, even though, naturally enough, the
image is only an image. In a similar way it is possible
to recognize a man once one has seen his portrait, even
though also in this case the image is not identical
with what it represents.

Luther takes none of these possibilities into account. To the contrary, he asserts that the "sign" or
"image" is identical with the reality itself. All the
words in the sentence "this is my body" are to be taken
literally, both "is" and "body". But how are we to understand this? In daily language we might say "the
young maiden is a rose", or, with Luther, "Christ is
a rose". According to Luther, the rose does not symbolize the maiden or Christ; rather, an identification is

implied. When Christ is called a "rose", "grapevine", "lamb", or whatever, these terms do not "mean" Christ or "refer" to Him. They are synonyms for Him; he is all of these things.[38] Should we object that Christ does not have red petals, thorns, and so forth, that is, things that pertain to a "natural" rose, Luther would reply that that is true enough, but that now we have used the expression of Christ, it has received a new significance. From now on the word "rose" covers both the flower and Christ, in the same sense as the word already includes roses which are carved in wood or sculpted in marble.

If this were not the case, or so Luther maintains, then language would not be able to live up to its intention. It would be mere riddletalk or code, requiring a "key" before we could understand it. A code always presupposes that there exists some other language which is the "right" one. If we play the spy and transform a message into figures or mathematical symbols, the intelligible sentence remains the "right" one, while the coded sentence merely refers to this sentence, the meaning of which is contained by the code. In fact, if the "right" sentence was in turn a code (that is, if the system resembled a collection of Chinese boxes), then it must also refer to another level of language at which the real and immediate meaning was accessible. Similarly, there are no echoes which are not echoes of something; nor are codes or signs possible which do not stand for something else, namely simple language.

Thus Luther is essentially claiming that language in general is not a code. Admittedly, language contains multitudinous possibilities for "inauthentic" speech, that is, such forms as irony, humor, satire, contradiction, paradox, images, metaphors, and so forth. However, these may not be understood to be codes. To the contrary, in the final analysis they are the means by which language explains itself and makes itself clear and intelligible. Language can create its own clarity. Clarity cannot be derived from something outside of language, nor is language merely a sign or code which refers to some reality which cannot be adequately described in words. For this reason there is some danger in distinguishing between "authentic" and "inauthentic" speech; one might be led to believe that "Achilles is brave" or "the girl is lovely" is more true than "Achilles is a lion" or "the girl is a rose". Both types of expression may be either true or false; the former is not more authentic, veridical, or immediate than the latter.

This was Luther's insight, in essence. Sentences like "this is my body" do not have referential or symbolic qualities; rather, they are assertions about reality. This is of the utmost importance for Luther: if it is not the case, then we shall have scant joy of the Word of God, for then God cannot really have revealed himself. As a result, the Gospel and the rest of Scripture would be a rebus requiring to be solved before we may perceive its true meaning. Luther finds this notion unacceptable, on the assumption that God has not merely revealed a fragment of himself, but the whole of his love. The Gospel is very close to man, indeed, as close as language itself. "The New Testament ... is the conferral of grace and the forgiveness of sins, that is, the true Gospel ..."[39] The Gospel does not <u>deal with</u> grace and forgiveness; it is identical with them.[40]

Luther is here touching on an insight which in modern times has been rediscovered and described in a different terminology than that of rhetoric. For example, the Danish theologian and author N.F.S. Grundtvig was able to speak of "the Word that creates what it names". It is this aspect of language that Luther, too, had perceived.

Around the middle of this century, English philosophers of language made the interesting discovery that not all words refer to something.[41] When one says "horse", one means a particular animal, or else the genus. In other words, the word "horse" refers to a non-linguistic reality (although this may be questioned, but it would not serve our purposes at this point to do so). On the other hand, when one says, "I promise, baptize, wed you", then one refers to a reality which lies outside of the expression. The expression itself creates the reality to which it refers. "I promise you" is itself the promise. Thus the sentence in question is not _about_ a promise; it _is_ a promise. The same is the case when one writes, "I hereby bequeath ..." One's last will and testament, complete with all its properties of inheritance, comes into being on this occasion. This is a speech act, or a performative utterance, to use the modern terminology. According to Luther, this is precisely what happens when we read the New Testament; it does not merely proffer God's love; rather, it bequeaths or bears witness to it. If it did not do so, it would have to refer to yet another New Testament capable of communicating the love of God.[42] In the same sense, "I love you" is not an announcement of some inner love, but is instead the expression and form of love. The New Testament _is_ the love of God.

Of course, Luther had no notion of modern Anglo-Saxon linguistic philosophy. His point of departure was that rhetoric which was revived during the Renaissance, and whose presupposition it was that language is able to communicate to its audience every conceivable type of

reality. Language, and in particular the sensuous features of it such as images, metaphors, and similes, is
able to make what is remote in terms of time and space
into something present and immediate. We encounter reality via the sensuous nature of language.

Now, in rhetorical terms there are no expressions
which merely refer to something. Simply in virtue of
the fact that it is uttered, every expression is performative. A statement always intends to change a situation in one way or another, whether this be by an-
nouncing, informing, entertaining, deluding, provoking
to awareness, or whatever.[43] The notion of some special
reality which can be isolated from its linguistic gar-
ments is foreign to both rhetorical praxis and theory.
"Reality" and "language" are not two different quantities; rather, language brings reality to its audience,
just as a power cable supplies the consumer with electricity. Of course, electricity is not more electric
at the power plant than it is in one's lamp (or whatever other metaphor one might choose).

Synechdoche

However, there still remains one major difficulty: how
can someone say "this is my body", when in fact he is
offering one a piece of bread? To this Luther rejoins
that grammar is capable of more things than logic is.[44]
The rhetorical and grammatical learning of the Scholastic tradition included a figure of speech called synechdoche (lit. "co-understanding").[45] By this is meant
the fact that certain words or phrases are often said
on the presupposition that something is understood. Instead of explaining all that one does, one might simply
say "plastics", and thereby signify, not that one is
made of the stuff, but that one's trade has to do with

the fabrication and sale of certain polymers. Similarly, "man does not live by bread alone" is a phrase in
which "bread" is more than mere wheat, namely the entire material basis of human life.

In a similar fashion, it is possible to affirm that
"this is my last will and testament" while proffering
a piece of paper, although it is not the paper itself
which makes up the testament. Luther mentions that the
dove stands for the Holy Spirit, while the fire perhaps
symbolizes an angel.[46] "Symbolize" is perhaps too strong
a term in this context. Admittedly, synechdoche and
symbol may seem to resemble each other from an external
point of view, in the sense that both are examples of
"abbreviations", that is, one renounces the possibility
of saying everything and instead chooses to say something about only a part of the "reality" in question.
The decisive difference between these two modes of expression resides in the fact that synechdoche undertakes its "abbreviation" for reasons having to do with
the technique of communication. One "abbreviates" for
ontological reasons, that is, because the reality to
which the symbol refers simply cannot be exhaustively
formulated in terms of language. Thus one is compelled
to make do with the "abbreviated" expression, as was
suggested above in connection with the way of reading
texts which prevailed during the Middle Ages.

It would perhaps be appropriate to exemplify this
with the significance of the word "testament". This
word refers to both the conditions stipulated in the
testament as to the disposition of an inheritance and
to the piece of paper on which such dispositions have
been recorded. Thus when one says that "I cannot find
my (last will and) testament", the word is used in the
latter sense: it is the piece of paper, the document

itself, which is lost, and not the contents of it. If the document itself were to be lost, then in a certain sense it would no longer be valid, which means that the external form is not without a significance of its own. If my uncle's last will and testament has disappeared, then, barring a possible copy at the bureau of records, I shall not inherit his fortune. Thus the paper and the document are not symbols or signs of the will and testament; they are identical with it and without them the testament is not juridically valid.

On the other hand, though, it is clear that the paper is not itself the will and testament, which consists of its contents or meaning. But the contents are automatically understood when one searches for one's uncle's will (i.e., the paper itself). After all, one is not merely searching for a piece of paper, but for something of real potential value to oneself.

This analogy also applies to the sacrament of Communion. Its external form, consisting of bread and wine, corresponds to the testamental document, while its content, the body and blood of Jesus, correspond to the contents of the document. Nevertheless, without the bread and the wine, there _are_ no contents, for which reason Luther adheres to the notion of the Real Presence, that is, to the idea that Christ really is present in the Sacrament.

Therefore, when the Communion service reads "this is my body" and accompanies this statement with the manipulation of the bread, for Luther this is a synechdoche, rather than a symbol. The bread does not _refer_ to something else; rather, it automatically includes the notion of "body". Indeed, it _is_ body. As he says, "A sophist (i.e., a scholastic theologian) cannot bellieve this, but he who is familiar with the direct use

of the Scriptures it not mistaken, and it is easy for
him to understand. The "figure" of synechdoche rights
all things; (it is) that "figure" which governs powerfully, not only the Scriptures, but over all languages."[47]

   In other words, the synechdoche-"figure" does not
"refer" to anything; instead, it describes the relationship in question. In a similar sense, a handclasp
or a caress does not "signify" friendship or love, respectively. They are these things. In the same way, the
bread and the wine are the body and blood of Christ.

   In a certain sense, it can be said that synechdoche
is a metaphor. As previously mentioned, the term "plastics" may serve as a metaphor which includes far more
than the literal meaning of the word. The question is,
then, why do we not use more precise language? Indeed,
why do we use figures and metaphors at all? The answer
is, because we cannot avoid doing so. It would be entirely too tedious - and even pedantic - to list the
co-implicates of the word "plastics". A single short and
well chosen word says what is intended far better than
a great many words can do. The metaphor is accessible
and readily intelligible. The concept in question is
both illustratively described and defined merely by referring to an important aspect of it. One "gets the
drift" immediately, so that the meaning is easily recalled. Thus the real question is whether it is at all
possible for language to function or even to exist without the formation of metaphors. Once again, Luther "is
delighted that the Holy Scriptures make extensive use
of such grammatical figures as synechdoche, metalepsis,
metaphor, hyperbole, and so on; indeed, in no other
work do we find so many figures."[48] Similarly, he remarks that, "I do not know how it can be that figural

(i.e., metaphorical) speech has such power: it so powerfully enters the mind and moves it that every individual has a natural desire to hear or speak in metaphors.
Does it not sound much better to say that "Heaven announces the teachings of God" than that "the Apostles
proclaim the Word of God"?"[49]

The Five Senses

According to Luther, we humans live within our five
senses because we have to have something to cling to;
in his Greater Catechism he adds[50] that, "yes, and it
has to be something tangible in order for us to grasp
and comprehend it with the senses and thereby to take
it into our hearts.[51] So saying, Luther in reality reproduces one of the basic rules of rhetoric, namely,
that if one wants someone to understand something, one
has first to get them to imagine it.[52] Of course, it
is precisely this function which is the nature of the
linguistic figures. Luther is fully aware of this, as
he bases his argumentation on Horace's definition
in the Ars Poetica of trope and metaphor.[53]

To put it another way, when one says that "Christ
is a rose" or that "this is my body", we have to do
with metaphors which speak veridically, not inauthen-
tically. Like the humanism of his day, Luther regarded
language as the bearer of reality. For him, Adam's nam-
ing of the animals in Genesis 2,19 was not a matter of
attaching random designations to the various creatures;
instead, he conferred their real qualities on them.
Luther goes on to explain very lucidly how even the
most powerful animals are obliged to behave in accordance with the names bestowed on them by Adam. The ability of language to bring reality along in its train is
quite plain.[54]

Luther likewise maintains that all of the sufferings
of Christ were entirely in vain if we were not in possession of the Word about them: "Because even if Christ
had been given on our behalf and crucified 1000 times,
it would have been in vain, had not God's Word arrived
and communicated it and presented it to me, saying,
'this is to be yours; take and keep it'."[55] This corresponds to the humanistic discovery that the essence
of history is not what once took place, but what is recounted. History is not fact, but narrative.[56]

A factor which contributes to the clarity of language is the alienation which many linguistic figures
bring about. With the aid of both allegories and metaphors, one relates something familiar in a new and un-
familiar way.[57] This phenomenon frequently bears the
German loanword Verfremdung, although this is a device
which indicates that we do not regard this phenomenon
as a natural part of the essence of language. Its goal
is to make the listener stop and turn his attention to
some new expression, the newness of which helps to create new comprehension. This is what Luther does when
he calls Christ a rose or the Pope a Judas, or uses one
of the countless comparisons, metaphors, allegories,
and so forth which characterize his language. Moreover,
this is not merely "popular" language, since Luther is
quite familiar with the theoretical background of such
usage and employs it consciously.[58]

The idea of coercing language to its breaking point
is, of course, to get the audience to understand the
importance of the message; it is forced onto them, so
that they cannot avoid it. Luther expresses this with
the phrase pro nobis, "for us". In short, what is said
is not merely a matter of information, but a personal
announcement of cardinal importance. Most scholars cor-

rectly acknowledge the importance of this aspect of Luther's theology, although they usually are not aware
that the frame of reference of this concept is that of
rhetoric. This is therefore not a special category resulting from Luther's unusual theology, but the reverse:[59] his theology is predicated on one of the general presuppositions of communication. Everything that
really is of importance must be communicated in "pro
nobis" or "für sich" categories. One may compare Søren
Kierkegaard's remark to the effect that the New Testament is to be read as if it were a letter from one's
lover. It is a communication which has only the most
intense interest of the recipient. In rhetorical terms,
one would say that one makes use of the high rhetorical
or stylistic level.

Now, if language, with all of its various resources
is of such great significance for preaching, then knowledge of language must be of decisive significance for
both the preacher and his audience. I do not mean language understood in a modern philological sense, but to
language in all its - rhetorical - depth of expressiveness. As Luther emphasizes, "Although faith and the
Gospel may be proclaimed by quite ordinary priests with
particular linguistic abilities, they nevertheless become too stagnant and inadequate, so that at last one
becomes quite tired of them, and the whole falls to
the ground. But where such linguistic abilities are
present, they become fresh and alive, the Bible is revived anew, and faith is continually renewed with new
words and works."[60]

The Clarity of Scripture

Of course, if language is able to express all that it
intends, then Luther is forced to conclude that the

Bible is clear. In his pamphlet On the Freedom of the
Will Erasmus had found an example in Rom 11,33: "O the
depth of the riches and wisdom and knowledge of God!
How unsearchable are his judgements and how inscrutable
his ways!" Erasmus took this to mean that there are
some passages in the Bible which are so obscure that
we cannot penetrate their profundity.[61] Luther asserts
that this cannot be correct: the Bible is quite clear,
since it deals with Christ from one end to the other,
both explicitly and in metaphors and typologies. "If
you take Christ away from the Scriptures, what do you
find in them? All that the Scriptures contain and intend is indeed clear and plain, although certain passages are obscure because we do not know the words
(that is, their meaning and grammar). But if one knows
that the contents of Scripture are illuminated by the
clearest light, then it would be foolish and godless
to speak of obscurity for the sake of a few unclear
passages ..."[62]

Like all other language, the Biblical text does not
intend to veil or conceal. It is clear and impossible
to mistake; the love of God is communicated to us un-
forged and unambiguously. Therefore even the Incarnation may be understood as a linguistic event: "If one
does not take the Word of God directly (i.e., at face
value), one might just as well deny that Christ is
God".[63] If one does not believe in the Word, then neither does one believe in Christ himself. Christ became
man, or, to put it more powerfully, Christ became a
sinner: "When Christ became the victim of our sins, in
metaphorical terms he became sin". Our sins were therefore really transferred (= metaphor) onto Christ.[64]

The above remarks apply to external clarity. Internal clarity is a different matter, since the conviction

of the heart does not always correspond to the external appearance. Man resists the Word because of his self-ishness and evil, but one cannot criticize the Word of God for this: "It would be equally frivolous to com-plain about the sun on a dark day, if one covers one's eyes or goes into a dark room and conceals oneself."[65] This means that understanding entails two aspects. It is one thing for the text in question to be clear and intelligible; it is quite another for one to accept what has been said and to make it one's own. In other words, if the Word does not somehow penetrate the indi-vidual and so become affectus (see above, pp.105) then the individual himself will not obtain clarity. Man is possessed by evil and selflove which resists the clari-ty of the Gospel.

Where is the Holy Spirit?

From all this it will be apparent that language is able to express anything and everything; it is likewise clear that language has a monopoly on communication. The pre-supposition of all communication is sense perception, and language is able to make the sensual world intel-ligible. The following statement would seem to be valid: the more important a matter is, the clearer it must be described.

This monopoly signifies that the only possibility of expression for the Holy Spirit resides in language, or, as it has been said, spiritus latet in littera, the spirit is concealed in the letter. Although this thought was frequently adumbrated by Luther, posterity has had some difficulty in grasping it. This applies to, among others, a contemporary scholar like the Danish research-er, R. Prenter,[66] who writes: "the presupposition for our understanding the words is that one must be in possession of the spirit".[67] Prenter insists that one must first have cognito rerum (knowledge of the things) before one can attain to cognito verborum (knowledge of the expressions). This is a good example of how a spiritualistic way of thought often accompanies - and creates - a nominalistic understanding of language.

Thus for Luther the Word and the Spirit are inseparable. In the course of his career Luther continued to emphasize this fact, as is above all evident in his polemics concerning the sacraments, which forced him to chisel out his formulations in detail.[68] One of the other Reformers, Zwingli, claimed (incidentally in broad agreement with ecclesiastical tradition) that the finite cannot contain the infinite, finitum non capax infiniti. This statement is usually construed so as to imply that the Spirit is able to communicate itself to man through other channels than the Word. Luther found it possible to subtract the non from this statement: the finite may very well contain God's infinite Spirit:[69] "The external things (scil. the Word and the sacraments) must precede while the internal ones (scil. the Spirit and faith) must follow, coming as they do from the external things. He has determined not to give any man the internal gifts except through the exernal ones. He does not communicate to anyone faith and the Spirit without the external words and signs."[70]

In reality, it is a matter of taking the Incarnation seriously. According to John 1,14, the Word became flesh and dwelt among us. Does this not signify that God thereby declared his love for us in our own language, exhaustively and unmistakably? The Incarnation binds us permanently and unalterably to the external word and external signs.

There is no "naked God" (deus nudus) whom we may approach directly. Therefore Luther is able to make fun of mystics and enthusiasts who sit around, bored, and wait for the Spirit to come upon them.[71] Of course, it is possible to object that in the very notion of the Incarnation the idea is present that a different and higher reality lies behind the one we do understand. God is something else and more that his appearance to us. However, this does not take us beyond the realm of language, since it is entirely possible to state, by means of language, that there is something about which we cannot speak. Luther calls this aspect of God the hidden God,[72] by which he means God as he exists beyond his Word. It is only in and through God's Word that we know him; otherwise, he remains hidden: "God does much that he does not reveal to us in his Word ... we must adhere to his word, and turn away from his unsearchable will ... Moreover, who is actually able to conform himself to a completely unsearchable and unknowable will?"[73]

Thus the idea of the Incarnation presupposes that there is more to God than he has permitted to be revealed, but the nucleaus of this idea is the assumption that God has told us all that he intended to say through his Word.

Textual Intentionality

One of the important conclusions of Renaissance humanism was that in reading a text it was important to get a grasp on its intention, or scopus, that is, the purpose for which it was written or narrated.[74] This might seem to be a commonplace, although it is no easy matter even today. During the Renaissance it was assumed that a text attempts to represent itself as a unity. For this reason Renaissance scholars avoided subdividing

texts into sections, verses, or individual terms, as
interpreters preferred during the Middle Ages. Such
fragmentation was earlier thought to be a reasonable
approach, since the text was held to be a mere symbol,
so that each verse could conceivably contain its own
deeper significance unrelated to the surrounding context.

On the other hand, if one regards the text as a unit,
then all of its parts become elements in a particular
context, in which they all conjoin to achieve a definite goal. If a story has a particular plot or point,
it would be meaningless to read its individual sections
in isolation. In other words, scholars attempted a literary reading of the text, in which such features as
composition, genre, stylistic devices, and so forth
are all seen as together serving a collected whole. Of
course, the means of achieving such analysis are all
"literary", that is, rhetorical and poetical, since the
Bible itself is a literary text the nature of which is
both poetical and rhetorical. The "literary" aspect applies not only to the external form of the text, but
of course also to its contents, that is, its theology.

In this sense Erasmus was able to claim that "the
most distinguished task (scopus) of the theologian is
to retell the Holy Scriptures so as to clarify what
faith is and not to concern himself with frivoulous
matters. He is to speak seriously and effectively of
piety, so as to produce tears and to kindle the hearts
(of the audience) towards heavenly matters."[75] For his
part, Luther maintains that the scopus of the Bible
is Christ, in the sense that he is the collective focus
in the light of which all of the various parts of the
Bible are to be interpreted (see the section above on
the clarity of the Scripture). While there are many

differences between Erasmus and Luther, the structure
of their thought is identical, in that both seek to
find that which is truly central and important in the
Bible. One might say that this is a typically literary
way of reading a text; moreover, it is also contagious,
as it also has implications for the concept of faith.
The Danish scholar Leif Grane has pointed out that for
Luther _fidei intellectus_, the understanding of faith,
is not subjective or meditative. Rather, it means simply to understand the text in question on the basis of
its own intention.[76] Thus faith, too, becomes a "literary" concept, a textually determined phenomenon over
which the thinking subject has no control.

It will be evident that scopus-reading is identical
with contextual reading: it is impossible to understand
without seeing a text in conjunction with both its immediate surroundings and its place in the totality. Verses
and chapters are to be understood on the basis of the
surrounding verses and chapters and, if necessary, on
the basis of the Bible as a whole. Luther remarks that
"if the words in one passage are unclear, yet they are
both clear and intelligible in another".[77] Thus one is
not to entrench oneself in one passage in order to allow it to interpret itself. This applies not only to
the Bible, the truth value of which cannot be exceeded
by other works, but to all other texts as well. Furthermore, as we have seen, the basic reason for this
is fundamentally philosophical: a statement does not
"signify" something; it in fact creates the truth. And
the nature of language is such that it works by context,
including words, sentences, and figures. In this way
the phenomenon of metaphor points to the fundamental
structure of language: linkage and context. Of course,
what is true of language in general is also true of in-

dividual texts. Therefore the language and the text -
the Bible included - are their own interpreter.

No to the Quadriga

These insights enable us to approach more closely Luther's rejection of the quadriga, the fourfold sense
of Scripture (see above, pp.172). One might be inclined
to expect that Luther was an adherent of the literal
sense, as most scholars have indeed held, including
such a well known scholar as Ebeling.[78]

However, when we use such words as "historical",
"literal" or "historico-literal" of the Bible or of Luther's understanding of it, modern sensibilities have
trouble following the thread. For us, history has something to do with facts; we have no possibility to go
behind the history and to say that in reality an event
is merely a circumlocution for something else.

A special variety of the allegorical interpretation
is the typological interpretation, according to which
a given historical event may be seen as an allegory
on another historical event. The one is a sort of prototype of the other. Thus, for example, Napoleon is a
sort of allegory of Hitler: although Napoleon's life
took place within a particular historicl context, it
receives its real significance via the fact that it
points forward to Hitler.

This type of interpretation is quite common in the
Bible and in Christian exegesis. For example, Moses and
David are in some passages regarded as prototypes of
Christ. For this reason in Acts 2 the Apostle Peter is
able to give a speech on the occasion of the first public manifestation of the Christian congregation. Here
he maintains that in Psalm 16 in the Old Testament it
is not really David who is speaking, but Jesus, who

spoke through the words of the psalm already long before his own birth.

This sort of interpretation is quite unintelligible in terms of our understanding of history. We do not agree with Peter's interpretation; nor can we accept that Napoleon is a circumlocution for Hitler. It will always be possible to draw some more or less convoluted connecting line between historical figures or phenomena which are separate from each other in time, and so to demonstrate some sort of causal relationship. However, we are unable to imagine that one event derives its actual significance through another one. How could it possibly be meaningful to exchange time and place in this fashion, unless one happens to believe in reincarnation, or something similar?

Now, to Luther, this was no problem at all since, as we have seen, he maintained that the whole Bible speaks of Christ: "All parts of the Scriptures are to be understood as if they have to do with Christ, whether directly or metaphorically."[79] As far as I can see, the solution to the problem of making Luther's understanding of Scripture intelligible or acceptable to us lies in the conclusion that in reality he did not insist on the literal meaning. But to draw this conclusion, we should also have to recognize that Luther accepted the fourfold sense of Scripture, since the sensus literalis only makes sense within this framework. But what in fact occurred was that Luther not only did away with the three allegorical senses of Scripture, but with the whole quadriga, including the literal sense. Luther had de facto only a single concept of Scripture, one which permitted typologies (e.g., between the Old and the New Testaments), metaphors, allegories, and so forth. But he insisted that whether the meaning

of the text was immediately accessible or more subtle,
it was in any case invariably precise and thus not amen-
able to multiple interpretations.

In modern times Luther's understanding of texts has
been reserved for the understanding of fictional literature. Thus we are prepared to acknowledge that an author may do what God, according to Luther, has done in
"writing" the Bible: he has exceeded the limitations
of time, space, and the laws of nature by allowing characters and actions which are not immediately related
to reflect on one another. We do not restrict this ability to exceed such limitations to fairy tales or myths
in which time and space and events are determined by
the plot, instead of by considerations as to what is
"realistically" possible. Even "realistic" novels and
films contain these sorts of departures from the "normal" order. They also contain imposing improbabilities,
such as entering into the characters, so that we may
see what they are thinking or feeling. Also, we may
note that the author, whether he is the omniscient author or the no less fictive "I", is better informed
about his world than is possible for mortal man. The
interpretation of novels and narratives utilizes as a
matter of course such concepts as typology and allegory
in the attempt to reveal narrative structure. For example, any decent Western contains a number of situations (such as saloon brawls) which are intended both
to anticipate prototypically the final contest between
hero and villain and to develop the suspense of the audience en route to the dénouement.

I mentioned previously that Luther had a literary
approach to the Bible, and in consequence of this necessarily also a literary understanding of faith. In
spite of this fact, he had no difficulty in imputing

truth to the Bible. To the contrary, he shared the viewpoint of Renaissance humanism on this point to the effect that the more effective a communication or text
is, the more "real" it becomes. Naturally, our own concept of reality is quite different from Luther's. We
are prone to exclude all that is fictional and limit
ourselves to what is factual. Accordingly, if God did
not really create the world in six days, then the first
Creation Narrative of Genesis cannot be factual for us.
It is presumably one of the reasons for the crisis of
modern theology that we insist on this rigid distinction between the factual and the fictional. The "solution" adopted by theology has been to reintroduce a
theory of multiple interpretation: a) a type of historical-critical exegesis conducted along scientific lines,
and which is generally of no utility outside of the institutions of higher learning which practice it. Neither the proclamation of the Church nor religious instruction in the schools seem to be able to benefit
from it. b) A dogmatic and confessional actualization
of Christianity capable of being used in the proclamation of the Church. This corresponds to the sensus allegoricus of the quadriga of the Middle Ages. But in
our day this medieval approach is often found implaus-
ible, because it has fictional characteristics. c) Anthropological interpretation is also frequently maintained, that is, one which attempts to work out a specifically Christian morality. c) The reader may judge
for himself whether some interpretations corresponding
to the mystical interpretation are still propounded today.

What is new in the modern situation with respect to
that of the Middle Ages is that there is no longer any
connection between regarding the Bible as describing

factual situations (interpretation a) and the other modes of interpretation. This is exemplified by the fact that it is very difficult to relate the historical-critical and scientific study of Biblical texts undertaken at the universities and institutions of higher learning to the homelitic or normative use of the Bible. No matter what methodological basis underlies a modern interpretation, the interpretation will only be able to say something about the meaning of the text - but it will say nothing about whether or not it is true. This has been particularly stressed by the modern philosophers of existence. Rudolf Bultmann, who was both an extraordinarily sharpsighted exegete and one of the fathers of existential theology, distinguished very clearly between the need to relate oneself to a historical narrative with scientific objectivity and the need to relate to it existentially. It is scientifically possible to investigate the concept of God in the New Testament, while in existential terms one has merely the option to respond in faith to the Word of God. "In one's existence it is only possible to speak of Him in fear and trembling, in thankfulness and confidence."[80] Accordingly, or so Bultmann concluded, the results of scientific activity are actually of only secondary importance, and in a strict sense they can never really have anything to do with the Christian faith - much less form the basis for it.

In other words, there is a colossal gap between the univocal interpretation of the Renaissance and our modern multifacetted way of reading the Bible. As mentioned above, the humanists regarded the Bible as the greatest work of art of all times. They likewise regarded God as the first and greatest orator and poet,[81] a poet who naturally made use of all possible stylistic amenities.[82] Like other successful works of art, the Bible forces its reader to take up a special position, in this case with respect to Christ. This unmistakeableness has nothing to do with keeping a narrative at all times on one and the same plane, in the same style, or whatever. Divine Scripture is like an organ which has not just a single pipe, but a vast set of them.[83]

In consequence we may say that Luther's break with the quadriga was not a break with metaphor or allegory, but a rejection of the polysemeity (multiplicity of meanings) of Scripture, and thereby an attempt to assure man that in the quest for salvation he has something concrete to which to adhere. It is accordingly somewhat misleading to maintain that Luther returned to a historical or literal way of reading the Bible. It is misleading because the modern consciousness understands something quite different by "literal" and "historical" than people of the Renaissance - and Martin Luther - did. We have a different and much narrower concept as to what is possible and meaningful in the way of historical assertions than was the case in Luther's day. Today we affirm a very restrictive definition the concept of facticity; moreover, we are very prone to combine "facticity" with "truth", "value", and "meaningfulness" in such a way that the three last-named quantities are reduced to virtually nothing.

In place of this, as I have suggested, it would be more fruitful to regard the category of fiction as a useful key to the understanding of Luther's way of reading Scripture, since such an approach permits a concept of "text" in which such features as "meaning", "truth", "attitude", and so forth may thereby come into their own. In a certain sense, even this suggestion does not make the path to Luther any easier for modern

man. We have a fundamental suspicion of everything which
is "just invention", that is, which is not fact. On the
other hand, perhaps the way of reading texts promulgated by Renaissance humanists - and Luther - may help us
to question our understanding of reality and language.
It may serve to remind us that meaning and truth come
to us before we have managed to take a position with
respect to them, that is, that faith always precedes
knowledge. Attitude and personal engagement always precede criticism and analysis, or, to put it another way,
we may be able to see that our knowledge and opinions
are not primarily founded on evidence as to what is
actually the case. Rather, they are based on and are
structured by those narratives and stories - from the
greatest epic works to the smallest narrative units,
such as metaphors, [84] which we hear and which we have
also been absorbed by - and into. This is the case with
pistis (faith) which is the fundamental basis of our
knowledge. Furthermore, if this is the case, then epistemological laws are of a rhetorical and literary character. This was the discovery the Luther of the Renaissance made while reading his Bible. By peering over
Luther's shoulder, modern readers of the Bible - and
of other texts - might find some food for thought.

The Battle with the Serpent

Luther's struggle with the fourfold interpretation may
be profitably studied on the basis of a particular topos
which was actual during the Renaissance. The legendary
Hercules (Greek Herakles) figured prominently at the
time in literary works. His 12 mighty deeds and misad-
ventures were retold, reworked, and actualized in numerous forms. In a contemporary etching, Luther himself
was depicted as the "German Hercules", murderously

slashing away at the theologians of the Middle Ages.[85]
Now, one of Hercules' many accomplishments consisted
of killing the many-headed Hydra of Lernia. As each of
its 9 heads was chopped off, 9 more grew back in its
place, until at last Hercules succeeded in subduing it
with the aid of a forest fire, by means of which he
cauterized the neck stumps so that new heads could not
grow back.[86] The humanists of the Renaissance regarded
Hercules to be their particular hero because of his
battle with the Hydra, as the monster in question had
come to symbolize the type of academic debate which had
been so popular during the Middle Ages.[87] The humanists
never tired of ridiculing the Scholastic debates at the
great universities, and even the Danish dramatist and
historian, Ludwig Holberg, once drew in his Erasmus
Montanus a caricature of a Scholastic hero.

The burden of this criticism of Scholasticism was
that the Scholastics were mainly concerned with trivialities. Of course, we are still familiar today with the
discussion as to how many angels were capable of danc-
ing on the head of a pin, but the humanists regarded
it as even worse that the dialectical discussions of
the Scholastics were seemingly endless, and therefore
also without issue. Just as each head of the hydra was
replaced by 9 new ones, every time a Scholastic "solved" a problem it was replaced by 9 new ones. The humanists felt that there was time for this sort of academic
discussion when one did not otherwise have anything important to do, and when one did not feel that reaching
any sort of conclusion was important. In other owrds,
they felt that such scholarship lacked personal engagement and real interest in the problems in question.

Erasmus of Rotterdam wrote an enjoyable description
of the futile hairsplitting of the academic world in

his work, In Praise of Folly: "They (the theologians) spread newly invented words and monstrous technical expressions around them. Also, they explain the secret mysteries in any way they please: how the world was created and organized; through which channels original sin is inherited; in what way, to which extent, and at what time Christ developed in the womb of the Virgin ... But all of these things are trivialities. There are other questions which they regard as important, which are, as they say, worthy of enlightened theologians, and which arouse them when they encounter them: did the divine conception take place at a particular time? Are there a number of filiations (son-becomings) within Christus? Is it possible to say that the Father hates the Son? Would it be possible for God to take the form of a woman, devil, donkey, pumpkin, or stone? - and if He chose a pumpkin, would He have been able to perform miracles, or be crucified, or ... It is altogether so extremely learned and difficult that I believe that even the Apostles themselves would have to have had the aid of another Spirit, if they wished to take on this new litter of theologians. St. Paul may well have been able to bear witness to the faith; nevertheless, when he says that "faith is a confidence in something hoped for, a conviction about something not seen", this would not really satisfy the doctors. He has also borne wonderful witness to love in his First Letter to the Corinthians, ch. 13, but he neither analyzed it nor defined it in true dialectical fashion ..."[88]

The humor of Erasmus' remarks should not be allowed to obscure the fact that he means them quite seriously. Erasmus' is probably not a terribly exaggerated picture of the type of discussion undertaken by contemporary theologians, who had inherited it from the Middle Ages.

Furthermore, the text quoted above offers a vivid impression of the aversion of Erasmus and other humanists
to this sort of theological work. Erasmus expressed
this aversion without irony in his "Methodus" (directory), which instructs us as to how we are to read the
New Testament. Here he advises us to ignore the countless trivial problems with which the theologians were
concerned, since, "Neither their number nor their extent has any end in sight, since, like the hydra, for
each one that is lopped off, innumerable others grow
to take their place".[89] Erasmus also notes that there
are many problems about which we need to know nothing,
since what is important is whether we adhere to "Christian philosophy", that is, to the love and teachings of
Christ.

One finds a similar train of thought in Luther's
work, not as far as the contents of the various theological conceptions are concerned, but as far as their
method is concerned. Luther, too, battles against the
"hydra" in a variety of ways.[90] Among other things, he
objects strenuously to that academic "scepticism" which
requires one to have a remote and relaxed attitude towards things which ought rightly - on his view - to require the utmost seriousness. This criticism is also
directed at Erasmus, among others, since he had maintained that we should allow those questions to remain
open for which we have no answers.[91] Luther was suspicious of this, and saw it as a sign of "scepticism" in
Erasmus.[92] This accusation was as unjust as was Luther's
generally increasing anger towards Erasmus.[93] Nevertheless, it is an indication of Luther's fear that relat-
ivization and nuance could detract from the seriousness
of the matter.

On the question of the clarity of the Scriptures,

Luther scented certain aspects of the "hydra" in the work of the Louvain theologian, Latomus, who doubted that the sense of Scripture was so univocal that it could serve as the sole rule of faith. In Luther's eyes, it was not a question of a variety of "opinions", but of the very truth about Christ.[94] Latomus had referred to the pictural character of the Bible, meaning, as discussed previously, that everything in it symbolizes something else. Of course, as mentioned above, this would mean that in a symbolic way everything refers to something else. Such symbolization would accordingly entail that the expressions would require interpretation, and this would in turn imply the possibility of multiple interpretations. In this sense, the rejection of the fourfold sense of Scripture becomes a sort of battle against the "hydra". A symbol contains an endless series of possible meanings; it is not ambi-, but poly-valent. The text becomes uncertain, which would ultimately mean that it would be up to the interpreter to decide which meaning he preferred.

It was precisely this situation which Luther feared, as he regarded its theological consequences to be fatal. In the final analysis, the view in question suggests that everyone could become the author of his own salvation or, to put it another way, he sensed a danger of subjectivizing the object of faith. To put it briefly, the entire anthropology and theology which was described back in chs. 6 and 7 would disintegrate. This acknowledgement brings us to the decisive aspect of the "hydra" metaphor. If we take the interpretation of texts as an example, according to Luther and the humanists it was only in the light of a fallacious interpretation that a Scriptural text can be said to offer a plethora of possible interpretations, since in reality its sense is univocal.

Thus the responsibility for the misapprehension of the text is shared by the interpreter and his method. In a similar way, the multitudinous problems detected by the Scholastic method of discussion do not reflect anything substantial; they are merely the result of the love of discussion of the philosophers and the theologians. Their futile debates enabled them to create for themselves a hydra-headed universe. But who, then, was the "hydra"? Naturaly, it was the interpreters, the quarrelers and debaters: in a word, man himself. As Luther says, the whole approach was "smooth and unstable"; it "turns and squirms in a thousand directions".[95] And this is how it is whenever man attempts to discover the truth on his own authority.

Now, if man is to be characterized as a something which is capable of thinking and acting of his own accord, then it would be meaningless either to call him a sinner through and through or to describe him as totally dependent on the action of grace. It is accordingly necessary to equip man with free will, i.e., so as to be able to choose between good and evil, and to be able to contribute to his own salvation, however much or litte.

Now, Luther regarded this as an illusion, as a "fool's folly". To him the idea that man himself would be able to discover the truth was just as absurd as the notion that a mirror could decide for itself what it should reflect. As H.G. Gadamer has put it, "Wir kommen gleichsam zu spät, wenn wir wissen wollen, was wir glauben sollen".[96] ("We are, as it were, too late, when we would think to know what we ought to believe"). In other words, faith precedes understanding; for Luther, as for Gadamer later, this was not merely a theological claim, but an epistemological one. If it were possible to con-

ceive of an intellect which was not bound by faith and
conviction, it would roam about with no idea as to where
it should turn. Of course, this notion is purely con-
jectural; the reality is quite different. In reality,
the individual who believes himself to he "himself" is
bound by sin, since it is his fascination with his own
mirror image, that is, his self-love or egoism or be-
ing-mired-in-one's-own-being, which takes control and
governs such an individual - his reason included. Man's
so-called plain common sense (sensus communis) is, in
the last analysis, governed by his selfishness. Therefore this faculty is unable to understand the depths
to which sin penetrates, so that it adheres to the superficial understanding of man as not sinful in any radical sense.[97] This brings us back to the model of the
pack-animal again; if either the devil or one's selfhood (the difference is negligible) sits in the saddle,
then the reason will be subject to the rider's prompt-
ings. Therefore the many efforts of the "hydra" are not
mere shadow-boxing, but the work of the devil and accordingly are also the devil's rejection of God and His
Word.

Conclusion

We have arrived at the end of our journey. I have not attempted to provide an exhaustive description of Luther's conceptual universe. Many important features have not even been touched on, and in this connection it will be necessary simply to defer to the extensive literature in many languages on Luther which the academic world has provided. To put it mildly, Luther is not exactly an unexamined phenomenon as far as both serious academic and more popular study are concerned.

The present examination has confined itself to a review of a few important aspects of Luther's understanding of how the mediation of knowledge takes place. Nowadays we call this ambit the field of "communications theory". However, this phrase is scarcely applicable to Luther, since his own version of this field entails a particular understanding of man, one which embraced an anthropology together with its attendant epistemology and psychology. These features are not ordinarily encompassed by the modern term "communications theory", a term which suggests only that a particular contents are present which are to be communicated in one way or another. Thus we have "merely" to do with communication. This "merely" is extremely characteristic of the modern sensibility, and if we were to transfer it to the period of the Renaissance, this meant the field of rhetoric, and in these pages I have attempted to show how such central Lutheran concepts as faith, will, and the understanding of Scripture can be adequately understood using rhetoric as one's frame of reference. In so doing, this study depicts Luther as a child of his times, rather than as an atemporal genius with no roots whatsoever. He becomes one with his own historical period. By the same token, it is hoped that this study has

succeeded in emphasizing the fact that Luther's understanding of the "dialectic of mediation" differs import-
antly from our own. If this is not acknowledged, we shall
seriously misunderstand the world of Luther's ideas.
This is not only important for a correct reading of Luther's writings. It may also serve as a starting point
for a discussion of the relationship between Renaissance
humanism and the Reformation. The guiding insight in
this connection has been the recognition that the Reformation was the child of the Renaissance, which explains
the subtitle of this work: "knowledge and mediation during the Renaissance".

Nevertheless, I should like to adumbrate some of these
questions in all brevity: how was it possible for the
Reformation movement to enjoy a success that is without
parallel in history? Admittedly, there were numerous
good reasons for this phenomenon whose bases were economic, ecclesiastico-political, theological, and so forth.
But I should like to suggest that at least one contributory cause was the fact that the ground had been so
weel prepared by Renaissance humanism that in a certain
sense it could be maintained that Luther did not say anything that was really new. I should like to stress that
I am not saying this in order to denigrate Luther's originality and independence. Nevertheless, Luther's creative contribution could to a significant extent be described as an emphasis and bringing to fruition of motifs
which were implicit in the humanism of the Renaissance.

To contemporaries of Luther who were conversant with
the type of epistemology and life-style inherent in the
then-prevalent humanism, Luther's proclamation must have
seemed immediately recognizable. Indeed, many humanists
did not hesitate to support the "German Cicero"; of
these, Philip Melanchton was merely the best known fi-

gure but by no means the only one. It was often the humanists who argued on behalf of the Reformation in the
city councils, and who strove to convince their members
to adopt the new form of worship.[1] In this connection
the conflict between Luther and Erasmus has been allowed to misrepresent considerably the relationship between
humanism and the Reformation.

In addition to these historical questions, it would
be appropriate to pose a more theoretical one: was Luther right? Was the understanding shared by him and his
contemporaries of man and communication more realistic
and adequate to describe the phenomena in question than
our own? Luther played down the significance of the subject and emphasized instead the ability of language,
that is, of communication, to create and shape man's
being. Was this not more realistic than the contemporary cult of personality and self-identification, a tendency which has recently been characterized as narcissistic (i.e., self-reflection), and which in its contemporary form is not merely a psychological, but also
a sociological phenomenon?[2]

In other words, we have to do with answers to such
fundamental questions as "who am I?" and "what is truth?"
A theological way of stating the problem would be to ask
whether it is possible to express the Christian proclamation on the terms provided by a "narcissistic" anthropology. Are such concepts as "faith", "salvation", "grace",
"sin", and so forth in any way meaningful, if man is
regarded as the absolute center of his own existence?
Or is an anthropology along the lines envisioned by Luther in reality a presupposition for a meaningful proclamation of the Christian message? The answers to these
questions could be held to be particularly relevant to
a Church that styles itself "Evangelical Lutheran."

Notes

1. Renaissance and Reformation

1. Delio Cantimori, Zur Geschichte des Begriffes "Renaissance", in: Zu Begriff und Problem der Renaissance, A. Buck, (ed.), Darmstadt, 1969,

2. Konrad Burdach, Reformation, Renaissance, Humanismus, Leipzig, 1926, repr. Darmstadt, 1963, pp. 1ff.

3. Cf. (ed.) August Buck, Zu Begriff und Problem der Renaissance, Darmstadt, 1969 (= Wege der Forschung 204). Eine Einleitung, p. 15. Moreover, our concept of "renaissance" is not only to be traced back to Michelet, but probably in equal measure to J. Burkhardt, a friend of Nietzsche whose understanding of the period concentrated on the concept of the self-creating individual with a strong will, the man who liberates himself from all norms and authorities and accordingly is able to live entirely "aesthetically", i.e., as his own creative center. See Die Kultur der Renaissance in Italien, 1860.

4. Burdach, op. cit., p. 10; Buck, op. cit., p. 7.

5. H.-G. Gadamer, Wahrheit und Methode, 1965.

6. Of course, it will be impossible here to present an exhaustive picture of this way of writing history. As a representative example, I should like to mention Enno van Gelder's The two Reformations in the 16th Century, The Hague, 1961. In spite of a stillborn effort to see some connection between the great (humanistic) reformation and the little (ecclesiastical) one, the latter proved nevertheless to be a blind alley with respect to the former.

7. K.E. Løgstrup, "Viljesbegrebet i De servo arbitrio", Dansk Teologisk Tidsskrift, 1942, pp. 129ff., quoted with approval by L. Grane, Protest og Konsekvens, København, 1968, p. 214.

8. In recent years, an entire literature has sprung up around the theme of the Folie et déraison à la renaissance, and related subjects. The phrase was the title of a colloquium held in 1973, the contributions to which were published in Brussels in 1976.

2. The Tripartite Man

1. Bruno Snell, Die Entdeckung des Geistes, Hamburg, 1955.

2. Cf. D. Ross, Aristotle, pp. 154ff.

3. D.W. Robertson, A Preface to Chaucer, Princeton, 1962.

3. The Undivided Man

1. Cf. e.g., Svend Bjerg, Den kristne Grundfortælling (The Christian fundamental Story), Aarhus, 1981, and (ed.) H.C. Wind, Religionen i Krise (Religion in Crisis) København, 1980, the section on "Viljens frihed" (the freedom of the will) (by Jan Lindhardt).

2. Cf. the thorough discussion of the way modern scholarship has dealt with Luther's relationship to mysticism, in: Luther and the Mystics. A re-examination of Luther's spiritual experience and his relationship to the mystics; Minneapolis, 1976, Part I, pp. 25-130.

3. Luther's preface indicates that he did not count the phenomenon as mysticism, but as "theology"; cf. WA, 1.379.

4. Erich Vogelsang, Luther und die Mystik, Lutherjahrbuch, 1937, pp. 32-54.

5. Aurelius Augustinus, Confessiones, IX, 10; English Trans., Edinburgh, 1876 (ed. by J.G. Pilkington, M.A.).

6. Cf. Heiko A. Obermann, Simul gemitus et raptus: Luther und die Mystik. Kirche, Mystik, Heiligung und das Natürliche bei Luther. Vorträge des Dritten Internationalen Kongress für Lutherforschung, ed. Ivar Asheim, Göttingen, 1967, pp. 20-59.

7. Johann Tauler, Predigten. Vollst. Ausgabe. Übertr. u. hrsg. von Georg Hoffmann, Basel/Wien 1961.

8. Oberman, op. cit., p. 5.
9. De secreto conflicto curarum mearum. Petrarca, Prose, 1955, pp. 22ff.; cf. Morris, Petrarch and his World, London, 1964, pp. 192ff.

10. Cf. Jan Lindhardt, Rhetor, Poeta, Historicus, Leiden, 1979, Ch. 5, Gott und Mensch, pp. 66ff.

11. This argument derives from St. Thomas Aquinas; cf. Harry J. McSorley, Luthers Lehre vom unfreien Willen, München, 1967, pp. 135ff.

12. King Lear, Act I, sc. ii, v. 132ff.

13. Keith Thomas, Religion and the Decline of Magic, London, 1970, pp. 283ff.: Astrology. Cf. also Eugenio Garin, Medioevo e Rinascimento, Bari, 1961, pp. 170ff. Astrology was suppressed during the Middle Ages, while it apparently had free rein during the Renaissance.

14. E. Panofsky, The Life and Art of Albrecht Dürer, 4th ed., Princeton, 1971, pp. 157ff.

15. Keith Thomas, op. cit.

16. This problem has been extensively discussed by Leif Grane in Contra Gabrielem, Luthers Auseinandersetzung mit Gabriel in der Disputatio Contra Scholasticam Theologiam 1517, København, 1962.

17. Cf. Marjorie O'Rourke Boyle, Erasmus on Language and Method in Theology, Toronto, 1977.

18. Pico della Mirandola attacked rhetoric and so came into conflict with the humanist Barbero. Their correspondence has been

published by Quirinius Breen, Christianity and Humanism. Studies in the History of Ideas. Michigan, 1958, pp. 1-38. Melanchton did not believe that Barbero defended rhetoric well enough, for which reason he, too, wrote a defense of it in 1558; cf. Breen, pp. 39ff.

19. On the artes liberales system, see H.I. Marrou, Histoire d'éducation dans l'antiquité, 6th ed., Paris, 1965. During the late Middle Ages, the teaching of rhetoric went into decline at the universities; cf. Olaf Pedersen, Studium Generale, København, 1979, p. 282.

20. Cf. R.W. Lee, Ut Pictura Poesis. The Humanistic Theory of Painting, N.Y., 1967.

21. A good recent account of this is provided by Ronald Witt, Coluccio Salutati and his public Letters, Genéve, 1976.

22. Alberto Mussato was the first to receive the poet's crown of laurel. On the coronation of Petrarch, see M. Bishop, Petrarch and his World, London, 1964, pp. 164ff. It later became a fixed phrase of the humanists to speak of the "three crowned heads", i.e., Dante, Petrarca, and Boccaccio. To his great regret, however, Dante was never crowned, although both he and posterity thought he deserved to be.

23. H. Lausberg, Handbuch der Rhetorik I-II, München, 1960. a short account of some of the basic concepts of rhetorical theory, as well as of their epistemological consequences, has been provided by Jan Lindhardt, Retorik, København, 1975.

24. Aristotle, Ars Poetica, 23.

25. See the introduction by Jørgen K. Bukdahl, with references, in: ed. Malthe Jakobsen, Sprog og Virkelighed (Language and Reality), København, 1974.

26. Cf. Jan Lindhardt, Middelalderens (og Renæssancens) Bibeludlægning (The Exegesis of the Middle Ages (and the Renaissance)) Fønix, 3 (1979) pp. 200-213.

27. Institutio oratoria, Bk. VI. i-ii.

28. Quoted from The older Sophists, ed. Rosamond Kent Sprague, Columbia S.C., 1972. On the connection between the Renaissance and Greek sophistry, see Nancy Struver, The Language of History, Princeton, 1970.

29. Helmut Junghans, Der Einfluss des Humanismus auf Luthers Entwicklung bis 1518, Luther-Jahrbuch, 1970, pp. 37-101. In a lecture held at the University of Copenhagen in 1979 entitled Initia GLoriae Lutheri, Junghans pointet out that not only were Luther's past and contemporary society influenced by rhetoric, but also that Luther's very posterity was formed by the rhetorical-humanistic bon mots of the day. He was primarily praised as a great preacher, who had the power of the word in his gift, "ein Prediger Held". He was further called Apollo, Hercules,

and Cicero, and even received the typically humanistic predicate, "extremely learned". In fact, the entire ideology of the liberator, that is, Luther as Eleutherius, the one who is free - and thus a liberator - with respect to political and religious matters, was also a classical topos of the rhetorical schools.

30. Cf. Lewis W. Spitz, The religious Renaissance of the German Humanists, Cambridge, Mass., 1963. Idem, Headwaters of the Reformation, Studia Humanitatis, Luther Senior et Initia Reformationis, in: Luther and the Dawn of the Modern Era, Studies in the History of Christian Thought, Vol. VII, pp. 89-116.

31. Headwaters of the Reformation, op. cit., pp. 103ff.

32. Ulrich Nembach, Predigt des Evangeliums, Luther als Prediger, Pädagog and Rhetor, Neukirchen, 1972.

33. I find somewhat unlikely Nembach's thesis, according to which Luther made especial use of Quintilian's analyses of political speeches to popular assemblies as particularly suitable for describing the situation of the sermon, as well as its structure and audience. Nevertheless, this does not alter the fact that Nembach has clearly demonstrated that Luther was quite dependent on Quintilian; cf. op. cit., pp. 133ff.

34. Birgit Stolt, Docere, delectare und movere bei Luther. Analyse an Hand der "Predigt, dass man Kinder zur Schule halten solle"; cf. Wortkampf, Frühneuhochdeutsche Beispiele zur rhetorischen Praxis, Frankfurt a.M., 1974, pp. 31-77.

35. Birgit Stolt, Studien zur Luthers Freiheitstraktat mit besonderer Rücksicht auf das Verhältnis der lateinischen und der deutschen Fassung zu einander und die Stilmittel der Rhetorik. Stockholm, 1969.

36. Klaus Dockhorn, Luthers Glaubensbegriff, Linguistica Biblica 21/22 (1973) 19-39.

37. I have personally attempted to sugggest some reasons for the displacement of rhetoric; see Retorik, op. cit., Ch. 7.

4. From Accidia to Melancholy

1. General background on the concept of accidia is to be found in Siegfried Wenzel's Accidia in Medieval Thought and Literature, North Carolina, 1967; and in Susan Snyder's The Left Hand of God: Despair in Medieval and Renaissance Tradition, Studies in the Renaissance, 12 (1965) 18-59.

2. Wenzel, op. cit., pp. 4ff.

3. Snyder, op. cit., pp. 21ff.

4. Snyder, op. cit., pp. 31ff.

5. De secreto conflictu curarum mearum, in: ed. G. Martellotti

and P.G. Ricci, Fr. Petrarca, Prose; La letterattura italiana, Storia e Testi., Milano-Napoli, 1955. A study of this text is to be found in : Morris Bishop, Petrarch and his World, London, 1964, pp. 192ff. See further Oscar Giuliani, Allegoria retorica e poetica nel Secretum del Petrarca, Bologna, 1977.

6. Leif Grane (Modus loquendi theologicus, Luthers Kampf um die Erneuerung der Theologie (1515-1518), Acta Theologica Danica, Vol. XII, Leiden, 1975) carefully demonstrates the way Luther incorrectly reads St. Augustine in the interests of arriving at a different totality than that intended by Augustine. See also my own remarks on Grane's book in Fønix 2 (1978) 129-139 ("Om at tale historisk").

7. Fr. Petrarca. Prose, op. cit.; the Secretum is on pp. 22-214, Citat, p. 34.

8. Ibid., p. 40.

9. Bk. VIII, Jff.

10. Petrarca, Prose, p. 42.

11. For Augustine's analysis of Petrarch's unenviable situation in Prose, op. cit., p. 68; see further Charles Trinkaus, in Our Image And Likeness, op. cit., Vol. I, Ch. I: Man between Despair and Grace, pp. 3ff.

12. Bk. IX, 10.

13. Cf. Ch. Trinkaus, op. cit., pp. 30ff.

14. Jerrold E. Seigel, Rhetoric and Philosophy in Renaissance Humanism. The Union of Eloquence and Wisdom, Petrarch to Valla. Princeton, 1968; see esp. Ch. 2: Ideals of Eloquence and Silence in Petrarch, pp. 31ff.

15. Cf. Jan Lindhardt, Retorik, on Augustine, pp. 109-111.

16. Charles Trinkaus, The Poet as Philosopher. Petrarch and the Formation of Renaissance Consciousness. London, 1979; see esp. Ch. II: Petrarch and the Tradition of a Double Consciousness.

17. R. Klibansky, Erw. Panofsky and Fr. Saxl, Saturn and Melancholy, London, 1964, pp. 234ff.

18. Jan Lindhardt, Rhetor, Poeta, Historicus, Acta Theologica Danica XIII, Leiden, 1979, pp. 93ff.

19. Cf. Klibansky, Panofsky, Saxl, op. cit., pp. 217-276.

20. E. Panofsky, The Life and Art of Albrecht Dürer, Princeton, 1971, p. 161. See also Klibansky, Panofsky, Saxl, op. cit., pp. 284-400.

21. Klibansky, Panofsky, Saxl, op. cit., p. 259.

22. E. Panofsky, A. Dürer, op. cit., p. 166.

23. Quoted in Klibansky, Panofsky, Saxl, op. cit., p. 218.

24. Robert Burton, The Anatomy of Melancholy, Abridged and Edited by Joan K. Peters, Milestones of Thought, New York, 1979, p. 6. This is an introductory poem in which Burton attempts to account for his conclusions.

25. Quoted in Klibansky, Panofsky, and Saxl, op. cit., p. 230.

26. WA Br. 1,514ff.

27. See e.g., Otto Scheel, Dokumente zu Luthers Entwicklung, Tübingen, 1929, Dokument nr. 247, p. 97.

28. Cf. Lars Bo Bojesen and Jan Lindhardt, Samvittigheden (Conscience), København, 1979, pp. 80ff.

5. Luther's Understanding of Faith

1. Klaus Dockhorn, Luthers Glaubensbegriff und die Rhetorik. Linguistica Biblica 21-22 (1973) 30.

2. Cf. e.g., Peter Søby Kristensen, Kommunikation, København, 1975, pp. 30ff.

3. WA 10, I, 1.183. There is a wealth of useful references and quotations in Thestrup Pedersen's Luther som Skriftfortolker I, En studie i Luthers skriftsyn, hermeneutik og eksegese, pp. 107ff.

4. "Rhetoricatur igitur Spiritus Sanctus iam, ut exhortatio fiat illustrior", WA XL, 3; Cited in Klaus Dockhorn, Luthers Glaubensbegriff, op. cit., p. 30. Students of Luther often seem tempted to suppose that in Luther's work the Word of God is something different from the ordinary human word. See Thestrup Pedersen, op. cit., pp. 111ff.

5. WA 10, I, 1.183.

6. Erich Auerbach (Sermo humilis, in: Literatursprache und Publikum in der lateinischen, Spätantike und im Mittelalter, Bern, 1958) has pointed out in conjunction with his analysis of Augustine's De doctrina christiana, which deals with the Christian rhetorician, that there need not necessarily be any direct or simple relationship; to the contrary, there is a relationship of tension between res (subject) and verba (expression) in Christian tradition. What came to characterize Christian preaching was the sermo humilis (humble sermon or speech), in which the ideal was to speak in a humble and simple way of the most elevated topic of all, namely the Gospel of Christ. The idea underlying this tension is the notion that it is impossible to proclaim God's speech directly in human words, so that one does best to do so in a modest form. See further my Retorik, København, 1975, pp. 116ff. Luther adopted many of the stylistic elements of this sort of sermon; cf. B. Stolt, Studien zur Luthers Freiheitstraktat, Stockholm, 1969, pp. 129ff.; but he did not adopt the stylistic theory on which it was based. He assumed that God was able to say whatever he wanted in human language.

7. This will be examined more thoroughly with special attention to the reading of Scripture in Ch. 7.

8. According to St. Thomas, the Scriptures detach their language from time and space; cf. Peter Meinhold, Luthers Sprachphilosophie, Berlin, 1958, p. 47.

9. K.O. Apel, Die Idee der Sprache von Dante bis Vico, Archiv für Begriffegeschichte 8, Bonn, 1963, p. 69. See also Peter Meinhold, Luthers Sprachphilosophie, op. cit., Ch. VI: Luthers Stellung innerhalb der christlichen Sprachphilosophie, pp. 45ff.

10. Lorenzo Valla, Whose works Luther had read, was one of the most acute critics of Scholastic philosophy. Valla emphasized that concrete things had to be one's point of departure if one wished to get anywhere with such concepts as Ens (being), aliquid (something), unum (unity, the One), verum (the True), etc.; cf. E. Grassi, Humanismus und Marxismus, Hamburg, 1973, pp. 231ff.

11. In Praise of Folly, translated by Clarence H. Miller, New Haven and London 1979, p. 94.

12. Quoted from Jørgen Fafner, Retorik, København, 1977, p. 45.

13. William J. Kennedy, Rhetorical Norms in Renaissance Literature, New Haven and London, 1978; however, see also Brian Vicker's critical discussion of this work in Rhetorik, Ein Internationales Jahrbuch, Vol. 2, 1981, pp. 106-111.

14. Cf. E.R. Curtius, Theologische Poetik im italienischen Trecento, Zeitschrift für röm. Phil., 1940, p. 1-15; and Gregor Müller, Bildung und Erziehung im Humanismus der italienischen Renaissance, pp. 130ff., and 357.

15. Erasmus of Rotterdam, Methodus, in: Ausgewählte Schriften, Vol. III, pp. 38-76, and esp. pp. 48ff. In this connection, humanism made use of patristic scholarship. See J. Dyck, Ticht-Kunst, Bad Hamburg, 1966, and Jan Lindhardt, Rhetor, Poeta, Historicus, Leiden, 1979.

16. Erasmus felt that the "ruined" Holy Spirit could be restored by working through the relevant criteria of language, such as grammar and rhetoric. It would probably not be possible to say more strongly that the Spirit is bound to the word. Cf. Erasmus' Apologia, Ausg. Sch. III, p. 96.

17. Quoted from Peter G. Sandstrom, Luther's Sense of Himself as an Interpreter of the Word to the World, Amherst, Mass., 1961, Sanderson has borrowed the statement from Painter, Luther on Education, 1889, which was unfortunately not available to me.

18. W. Joest, Ontologie der Person bei Luther, Göttingen, 1967, p. 288. K.E. Løgstrup (in Religion, 1976) has formulated the same insight very precisely in terming the sense of hearing "the compliant sense". Hans Blumenberg (Die Licht als Metapher der Wahrheit, Studium Generale 10/7 (1957) 432ff.) points,

among other things (p. 440) to the tradition which maintained that what one happened to hear was ineluctable, inescapable.

19. Cf. WA 43,72, and also H.O. Oberman, Simul gemitus et raptus, op. cit., who claims that Luther repeatedly warns against the possibility of direct mediation between God and man.

20. WA 57 H,138; cf. Joest, op. cit., p. 288.

21. WA 57 H,138, pp. 20ff.

22. Cf. Lars Bo Bojesen and Jan Lindhardt, Samvittigheden (Conscience), København, 1979, pp. 76ff.

23. Emil Brunner, Die Mystik und das Wort, 1921, p. 188.

24. Cf. Sigfrid v. Engeström, Luthers trosbegrepp. Med särskild hänsyn till försanchaalandets betydelse, Uppsala, 1933, who shows both correctly and with a wealth of examples that this cannot possibly adequately characterize Luther's thought; see esp. pp. 181 and 200.

25. Preface to St. Paul's letter to the Romans, Erlangerausg.1854, bd. 63.

26. Undervisningsvejledning for folkeskolen. Betænkning nr. 260, 1960, p. 112. (Teaching guidance for primary school. Report nr. 260, 1960, p. 112.)

27. The ideas in question are to be found in Thomas Aquinas, Summa Theologica, Secunda secundae, quaestio IV, art. 1-4.

28. On good works, see WA 6.

29. Which is naturally not to say that the reception of the word is not dependent on the presuppositions of its audience. If one's words should happen to fall on stoney ground (cf. Mk 4), one should not expect any reaction. However, this does not entail that the listener decides for himself whether he will accept the word or not. See also Ch. 6, n. 19.

30. S.v. Engeström (Luthers trosbegrepp, op. cit., 1933, excursus pp. 228ff.) examines these concepts in detail.

31. For the "Sensus proprius" see Luther's commentary on Romans 3,20 in WA 56; See also R. Prenter, Den unge Luthers teologi (The Theology of young Lutner), rorelæsninger ved Aarhus Universitet i forårssemesteret, 1956 (duplicated), pp. 82ff., and R. Schwarz, Fides, Spes und Caritas bei jungen Luther, Berlin, 1962, p. 136.

32. Since understanding is "pathetic", understood in the sense of overshadowing everything else, it need not be cast in the highest of the rhetorical styles; see above, n. 6.

33. Cf. Jan Lindhardt, Retorik, op. cit., pp. 82ff.

34. Engeström, op. cit., p. 175; "Nullus enim loquitur digne nec audit aliquam Scripturam, nisi conformiter ei sit affectus,

　　　ut intus sentiat, quod foris audit et loquitur, et dicat: Eia
　　　vere sic est." WA 3,549, Dictata super Psalterium 1513-15 (on
　　　Psalm 86).

35. WA 3,548 (Engeström, op. cit., p. 181).

36. WA 6,216.

37. WA 2,588 (Commentary on Galatians).

38. Commentary on Romans 8,3, WA 56,356.

39. On Good Works, WA 6,206.

40. Cf. Schwarz, Fides, Spes und Caritas, op. cit., p. 190.

41. Katolsk Katekismus for det apostolske Vikariat Danmark, 1932.

42. Luther broke with false modesty already in his Commentary on
　　　Romans, WA 56,471ff. Cf. also David Löfgren, Die Theologie der
　　　Schöpfung bei Luther, Göttingen, 1960, pp. 283ff.

43. Cf. Engeström's account of the views of a number of theologi-
　　　ans and Luther scholars on the significance of the affections.
　　　Brunner fiercely denies their significance; this is dismissed
　　　by Engeström on pp. 181 and 206. On Karl Barth, see p. 207.
　　　In order to avoid involving the empirical subject - with his
　　　actual psychological equipment - in salvation, Loewenich (The-
　　　ologia Crucis) and Elert (Morphologie der Luthertums, I, Mün-
　　　chen, 1952) found it necessary to invent a transcendental sub-
　　　ject (!) capable of possessing complete righteousness, which,
　　　of course, the empirical subject never can. Cf. Engeström, pp.
　　　230ff. According to Loewenich, to believe in God is something
　　　quite different than to experience him (p. 203). Even more re-
　　　cent students of Luther evince this fear of psychology. For
　　　example, it is important to R. Prenter (Der barmherzige Rich-
　　　ter. Iustitia dei passiva in Luthers Dictata super Psalterium
　　　1513-15, Acta Jutlandica XXXIII, 2, Aarhus, 1961) that the
　　　"experience in the tower" (when Luther is thought to have made
　　　his fundamental acknowledgement of the need for reformation)
　　　not be understood psychologically: "Man darf in den Dictata
　　　nicht nach der psychologischen Form, sondern nur nach dem the-
　　　ologischen Inhalt des Turmerlebnis fragen" (p. 57 and passim).
　　　Similarly, G. Ebeling, (Luther. Einführung in sein Denken, Tü-
　　　bingen, 1964) shows how Luther broke with the Aristotelian
　　　psycho-scholastic psychology (pp. 96, 172, 175), but he re-
　　　gards this as a purely theological break, and has no awareness
　　　of the　fact it was predicated upon a different psychology.
　　　Even Leif Grane, Modus loquendi theologicus, Leiden, 1975,
　　　seems to be suspicious of psychology; cf. Jan Lindhardt, Om
　　　at tale historisk (About speaking historically), Fønix 2(1978)
　　　137.

44. See the commentary on Isaiah 53 in WA 40,III,738; cf. Enge-
　　　ström, op. cit., p. 179.

45. Engeström, op. cit., p. 180.

46. Engeström, excursus, p. 226.

47. Luther rejected the theologica mystica, which preached the
    verbum increatum (the uncreated, i.e., the in-audible, un-read-
    able and eternal word which is communicated directly by the
    Holy Spirit) in favor of the theologia propria (the true theo-
    logy), which he held to be communicated by means of the verbum
    incarnatum (the incarnate word). See WA 9,98; cf. Obermann,
    op. cit., p. 33.

48. On Luther's struggle in the monastery, see e.g. Roland H.
    Bainton, Here I stand, A Life of Martin Luther, N.Y., 1950,
    Ch. II-III.

49. Knud Hansen, Gudsbilledets frugter at bære, Præsteforeningens
    Blad, 69 (1979) pp. 373ff. and 381.

50. Preface to Romans, op. cit.

51. R. Schwarz, Fides, Spes und Caritas ... op. cit., p. 122.

52. From "On the Freedom of a Christian", WA 7,32.

53. Ibid., WA 7, 36.

6. The Enslaved Will

1. WA 18,716.

2. De civitate dei XI,18; cf. Josef Kopperschmidt, Rhetorik und
   Theodizee. Studie zur hermeneutischen Funktionalität der Rhetorik bei Augustin. Kerygma und Dogma 17 (1971) 273-291.

3. De corruptione et gratia; cf. Gotthard Nygren, Das Prädestinationslehre in der Theologie Augustins. Eine systematisch-teol-
   ogische Studie, Lund, 1956, p. 80.

4. On St. Thomas, see Harry J. McSorley, Luthers Lehre vom unfreien Willen nach seiner Hauptschrift De Servo Arbitrio im
   Lichte der biblischen und kirchlichen Tradition, München, 1967,
   pp. 126-176.

5. Thoroughly explored by Leif Grane in: Contra Gabrielem, Luthers
   Auseinandersetzung mit Gabriel Biel in der Disputatio Contra
   Scholasticam Theologiam 1517, København, 1962.

6. See Die Religion in Geschichte und Gegenwart, Tübingen, 1962,
   Vol. 6, Col. 1722 (art.: "Willensfreiheit").

7. Cf. W. Lesowsky's introduction in: ed. W. Welzig, Erasmus of
   Rotterdam, Ausgewählte Schriften, Darmstadt, 1969ff., Vol. 4,
   pp. VII-XXX.

8. The title in question is Assertio omnium articulorum. M. Lutheri per bullam Leonis X. novissinam damnatorum. 1520; cf.
   WA 7,91ff. Here Luther affirms that he must insist on the cor-
   rectness of 41 articles, of which particularly art. 36 has to
   do with the question of free will.

9. Op. cit., p. 8.

10. WA 18,783.

11. K.E. Løgstrup, Viljesbegrebet i De Servo Arbitrio (The Concept of Will in De Servo Arbitrio), Dansk teologisk Tidsskrift, 1940, pp. 129-147.

12. "Or, if one whould still not understand what I am saying, then we shall introduce a necessity which by force compels one to perform an act - and yet another necessity, which infallibly manifests itself at the appointed time. Whoever is listening to us will recognize that we are speaking of the latter, and not of the former; in other words, we are not asking as to whether Judas became a traitor of or contrary to his own will, but as to whether it had ineluctably to occur at the time preordained by God that Judas wilfully betrayed Christ." WA 18, 720-721; quoted by Løgstrup, op. cit., p. 140. In other words, there is no question of any external force (coactio) to which man must submit against his will, but of an internal necessity behind which is, in the last analysis, God.
   It is a commonly-held view in most of the literature on Luther that he felt that with respect to God man's will was unfree, whereas it was free with respect to other men. Some of Luther's statements could be construed to mean this, but wrongly so. In one passage Luther speaks of two kingdoms, in one of which man is a slave, namely, with respect to God, while he is free in the other. However, the latter has nothing to do with the freedom of the will as this concept has been traditionally understood; rather, it corresponds to what Luther says in On Christian Freedom: "A man is a free lord over all things", that is, because all commandments and so forth have disappeared; no legalistic demands exist from God's side. A corresponding statement describes the enslaved will: "The Gospel has left the power of decision in our own hands so that we may rule over things and exploit them as we will." (WA 18, 672). Thus we are free of the compulsion of the Law (Luther explicitly mentions Moses and the Pope in this connection), but, of course, this has nothing to do with the concept of the will itself or with the question as to whether man is free in an anthropological sense.
   Another way in which scholars have attempted to demonstrate the idea of the freedom of the will in Luther's thinking is characterized by such remarks as the following: "We know that man has been installed as lord over that which is beneath him. He has all rights and his free will over all such things." (WA 18,781). But this passage, too, is unsuitable to prove the notion of free will in Luther's thought. A non-commissioned officer is not free simply in virtue of the fact that he is able to order his troops about. Nor does a result cease to be a result of something, just because it is itself also the cause of something else. A thing which has been produced by some-

thing else does not stop being a produced thing just because
it is able to produce something itself.

Finally, scholars have pointed to Luther's remark that there
are relationships among men which are indifferent or neutral,
in contradistinction to the situation between man and God (WA
18,768).

Here I would point to the teaching about the
various rhetorical levels of style. Relationships between men
may often be conducted in the low style, while man's relationship has to be conducted in the highest one.

13. WA 18,750.

14. WA 18,636.

15. From Operationes in Psalmos, WA 5,177.

16. See the literature mentioned in Ch. 7, n. 88.

18. WA, 40, I, 286.

19. Of course, there is some sort of presupposition, since faith
    is not a matter pertaining to plants or animals, but to men.
    The receptivity of men entails, among other things, that they
    may be affected by things outside of them: "Heaven was not
    created for geese."; cf. WA 18,636.

20. De servo arb.; WA 18,747.

21. WA 3,431.

22. Quoted in Söderblom, Tre livsformer: Mystik, förtröstad, vet-
    skap, Stockholm, 1923, pp. 23ff.

23. WA 18,696.

24. WA 40, I, 546.

25. WA 40, I, 283ff.

26. WA 7,25.

27. WA 40, I, 288.

28. WA 18,747.

29. WA 57, I, 147.

30. H. Lausberg, op. cit., §§ 410-426.

31. Eckhard Kessler, Petrarca und die Geschichte, München, 1979;
    see esp. the section entitled "Viri illustres als Gegenstand
    exemplarischer Geschichtsschreibung", pp. 102ff.

32. See the section on Historie in: Religionen i Krise, ed. H.C.
    Wind, København 1980, Vol. 2, p. 32ff.

33. Many Luther scholars have misunderstood this feature; an exam-
    ple is Østergaard-Nielsen, who denies that Luther regarded

Christ as an <u>exemplum</u> (H. Østergaard-Nielsen, Scriptura sacra
viva vox, København 1957, pp. 153ff.) It is correct that Luther rejected the medieval teaching on the <u>imitatio Christi</u>,
i.e., the notion that it was a Christian duty to imitate the
moral behavior of Christ here on earth and to wander about as
he did; in short, the idea that Christ should be regarded as
a moral example. But it would be a serious misunderstanding
of the concept of the <u>exemplum</u> so to restrict it. The fact of
the matter was that the idea entailed that that which was depicted as the hearer's own <u>exemplum</u> had also to be his own
present reality. Thus it would have been more than passing
strange if Luther had rejected the idea of the <u>exemplum</u> - which
in fact he did not; quite the contrary.

34. Cf. D. Walther von Loewenich, Luther als Ausleger der Synop-
    tiker, München, 1954, pp. 12ff., who provedes a number of il-
    lustrations of the idea of the <u>exemplum</u> in Luther's thought.
    See further Joest, op. cit., pp. 365 and 382.

35. Erasmus, Diatribe, Ausg. Sch. IV, pp. 118ff.

36. Mt. 19,21; Erasmus 74.

37. Lk. 9,23; Erasmus 74.

38. 1. Kor. 9,24; cf. Erasmus 83.

39. WA 18,673.

40. 18,679.

41. WA 18,672.

42. WA 18,727.

43. WA 18,710ff.

44. See the rejection of the Scholastic teaching on the idea of
    double necessity in WA 18,616 and 720ff.

45. WA 18,717.

46. Cf. G. Ebeling, Luther, Einführung in sein Denken, Tübingen,
    1964, p. 15.

47. WA 56,352.

48. WA 56,343.

49. WA 56,288.

50. W. Joest, Ontologie der Person bei Luther, p. 268.

7. Use of the Bible

1. Cf. Fr. Kropatscheck, Das Schriftprinzip der lutherischen Kirche, Leipzig, 1904, pp. 436ff.

2. Cf. Birgit Stolt, Studien zur Luthers Freiheitstraktat mit be-
   sonderen Rücksicht auf das Verhältnis der lateinischen und der
   deutschen Fassung zu einander und die Stilmittel der Rhetorik,
   Stockholm, 1969, pp. 119ff.

3. Sendbrief von Dolmetschen, in: WA 30,2,632-646.

4. Jan Lindhardt, Rhetor, Poeta, Historicus, Studien über rhetorische Erkenntnis und Lebensanschauung im italienischen Renaissancehumanismus, Leiden, 1979, pp. 113.

5. Bruno Migliorini, Storia della Lingua Italiana, Firenze, 1962.

6. However, the whole service did not take place in Latin; usually, the sermon was held in the vernacular, Sermons were sometimes quite "popular", particularly if the preachers were members of the mendicant orders (especially the Franciscans). Considerable rhetorical abilities were often demonstrated on these occasions. See e.g. C.S. Baldwin, Medieval Rhetoric and Poetic, N.Y., 1959; further, A.F. Nørager Pedersen, Prædikenens idéhistorie, Copenhagen 1980.

7. Erasmus, Ratio seu compendium verae theologiae, in: Ausgew. Schriften III, Darmstadt, 1967, p. 152.

8. With the single important difference that historical critical research is not concerned with whether the message is true or not.

9. H.-G. Gadamer, Wahrheit und Methode, 2. ed. Tübingen, 1965, pp. 284ff.

10. Thus in the preface to the Epistle of James is referred to as a "trashy letter".

11. A. Buck, Zu Begriff und Problem der Renaissance. Eine Einleitung; and Delio Cantimori, Zur Geschichte des Begriffes "Renaissance"; both published in: ed. v.A. Buck, Zu Begriff und Problem der Renaissance, Wege der Forschung, Vol. 204, Darmstadt, 1969. See also A. Campana, The Origin of the Word "Humanist", in: Journal of the Wartburg and Courtauld Institutes, 1948, pp. 60ff.

12. E.R. Curtius, Theologische Poetik im Italienischen Trecento, Zeitschrift für romanische Philologie, 1940, pp. 1ff; further, Jan Lindhardt, Rhetor, Poeta, Historicus, op. cit., Ch. 8, pp. 93ff.

13. See above, Ch. 4, n. 6. Further, William J. Bouwsma, Renaissance and Reformation, The two Faces of Humanism. Stoicism and Augustinianism in Renaissance Thought. Iternerarium Italicum. Studies in Medieval and Reformation Thought, editor, H.A. Oberman, Vol. XIV, Leiden, 1975, pp. 3-60.

14. One might compare Luther's way of reading the Bible with the so-called "New Criticism" which was so popular in the 50's and 60's of this century, since this approach, too, entailed that one read a text "internally". Of course, Luther was in at least this respect not in a polemical situation with his contemporaries, as the "New Critics" were, for which reason his principles are by no means as rigid.

15. See Nancy Struever, The Language of History in the Renaissance, Princeton, 1971.

16. WA 40,1, commentary on 663, verses 4,26.

17. Cf. Jan Lindhardt, Middelalderens og renæssancens bibeludlæg-ning (The Exegesis of the Middle Ages and the Renaissance), Fønix 3 (1979) 200-213, with references.

18. Anne Riising, Danmarks middelalderlige prædiken (The Danish sermon in the Middle Ages), Odense, 1967, p. 94.

19. Op. cit., pp. 103ff.

20. See Aurelius Augustinus, De doctrina christiana, Bk. I. In fact, it is an important problem for the Christian understand-ing of symbols that symbols may in fact obscure the things they are intended to represent. A roadsign which is fitted out with a large number of indicators may similarly be a poor sign, since the complexity may inadvertently shadow the intended meaning of the sign. One pays more attention to the symbol than to that which it symbolizes or, as Augustine put it, one pays attention to the creature, and not to the Creator. Thus, in the Christian imaginative universe, the way from the symbol to the reality is sometimes overlong. The symbol becomes "wrong" in relation to the thing symbolized. Consider, for example, the equation: the Cross of the Repentant Thief = the Love of God. St. Augustine held that this sort of paradoxical mode was the most appropriate way to use symbols; cf. above, Ch. 5.

21. Henri de Lubac, Exégèse mediéval. Les quatre sense de l'Écrit-ure, Paris, 1964, second part, II section: Les aires du sym-bole, pp. 149ff. and esp. p. 177.

22. On the conception of the allegory in conjunction with models and metaphors, see Max Black, Models and Metaphors, Ithaca, 1966.

23. See e.g., Søren Holm, Romantikken, København, 1972., esp. pp. 52ff. I have also personally attempted to suggest some ways in which Romanticism may be understood as a secularised vers-ion of the Christian concept of the workings of the Holy Spirit (cf. my Retorik, Ch. 8, pp. 100ff.).

24. Poetics, 22.

25. H.-G. Gadamer, Symbol und Allegorie, in: ed. E. Castelli, Uma-nesimo e Simbolismo, Padova, 1958, pp. 23ff. Gadamer defends his understanding of allegory further in Wahrheit und Methode, 2. ed., 1965, pp. 66ff.

26. Reissued in a single vol. in 1910; reprinted in 1963; it is to this edition I refer throughout. See esp. Ch. I, Die Echt-heit der Gleichnisreden Jesu, pp. 1ff., and Ch. II, Das Wesen der Gleichnisreden Jesu, pp. 25ff.

27. Ibid., p. 52. Among other things, Jülicher mentions that Ari-stotle (in: Rhetoric, III, 4) speaks of this distinction, but characterizes it as "small". Jülicher, however, regards it as decisive.

28. Ibid., pp. 55ff.; with a reference to Aristotle's Rhetoric III, 3, this is described as a riddle; cf. p. 38.

29. Ibid., p. 64.

30. Cf. G. Ebeling, Evangelische Evangelienauslegung, 1942, reprinted in Darmstadt, 1962, pp. 46-47.

31. Jülicher, op. cit., pp. 69ff.

32. Cf. Jørgen K. Bukdahl, Sprog og erkendelse. En historisk indledning (Language and Cognition. A historical introduction), in: ed. M. Jacobsen, Sprog og virkelighed (Language and Reality), København 1974, pp. 9-29; further, Jan Lindhardt, Retorik, Ch. 8, pp. 100ff.; and K.O. Apel, Die Idee der Sprache in der Tradition von Dante bis Vixo, 1963.

33. E.Thestrup Pedersen, Luther som Skriftfortolker, I. En studie i Luthers skriftsyn, hermeneutik og eksegese (A studie of Luther's understanding of Scripture, his hermeneutics and exegesis). København, 1959, p. 290. Thestrup Pedersen himself agrees with this, although he has a very differentiated understanding of the "goal" of the allegorical interpretation; cf. pp. 292ff.

34. As he promised, so he acted. Ebeling subsequently attempted systematically to demonstrate how Luther rejects the allegorrical interpretation, first in 1522 (p. 50), then in 1523 (p. 51), in 1524 (p. 53, in 1525 (p. 61), and so forth. However, closer examination reveals that Luther is not definitively rejecting this method; instead, he is protesting against parti-cular interpretation which he has encountered in the course of the tradition. There is no general rejection of allegory as such. Thus, for example, where Medieval interpreters interpreted workers in a vineyeard as representing various psychological characters, in 1523 Luther made an ecclesiastico-historical interpretation out of the same parable, one in which Adam, Noah, Moses, and other Old Testament figures represent the workers who are called, while the heathen are those who are summoned at the eleventh hour. Which is more allegorical? However, Ebeling also asserts that, "Begründete Preisgabe allegorischer Auslegung findet sich also im Anfang nur, wenn ein Anlass zur Polemik gegen papistische Auslegung vorliegt, die den Text zur Begründung irriger Dogmenverdrecht" (p. 51). However, matters were no different later on in Luther's career; Luther continued to allegorize ad libitum, if we are to believe Ebeling. Ebeling's conclusion (pp. 85-89) is a fine collection of contradictory statements. Ebeling inquires as to how Luther could bring himself to abandon allegory, only to admit later on (p. 87) that he did not do so. His best formulation is perhaps the following: "die Preisgabe der Allegorese um ihrer selbst willen ist durchweg stillschweigen" (p. 88). Obviously so, when it has in fact never been expressed.

    Ebeling later modifies his attempt to de-allegorize Luther. Thus he maintains that Luther's principle was that allegories had to lead from the physical to the spiritual, for which reason it was unacceptable of the Papists to make the Old Testament priesthood symbolize the Roman one: "Die Tendenz: vom Leiblichen ins Geistlichen gehört allerdings zum Wesen allegorischer Auslegung. Auch hier zeigt sich wie bei den andern Regeln: Luther bringt die Grundregeln allegorischer Auslegung nur zu reinere, konsequenter Anwendung" (p. 182). Ebeling provides us with a wealth of apposite quotations and useful materials, the significance of which remains in spite of the author's lack of understanding of the phenomenon of allegory and of Luther's use of it.

35. Hans Wernle (Allegorie und Erlebnis bei Luther. Basler Studien zur deutschen Sprache und Literatur, Bern, 1960) offers a more sophisticated understanding of Luther's use of allegory. In his section entitled Das Wort Luthers (pp. 66ff.), Wernle shows how Luther did in fact become increasingly critical of Medieval symbolism, but nevertheless retained it. Wernle is in particular aware that allegorization is no longer symbolism, but instead serves as a tool in the hand of the (either divine or human) author. "Die Allegorie bleibt also ... aber sie wird rhetorischer Ausdruck, den der Verfasser aus bestimmten Gründen frei wählt. Er will etwas mitteilen, er will auf bestimmte Weise verstanden werden, er will einen Eindruck erwecken" (pp. 82-83). Unfortunately, Wernle does not evaluate the positions of Ebeling or other recent scholars. To explain the fact that allegory nevertheless lost ground at this time, he points out that Luther had become more humanistic (pp. 86ff.) and that allegory as a tool was simply too weak. Luther intended to do battle, and Wernle holds that to this end "Erlebnis" was a better basis (pp. 104ff.). This theory is more remarkable than convincing.

36. The so-called doctrine of transubstantiation was promulgated at the Lateran Synod in 1215. The doctrine maintains that the substance of the bread is exchanged with the substance of Jesus, whereas its accidents, that is, such things as taste, appearance, and so forth, abide unchanged. The result thus continues to look like bread, but is in reality the body of Jesus. The basis for this view is a symbolic understanding of being; the bread becomes a sort of token of the presence of the divine body in a way similar to the way the literal meaning of Scripture contains the other three meanings within it.

37. This view, too, is symbolic, but there is further between symbol and reality than there is in the Catholic view (see the preceding note). The connection between the symbol and the thing symbolized is accidental, because the symbol is not a part, even a little one, of the reality.

38. Luther's theory of metaphor is developed in "On the Communion of Christ", WA 26,379ff. See also e.g. WA 26,384, where he points out that "ist" (is) always has to do with being, and not with meaning. Is this a rose? Yes, it is: the answer has to do with being, not meaning.

39. WA 26,468.

40. WA 26,437.

41. J.L. Austin, How to do Things with Words, Oxford, 1962.

42. On the Communion of Christ, WA 26,468.

43. To use Austin's phrase: every statement is not only illocution-
ary, but perlocutionary.

44. On the Communion of Christ, WA 26,443.

45. H. Lausberg, Elemente der literarischen Retorik, 3rd. ed.,
1967, §§ 192-201.

46. On the Communion of Christ WA 26,442.

47. In his tract, Wider die himmlischen Propheten ..., WA 18,188.

48. In his treatise Wider Latomus, WA 8,83.

49. Ibid., WA 8,84.

50. Ein Sermon von dem neuen Testament, d.i. von der heiligen Mes-
se, WA 6,357.

51. WA 30,1,215.

52. Jan Lindhardt, Retorik, Ch. 6, Elocutio, pp. 74ff.

53. On the Communion of Christ, WA 26,273; cf. Ars Poetica, v. 47-
48.

54. WA 4,290 (lecture on Genesis); cf. Peter Meinhold, Luthers
Sprachphilosophie, Berlin, 1958, pp. 42ff.

55. Wider die himmlischen Propheten, WA 18,202.

56. Salutati discovered that history does not arise from the events
themselves, but from the narrator; according to him, one re-
counts only "memorable" or "instructive" events; cf. my Rhetor,
Poeta, Historicus, p. 146.

57. Note Quintilian's remarks on the concept of inversio (= allegory) in Inst. Or. 8,6,44.

58. Cf. Ulrich Nembach, Predigt des Evangeliums, Neukirchen-Vluyn,
1972, p. 162. On Luther's relationship to Quintilian, see
ibid., p. 130ff.

59. Cf. e.g., Ebeling, op. cit., p. 276: "Die Aussagen der Schrift
über Gott wollen nicht verstanden sein als Aussagen über sein
Für-sich-sein, sondern als Aussagen über sein Für-uns-sein."
Note also Kjell Ove Nilsson (Simul. Das Miteinander von Göttlichem und Menschlichem in Luthers Theologie, Göttingen, 1966,
p. 285): "Christi Gegemwart in der Kirche is - pro nobis - im-
mer eine sakramentale Gegenwart im Wort, eine Inkarnation des
Wortes in äusseren Worten und Ueichen ..." Even generously considered, such statements are artificial, since they suggest
that this is a remarkable theological quality in Luther's work.

60. WA 15,42.

61. Presumably, Erasmus does not mean "places" (= passages), that is, verses or chapters, but topics (he uses adytum) which either can or ought not to be discussed. He includes the will among these, since he doubts that it is a fruitful subject. Cf. Erasmus, De libero arbitrio diatribe. Ausg. Schriften, Vol. IV, Darmstadt, 1969, pp. 10ff.

62. On the enslaved will; see WA 18,186.

63. Against the heavenly prophets; WA 18,186.

64. Against Latomus, 8,8,86: "Christus dum offeretur pro nobis, factus est peccatum metaphorice." This is reproduced in Luther's German (Ausg. Werke, Ergänzungsreihe, Vol. 6, p. 76) as follows: "da Christus für uns geopfert ward, ist er zur Sünde gemacht im bildlichen Sinne ..." The translation would be misleading if it led one to believe that sin was not "really" transferred to Jesus, but only "metaphorically".

65. On the enslavement of the will, WA 18,608.

66. Spiritus Creator, 2nd ed., 1946, p. 115: "If God himself does not speak to the heart at the same time the ear hears the external word, the latter remains mere human words and laws." The text which Prenter is here paraphrasing (WA 3,348) does not actually contain the midleading words "ear", "external word", or "heart". As Luther in fact says in the same passage, human language can indeed reach the heart, since it is "a good and sweet word", which God makes use of. Otherwise it may be freely admitted that Luther's usage, particularly in his earlier writings, sometimes gives evidence of Platonic influence, but this fact ought not to be allowed to distract us from his actual intentions.

67. Thestrup Pedersen, op. cit., p. 425.

68. A fine account of this is to be found in Peter Meinholdt's Luthers Sprachphilosophie, 1958, Ch. I: Die Einheit von Geist und Wort, pp. 11ff.

69. Cf. E. Metzke, Sakrament und Metaphysik. Eine Lutherstudie über das Verhältnis des christlichen Denkens zum Leiblich-Materiellen, 1948, in: Gesammelte Studien zur Philosophiegeschichte, Witten, 1961, pp. 158-201, and esp. 179ff.

70. Wider die himmlischen Propheten, WA, 18,136.

71. Ibid., p. 137.

72. Concerning which, see WA 18,683ff.

73. On the enslavement of the will, WA 18,685.

74. Cf. Jan Lindhardt, Middelalderen og Renaissancens Bibeludlægning, op. cit., pp. 210ff.

75. Ratio seu Methodus compendio perveniendi ad veram Theologiam (i.e., "Method by which one quickly achieves a true theology"), Ausg. Werke, Darmstadt, 1967, Vol. 3, p. 170.

76. Leif Grane, Modus loquendi theologicus, Acta theologica Danica, Vol. XII, Leiden, 1975, p. 65.

77. On the enslavement of the will, WA 18,606.

78. Evang. Ev. Auslegung, pp. 190 and 413.

79. "Oportet omnes scripturae loci de Christo intelligantur, sive aperte sive in figura", WA 15,413.

80. R. Bultmann, Wissenschaft und Existenz, Glauben und Verstehen, Tübingen, 1965-66, III, pp. 107-122.

81. See above, p. 93 and 169.

82. Luther thought that this was sometimes done for the sake of "beauty"; thus, for exemple, he held that in 4,2 St. Paul adds an allegory which really has no basis in conjunction with the Old Testament text. But he adds that it is permissible to show, "a beautifully painted picture". See WA 40,1.657. The metaphor of the painter was extraordinarily popular during the Renaissance; cf. R.W. Lee, Ut Pictura Poesis, New York, 1967, Ch. IV-V. However, Renaissance and rhetorical thinkers did not understand beauty as something which one merely adds, having no other effect; rahter, they maintained that beautification, illumination (= enlightenment) sheds new light on things.

83. Thus it is necesary to be a capable interpreter. "Not everyone is able to find allegories. It is all too easy to delude oneself, or to get an idea of which one approves, and which one thinks is accurate, and yet it may nevertheless be completely wrong." WA 40,1.

84. Cf. e.g., A.C. Danto, Analytical Philosophy of History, Cambridge, 1965; C.S. Lewis, "Is Theology Poetry?" in: Screwtape Proposes a Toast and other Pieces, Glasgow, 1977 (1st ed. 1959); Jan Lindhardt, Historisk forståelse og bevidsthed (Historical understanding and consciousness), in: ed. H.C. Wind, Religionen i Krise, København, 1980, Vol. II, pp. 32-41; W. Schapp, In Geschichten verstrickt. Zum Sein von Mensch und Ding, Hamburg, 1953; H. Weinrich, Erzählsstrukturen des Mythos. Literatur für Leser, Stuttgart, 1971; Amos A. Wilder, Theopoetic: Theology and the religious Imagination, Philadelphia, 1976; Svend Bjerg, Den kristne Grundfortælling, Aarhus, 1981.

85. See the illustration in R. Bainton, Martin Luther, 7th ed., 1980, p. 100.

86. Cf. Herbert Hunger, Lexikon der griech. und röm. Mythologie, Hamburg, 1974, p. 163. The same section describes the use of this motif in art and literature.

87. Cf. E. Panofsky, Hercules am Scheideweg, Leipzig, 1930; Eugene M. Waith, The Herculean Hero, in: Marlowe, Chapman, Shakespeare and Dryden, London, 1962. On Salutati's use of the hydra metaphor, cf. Jan Lindhardt, Rhetorik, op. cit., pp. 121ff. On the humanists and Scholastic philosophy, cf. P.O. Kristeller, Studies in Renaissance Thought and Letters, Rome, 1956.

88. In Praise of Folly (Laus Stultitiae), 53.

89. Methodus (guide), Ausg. Werke, Vol. 3, Darmstadt, 1967, p. 74.

90. I have not yet found the hydra in Luther's writings, but I would be willing to bet a good deal that it is in them somewhere; if it is not discovered shortly, then it will no doubt turn up when the Index to the Weimar addition appears.

91. This is a recurrent feature of his attitude towards the theologians of the Middle Ages; cf. Ratio seu Methodus, op. cit., p. 128. It might be added that not only Erasmus, but indeed all of antiquity and the patristic period rejected <u>curiositas</u>. Cf. E.P. Meiering, Calvin wider die Neugierde: ein Beitrag zum Vergleich zw. reformatorischen und patristischen Denken, Niewkoop, 1980; further, H.A. Oberman, Contra vanam curiositatem, Zürich, 1974, who shows how this opposition to "curiosity" is also part of Luther's theology.

92. "Spiritus sanctus non est scepticus" (the Holy Spirit is not sceptical). On the Enslaved Will, WA 18,605. As I have previously mentioned, the opposition between Erasmus and Luther has been very much exaggerated by the scholars who have concentrated on the collision between the two. On the other hand, it is not to be denied that this opposition really existed. Perhaps a useful model for characterizing the differences is that which M.A. Hanne Flebo has employed to distinguish Luther from Gadamer (En undersøgelse af mulige fællestræk mellem Luthers retoriske humanisme og H.-G. Gadamers filosofiske hermeneutik. (A study of possible common features of Luther's rhetorical humanism and H.-G. Gadamer's philosophical hermeneutics) Speciale ved Inst. f. Kristendomskundskab, Aarhus Universitet, 1980). This is to use the rhetorical stylistic levels of pathos (the highest) and ethos (the lowest) to describe Luther and Gadamer, respectively. "Ethos" could also be held to be a good characterization of Erasmus. He was no "sceptic" in any of the word's meanings, and his goal was as sophisticated and varied a methodological approach as possible. For those who feel that the purity of theology lies in its unity, this could be taken to be a sceptical approach, but it would hardly be fair to do so.

93. Luther particularly attacked Erasmus after his death in 1536, especially in his "table talks"; one can get some notion of the extent of this in M. Luther, Ausg. Werke, Ergänzungsreihe, Vol. 3, pp. 119ff.

94. Cf. Thestrup Pedersen, op. cit., pp. 339ff.

95. Cf. WA 23,244ff.; further, E. Metzke, Coincidentia opposito-
    rum, Witten, 1961, p. 170.

96. H.-G. Gadamer, Wahrheit und Methode, 2. ed., Tübingen, 1965,
    p. 465.

97. The idea is, for example, already present in the attack on La-
    tomus, WA 8,10ff.

Conclusion

1. Capito might be mentioned as an example; cf. James M. Kittelson, Wolfgang Capito: from humanist to reformer, Leiden, 1975.

2. Christopher Lasch, The Culture of Narcisism, N.Y. 1978.

Literature

Martin Luther's works are qouted from Martin Luthers Werke. Kritische Gesamtausgabe, vol. 1-58, Weimar 1883-1948 (later reprints). Abbreviated WA; succeeding figures indicate volume and page.

Secondary literature. Only titles referred to in the text are mentioned.

Apel, K.O.: Die Idee der Sprache von Dante bis Vico, Archiv für Begriffgeschichte 8, Bonn 1963.

Aristoteles: De poetica, Loeb classical Library.

Auerbach, Erich: Sermo humilis, in: Literatursprache und Publikum in der Lateinischen Spätantike und im Mittelalter, Bern 1958.

Austin, J.L.: How to do things with words, Oxford 1962.

Bainton, Roland H.: Here I stand. A Life of Martin Luther, New York 1950.

Baldwin, C.S.: Medieval Rhetoric and Poetic, New York 1959.

Bishop, Morris: Petrarch and his World, London 1964.

Bjerg, Svend: Den kristne Grundfortælling (The Christian fundamental Story), Århus 1981.

Black, Max: Models and Metaphors, Ithaca 1966.

Blumenberg, Hans: Die Licht als Metapher der Wahrheit, Studium Generale 10, Heft 7, 1957.

Bojesen, Lars Bo og Jan Lindhardt: Samvittigheden (Conscience), Copenhagen 1979.

Bouwsma, W.J.: Renaissance and Reformation. The two Faces of Humanism. Stoicism and Augustinianism in Renaissance Thought. Itinerarium Italicum. Studies in Medieval and Reformation Thought, ed. H.A. Oberman, Leiden 1975, p. 3-60.

Boyle, Marjorie O'Rourke: Erasmus on Language and Method in Theology, Toronto 1977.

Breen, Quirinius: Christianity and Humanism, Studies in the History of Ideas, Michigan 1958.

Brunner, Emil: Die Mystik und das Wort, Tübingen 1921.

Buck, August: Zu Begriff und Problem der Renaissance, Eine Einleitung, in: the composite volume of the same title, Wege der Forschung, vol. 204, Darmstadt 1969.

Bukdahl, Jørgen K. Indledning i: Sprog og virkelighed (Introduction, in: Language and Reality), ed. by Malthe Jacobsen, Copenhagen 1974.

Bultmann, R.: Wissenschaft und Existenz, in: Glauben und Verstehen, III, Tübingen 1966, p. 107-122.

Burckhardt, Jacob: Die Kultur der Renaissance in Italien, 1860.

Burdach, Konrad: Reformation, Renaissance, Humanismus, Leipzig 1926, Darmstadt 1963.

Burton, Robert: The Anatomy of Melancholy, Abridged and Edited by Joan K. Peters, Milestones of Thought, New York 1979.

Cantimori, D.: Zur Geschichte des Begriffes "Renaissance", in: Zu Begriff und Problem der Renaissance, published by A. Buck, Darmstadt 1969, p. 19-39.

Curtius, E.R.: Theologische Poetik im italienischen Trecento, Zeitschrift für römische Philologie 1940, p. 1-15.

Danto, A.C.: Analytical Philosophy of History, Cambridge 1965.
Dockhorn, Klaus: Luthers Glaubensbegriff, Linguistica Biblica 21/22, 1973, p. 19-39.
Dyck, Joachim: Dicht-Kunst, Deutsche Barockpoetik und rhetorische Tradition, Bad Hamburg 1966.

Ebeling, Gerhard: Evangelische Evangelienauslegung, 1942, reprint Darmstadt 1962.
Ebeling, Gerhard: Luther, Einführung in sein Denken, Tübingen 1964.
Elert, Werner, Morphologie des Luthertums I-II, München 1952.
Engeström, Sigfried v.: Luthers trosbegrepp. Med särskild hänsyn til försanthållandets betydelse (Luther's concept of faith), Uppsala 1933.
Erasmus Roterodamus (of Rotterdam): Ausgewählte Schriften: Lateinisch und deutsch, hrsg. von Werner Welzig, vol. 1-8, Darmstadt 1967-1980.
Erasmus of Rotterdam: The Praise of Folly (quoted from a Danish translation by Villy Sørensen, Copenhagen 1979).

Fafner, Jørgen: Retorik, Copenhagen 1977.
Flebo, Hanne: En undersøgelse af mulige fællestræk mellem Luthers retoriske humanisme og H.G. Gadamers filosofiske hermeneutik. (A study of possible common features of Luther's rhetoric humanism and H.-G. Gadamer's philosophical hermeneutics), Institut for Kristendomskundskab, Aarhus Universitet 1980.
Folie et déraison à la renaissance, Bruxelles 1976.

Gadamer, H.-G.: Symbol und Allegorie, in: Umanesimo e Simbolismo, published by E. Castelli, Padova 1958, p. 23ff.
Gadamer, H.-G., Wahrheit und Methode, 2nd ed., Tübingen 1965.
Garin, E.: Medioevo e Rinascimento, Bari 1961.
Gelder, Enno van: The two Reformations in the 16th Century, Haag 1961.
Giuliani, Oscar: Allegoria retorica e poetica nel Secretum del Petrarca, Bologna 1977.
Grane, Leif: Contra Gabrielem. Luthers Auseinandersetzung mit Gabriel Biel in der Disputatio Contra Scholasticam Theologiam 1517, Acta Theologica Danica IV, København 1962.
Grane, Leif: Protest og konsekvens (Protest and consequence), Copenhagen 1968.
Grane, Leif: Modus loquendi theologicus. Luthers Kampf um die Erneuerung der Theologie (1515-1518), Acta Theologica Danica, vol. XII, Leiden 1975.
Grassi, E.: Humanismus und Marxismus, Hamburg 1973.

Hansen, Knud: Gudsbilledets frugter at bære (The fruits of God's image to bear), Præsteforeningens Blad, 69, 1979, p. 373ff.

Hoffman, Bengt R.: Luther and the Mystics. A Re-examination of Luther's spiritual Experience and his Relationship to the Mystics, Minneapolis 1976.

Holm, Søren: Romantikken, Copenhagen 1972.

Hunger, Herbert: Lexikon der griechischen und

Joest, Wilfried: Ontologie der Person bei Luther, Göttingen 1967.

Jülicher, Adolf: Die Gleichnisreden Jesu I-II, Tübingen 1910.

Junghans, Helmut: Der Einfluss des Humanismus auf Luthers Entwicklung bis 1518, Luther-Jahrbuch 1970, s. 37-101.

Kemp, Peter: Sprogets dimensioner (The Dimensions of the Language), Copenhagen 1972.

Kennedy, William J.: Rhetorical Norms in Renaissance Literature, London 1978.

Kessler, E.: Petrarca und die Geschichte, München 1979.

Kittelson, James M.: Wolfgang Capito, From Humanist to Reformer, Leiden 1975.

Klibansky, R., E. Panofsky og F. Saxl: Saturn and Melancholy, London 1964.

Kopperschmidt, Josef: Rhetorik und Theodicee. Studie zur hermeneutischen Funktionalität der Rhetorik bei Augustin, Kerygma und Dogma, 17, 1971, p. 273-291.

Kristeller, P.O.: Studies in Renaissance, Thought and Letters, Rome 1956.

Kristensen, Peter Søby: Kommunikation (Communication), Copnehagen 1975.

Kropatscheck, F.: Das Schriftprinzip der lutherischen Kirche, Leipzig 1904.

Larsen, Holger: Træk af retorikkens historie i oldtidens Grækenland (Feataures of the history of rhetoric in ancient Greece), Nordisk Tidsskrift for Tale og Stemme, 3, 1968, s. 95ff.

Lasch, C.: The Culture of Narcissism, New York 1978.

Lausberg, H.: Handbuch der literarischen Rhetorik: Eine Grundlegung der Literaturwissenschaft, 2nd ed., München 1973.

Lee, R.W.: Ut Pictura Poesis. The Humanistic Theory of Painting, New York 1967.

Lewis, C.S.: Is Theology Poetry? Screwtape proposes a Toast and other Pieces, Glasgow 1977.

Lindhardt, Jan: Retorik, Copenhagen 1975.

Lindhardt, Jan: Om at tale historisk (About speaking historically) Fønix, 2, 1978, s. 129-139.

Lindhardt, Jan: Middelalderens (og Renaissancens) Bibeludlægning (The Exegesis of the Middle Ages (and the Renaissance)), Fønix 3, 1979, p. 200-213.

Lindhardt, Jan: Rhetor, Poeta, Historicus. Studien über rhetorische Erkenntnis und Lebensanschauung im italienischen Renaissancehumanismus. Acta theologica Danica, vol. XIII, Copenhagen 1979.

Loewenich, D. Walther v.: Luthers Theologia crucis, München 1939.

Loewenich, D. Walther v.: Luther als Ausleger der Synoptiker, München 1954.
Löfgren, David: Die Theologie der Schöpfung bei Luther, Göttingen
1960.
Løgstrup, K.E.: Viljesbegrebet De servo arbitrio (The concept of
will of De servo arbitrio), Dansk teologisk Tidsskrift 1942,
p. 129ff.

McSorley, Harry: Luthers Lehren vom unfreien Willen, Beiträge zur
ökumenischen Theologie, München 1967.
Marrou, H.I.: Histoire d'éducation dans l'antiquité, 6. udgave,
Paris 1965.
Meiering, E.P.: Calvin wider die Neugierde; ein Beitrag zum Ver-
gleich zwischen reformatorischen und patristischen Denken,
Niewkoop 1980.
Meinhold, Peter: Luthers Sprachphilosophie, Berlin 1958.
Metzke, E.: Sakrament und Metaphysik. Eine Lutherstudie über das
Verhältnis des christlichen Denkens zum Leiblich-Materiellen,
in: Coincidentia oppositorum. Gesammelte Studien Zur Philiso-
phiengeschichte, Witten 1961, p. 158-201.
Migliorini, Bruno: Storie della lingua italiana, Florence 1962.
Müller, Gregor: Bildung und Erziehung im Humanismus der italieni-
schen Renaissance, Wiesbaden 1969.

Nembach, Ulrich: Prediger des Evangeliums. Luther als Prediger,
Pädagog und Rhetor, Neukirchen 1972.
Nilsson, Kjell Ove: Simul. Das Miteinander von Göttlichem und
Menschlichem in Luthers Theologie, Göttingen 1966.
Nygren, Gotthard: Das Prädestinationslehre in der Theologie Augus-
tins. Eine systematische-theologische Studie, Lund 1956.

Oberman, Heiko A.: Simul gemitus et raptus: Luther und die Mystik.
Kirche, Mystik, Heiligung und das Natürliche bei Luther, Vorträge des Dritten Internationalen Kongress für Lutherforschung,
published by Ivar Adheim, Göttingen 1967, p. 20-59.
Oberman, H.A.: Contra vanam curiositatem, Zürich 1974.

Panofsky, E.: Hercules am Scheidwege, Leipzig 1930.
Panofsky, E.: The Life and Art of Albrecht Dürer, 4th ed., Prince-
ton 1971.
Pedersen, A.F. Nørager: Prædikenens idéhistorie (The history of
ideas of the sermon), Copenhagen 1980.
Pedersen, E. Thestrup: Luther som skriftfortolker, I. En studie
i Luthers skriftsyn, hermeneutik og eksegese (Luther as exegete,
I. A study of Luthers understanding of Scripture, hermeneutics
and exegesis), Copenhagen 1959.
Pedersen, Olaf: Studium Generale, Copenhagen 1979.
Petrarca, Fr.: Prosa, a cura di Martellotti e P.G. Ricci, La let-
teratura italiana, Storia e Testi, Milano Napoli 1955.
Prenter, R.: Spiritus Creator, 2nd ed., Copenhagen 1946.
Prenter, R.: Den unge Luthers theologi (The Theology of the young
Luther), lectures at the University of Aarhus, spring 1956,
duplicated.

Quintilian, M.F.: Institutio oratoria, Loeb Classical Library I-IV, London 1966-69.

Religionen i krise (Religion in Crisis), ed. by H.C. Wind, I-II, Copenhagen 1980.
Riising, Anne: Danmarks middelalderlige prædiken (The Danish sermon in the Middle Ages), Odense 1967.
Robertson, D.W.: A Preface to Chaucer, Princeton 1962.
Ross, D.: Aristotle, London 1923.

Sandstrom, Peter G.: Luther's Sense of Himself as an Interpreter of the World to the World, Amherst, Mass. 1961.
Schapp, W.: In Geschichten verstrickt. Zum Sein von Mensch und Ding, Hamburg 1953.
Scheel, Otto: Dokumente zu Luthers Entwicklung, Tübingen 1929.
Schwarz, R.: Fides, Spes und Caritas bei jungen Luther, Berlin 1962.
Seigel, Jerrold E.: Rhetoric and Philosophy in Renaissance Humanism. The Union of Eloquence and Wisdom, Petrarch to Valla, Princeton 1968.
Snell, Bruno: Die Entdeckung des Geistes, Hamburg 1955.
Snyder, Susan: The Left Hand of God: Despair in Medieval and Renaissance Tradition, Studies in the Renaissance, vol. XII, 1965, p. 18-59.
Spitz, Lewis W.: The Religious Renaissance of the German Humanists, Cambridge, Massachusetts 1963.
Spitz, Lewis W.: Headwaters of the Reformation. Studia Humanitatis. Luther senior et Initia Reformationis, in: Luther and the Dawn of the modern Era, Studies in the History of Christian Thought, vol. VII, published by H.A. Oberman, Leiden 1974, p. 89-116.
Stolt, Birgit: Studien zur Luthers Freiheitstraktat mit besonderer Rücksicht auf das Verhältnis der lateinischen und der deutschen Fassung zu einander und die Stilmittel der Rhetorik, Stockholm 1969.
Stolt, Birgit: Docere, delectare und movere bei Luther. Analyse an Hand der "Predigt, dass man Kinder zur Schulen halten solle", see Wortkampf. Frühneuhochdeutsche Beispiele zur rhetorischen Praxis, Frankfurt am Main 1974, p. 31-77.
Struever, Nance S.: The Language of History in the Renaissance. Rhetoric and Historical Consciousness in Florentine Humanism, Princeton 1970.
Söderblom, N.: Tre livsformer: mystik, förtröstan, vetskab, Stockholm 1923.
Sørensen, Villy: Den gyldne middelvej, København 1979.

Thomas, Keith: Religion and the Decline of Magic, London 1970.
Thinkaus, Charles: In Our Image and Likeness. Humanity and Divinity in Italian Humanist Thought, I-II, London 1970.
Trinkaus, Charles: The Poet as Philosopher: Petrarch and the Formation of Renaissance Consciousness, New Haven 1979.

Undervisningsvejledning for folkeskolen. Betænkning nr. 260. (Teaching guidance for primary school. Report nr. 260).

Vogelsang, Erich: Luther und die Mystik, Lutherjahrbuch 1937, p. 32-54.

Waith, E.M.: The Herculian Hero, in: Marlowe, Chapman, Shakespeare and Dryden, London 1962.

Weinreich, H.: Erzählstrukturen des Mythos, Literatur für Leser, Stuttgart 1971.

Wenzel, S.: Acidia in Medieval Thought and Literature, North Carolina 1967.

Wernle, Hans: Allegorie und Erlebnis bei Luther. Basler Studien zur deutschen Sprache und Literatur, Bern 1960.

Wilder, Amos A.: Theopoetic: Theology and the Religious Imagination, Philadelphia 1976.

Witt, Ronald: Coluccio Salutati and his Public Letters, Geneva 1976.

Østergaard-Nielsen, H.: Scriptura sacra, Viva Vox, Copenhagen 1957.

Index

abstraction 93
accidia 67, 75
Achilles 181, 185, 186, 187
ad fontes 169
Adam 203
affectus 35, 63, 106, 154, 207
Agricola 46
aisthetikon 21
Alberti, Leon Battista 46
allegory 159, 175, 179, 180, 181, 185, 186, 190, 192, 193, 194, 204
almanac 42
amor 26, 72, 126
Andersen, H.C. 138
anthropology 15, 39, 86, 100, 112, 115, 154
Antiquity 1
anxiety 112
Apel, K.O. 233, 243
Aristotle 20, 21, 22, 54, 97, 181, 230, 243
ars dictaminis 50, 51, 52, 59
ars moriendi 70
artes liberales 48
assertio 133, 134
astrology 39, 40, 43, 78
audire 98
Auerbach, Erich 233
Augustine 25, 27, 33, 34, 36, 37, 39, 71, 72, 73, 74, 75, 76, 77, 91, 92, 108, 124, 124, 126, 129, 150, 158, 171, 174, 179, 232, 237, 242
Aurelius Augustinus 229
Austin, J.L. 245

Bainton, Roland H. 237, 247
Baldwin, C.S. 241
Barth, Karl 111, 112
beast of burden 137
belief 108
Biel, Gabriel 129
Bishop, M. 230

Bjerg, Svend 228, 247
Black, Max 242
Blumenberg, Hans 234
Boccaccio 45, 51, 96, 230
Bojesen, Lars Bo 233, 235
Bonaventure 158
Bouwsma, William J. 241
Boyle, Marjorie O'Rourke 229
Breen, Quirinius 230
Bruni, Leonardo 45
Brunner, Emil 100, 235
Bruno, Giordano 6
Buck, August 228, 241
Bukdahl, Jørgen K. 230, 243
Bultmann, Rudolf 216, 247
Burdach, Konrad 4, 228
Buridanus, Johannes 136
Burkhardt 228
Burton, Robert 81, 232

Calvin 6
Campana, A. 240, 241
Cantimori, Delio 228
Capito, Wolfgang 249
Cassian 68
Catholic Church 114
Cave 19
China 168
choler 78
Christ 141, 142, 144, 151, 204, 212, 213
church 5, 8, 9, 70
Cicero 63, 119
Clairvaux, Bernard of 69
code 196
commune 50
communication 86, 87
communion 162, 201
composition 58
concilia 167
concupiscentia 25
Confessiones 76
confidence 108
confirmatio 52
contingency 129
Cross 179
crowning the poet 51
Crusade 49
cupiditas 26

Curtius, E.R. 234, 241
Cyprian 158

Danish People's Church 167
Dante 51, 230
Danto, A.C. 247
David 212
deadly sins 66
delectare 55, 63
delectatio 26
dementia praecox 66
desire 19
Deus nudus 98, 208
Devil 69
devotio moderna 37
dialectics 6
dialectical theology 100
Dionysios the Areapagite 33, 36
dispositio 94
Divine omnipotence 123, 126
dual potential 20
Dumas, Alexandre 138
Duns Scotus 97
Dürer, Albrecht 71, 80, 81, 151, 229, 232
dwarf 48
Dyck, J. 234

East Germany 160
Ebeling, Gerhard 11, 190, 192, 236, 240, 243, 244, 245
ecstacy 35
ego 17
Elert 136
elocutio 95
Engeström, S.v. 235, 236, 237
Enlightenment 8
enthusiast 164, 194, 195
Erasmus of Rotterdam 4, 5, 10, 11, 14, 44, 46, 93, 96, 119, 206, 210, 211, 219, 221, 226, 234, 240, 246, 248
ethos 56
exemplum 143
Exodus 150
exordium 52

experience 104
experientia 112, 113

facet of individual 24
Fafner, Jørgen 234
faith 86, 140, 141, 218
fear 112
feeling 23, 24, 104, 105,
    107, 108, 117, 148,
    154, 163
felix culpa 69
fides informis 102
Ficino, Marsiglio 46, 80,
    81
Flebo, Hanne 248
flesh 107
Florence 49
four fluids 42
freedom 29
Freud 111
frui-love 27
fundamentalist 164, 165
furor divinus 81

Gadamer, Hans-Georg 7,
    166, 223, 228, 241,
    242
Galilei 6
Garin, Eugenio 229
Gelder, Enno van 228
genus subtile 56
Gerson 113
giant 48
glossalalia 112
Goethe 182
Gorgias 60
gospel 11, 111, 146, 165,
    197
grammar 6
Grane, Leif 211, 229, 232,
    236, 237, 247
Grassi, E. 234, 248, 249
Greek culture 17
Grundtvig 116, 197

habitus 102, 103
haecæitas 93
Hansen, Knud 237
happiness 112
Hegel 4
Hercules 218, 219

hexis 21
historiography 144
history 169
Hitler 212, 213
Hoffman 36
Holberg, Ludwig 219
Holl, Otto 11
Holm, Søren 242
Holocaust 138
Holy Spirit 89, 91, 92,
    96, 107, 164, 175,
    195, 207
Homer 17, 181
humility 110
humor 55, 77, 78, 196
Hunger, Herbert 247
hydra 221, 222
Hyperaspistes 45

I, the elusive 17
identity 35, 137
individual man 26
intuition 91
intuitive observation 26
irony 196
Israelite 1
iudicare 98

Jensen, N.O. 100
Jerome 67, 158
Jesus 96, 115, 123, 157,
    174, 179, 184, 189,
    201
Joest, Wilfried 98, 154,
    234
Judas 125, 238
Jülicher, Adolf 184, 185,
    186, 187, 190, 191,
    242, 243
Junghans, Helmuth 61, 230
justification 115, 150,
    151, 154

Kabbalism 78
Kennedy, William J. 234
Kessler, Eckhard 239
Kierkegaard, Søren 205
Kingdom of God 188
Kittelson, James M. 249
Kopperschmidt, Josef 237

Kropatscheck, Fr. 240

Lasch, Christopher 249
Latomus 246, 249
Lausberg 53, 230, 239, 245
lawyer 58, 59
Lee, R.W. 230, 247
Lenin 168
Lesowsky, W. 237
Lewis, C.S. 247
Lindhardt, Jan 228, 229,
    230, 232, 233, 234, 235,
    236, 241, 242, 245, 246,
    247, 248
Loewenich, Walter von 193,
    236, 240
love 37, 112
Löfgren, David 236
Lubac, Henri de 242
Lutheran Church 167, 168
Lutheran Orthodoxy 164
Løgstrup, K.E. 11, 59, 136,
    228, 234, 238

Machiavelli, Niccolo di 4,
    46
magic 41, 162
Magnificent, Lorenzo the 46
Magnus, Albertus 158
mania 81
Manichean 75
Mao 168
marxism 47, 168
Marrou, H.I. 230
McSorley 229, 237
Meinholdt, Peter 246
melancholia 71, 78, 151
Melanchton, Philip 4, 6, 7,
    46, 226
Meierung, E.P. 248
memoria 95
metaphor 86, 92, 108, 153,
    169, 181, 182, 184, 185,
    187, 189, 190, 193, 194,
    196, 199, 204, 206, 211,
    218, 244
metre 95
Metzke, E. 246, 249
Michelangelo 5
Michelet 4, 228

Middle Ages 1, 2, 33, 37,
    107, 126, 170, 173,
    174, 175, 178, 179,
    192, 194, 210
"midday sermon" 67
Migliorini, Bruno 241
Milton 83
Mirandola, Pico della 46,
    229
monastery 84
Morris 229
Moses 62, 174, 212, 238,
    243
motus 148
movere 55, 63
Müller, Gregor 234
Mussato 45, 230
mysticism 31

Napoleon 212, 213
narcissistic 227
narratio 52
Nembach, Ulrich 63, 230,
    245
Neoplatonic 74
New Testament 14, 89
Nilsson, Kjell Ove 245
nominalism 190, 191
nous 21
Nygren, Gotthard 237

Oberman, Heiko A. 36, 229,
    235, 237, 241, 248
Occam, William of 38, 39,
    43, 91
Old Testament 67, 146
Ontologie der Person 240
oral 94, 95, 96
origin 68, 178
ornatus 53
otiositas 68

Panofsky 81, 229, 232,
    233, 248
papacy, papal, papist
    157, 159, 160, 167
parable 96, 189
parables of the Kingdom
    187
paradox 196
partitio 52

passion 22
pathe, pathos 21, 23, 56,
    88
Paul 33, 62, 69, 115, 140,
    142, 143, 146, 149,
    153, 161, 174, 247
Pedersen, A.F. Nørager 241
Pedersen, E. Thestrup 191,
    233, 243, 246, 248
Pedersen, Olaf 230
Pelagius 129
peroratio 52
perspicuitas 54
Peter 157, 213
Petrarch 5, 37, 45, 51,
    62, 71, 72, 73, 74,
    75, 76, 77, 80, 93,
    143, 229, 230, 232,
    239
philologist 10
philosophia Christiana
    73, 171
phlegma 78
Pietism 164
pistis 218
Plato 18, 19, 20, 46, 75,
    81, 90, 92, 124
pluralistic society 13
Plutarch 161
poetry 55, 95
polysemeity 217
pope 204, 238
praescientia 124
Praise of Folly 44, 93,
    220
predestination 39, 125
Prenter, R. 207, 235,
    236, 246
Prodigal son 69, 184
promise 198
prudentia 73
psalm 55
psychomachia 25
Purgatory 66

quadriga 173, 212
quidditas 93
quid utile 134
Quintillian 58, 63, 64,
    86, 88, 139, 230, 245

radio 87
"raptus" 35
reality 189
reason 19, 22, 171
receiver 87, 101, 103
reformation 3
regeneratio 3
renascentia 4
Renaissance 1, 2, 3, 4
renovatio 4
restauratio 4
resurrectio 3
resuscitare 4
Reuchlin 46
Revelation 129

rhyme 95
rhytm 54, 58, 94, 141
Riising, Anne 176, 242
rinascita 4
Robertson, D.W. 25, 228
Romanticism 180, 181, 182,
    190
Ross, D. 228
Rousseau 191

Salutati, Coluccio 38, 39,
    40, 45, 161, 245
salvation 119
Sandstrom, Peter G. 234
sapientia 73
Sappho 18
Satan 137, 152
Saturn 82
scepticism 221
Scheel, Otto 11, 233
Scherfig, hans 180, 181
scholastic 39, 97, 102,
    170
Schwarz, R. 235, 236, 237
scopus 210
scopus-reading 172
scriptura sui interpres
    156
secretum 75
secularization 8, 12
Seigel, Jerrold E. 232
self 18, 29
self-reflection 20
sensual appetites 19
sentire 104

shadow-pictures 20
Shakespeare 41
simile 189
simul justus et peccator
    151
sloth 67
Snell, Bruno 228
Snyder, Susan 230
social sciences 30
Socrates 19
Söderblom 239
sola scriptura 156, 163,
    165, 168, 170
song 55
speak 66
speech act 198
Spitz, Lewis W. 62, 230
Staupitz, Johannes von 62
stoic 72, 73
Stolt, Birgit 63, 230,
    240
Struever, Nancy 230, 241
style 55
suicide 70
symbol 178, 182, 183,
    190, 191, 192
synechdoche 199, 200

Tauler 35, 37, 113
tentatio tristitiae 84
tertium comparationes 187
Tertullian 158
Thomas Aquinas 90, 92,
    97, 102, 127, 128,
    150, 158, 229, 234,
    235, 237
Thomas, Keith 229
Tillich, Paul 183
tradition 158, 159, 160,
    165, 167, 170
transmitter 86, 87, 103
transubstantiation 194
tristitia 67, 69
trivium 62
typology 206

unio mystic 32, 33
uti-love 27

Valla, Lorenzo 38, 233
Venice 49

verbum increatum 99
Vergil 97
videre 98
vision 59
vita contemplativa 77
vita solitaria 77
Vogelsang, Erich 32, 229
voluntarism 38
Vulgate 67

Waith, Eugenio M. 248
Wartburg 159, 160
Weinrich, H. 127
Wenzel, Siegfried 230
Wernle, Hans 244
Wilder, Amos A. 247
will 19, 22, 37, 73, 76,
    119
Wise, Frederick the 159
Witt, Ronald 230
Wittenberg 160
word 89, 98, 140, 170,
    207
Worms, Diet of 159

Zwingli 6, 208

Østergaard Nielsen, H.
    239, 240

TEXTS AND STUDIES IN RELIGION

1. Elizabeth A. Clark, **Clement's Use of Aristotle: The Aristotelian Contribution to Clement of Alexandria's Refutation of Gnosticism**

2. Richard DeMaria, **Communal Love at Oneida: A Perfectionist Vision of Authority, Property and Sexual Order**

3. David F. Kelly, **The Emergence of Roman Catholic Medical Ethics in North America: An Historical-Methodological-Bibliographical Study**

4. David Rausch, **Zionism Within Early American Fundamentalism,1878-1918: A Convergence of Two Traditions**

5. Janine Marie Idziak, **Divine Command Morality: Historical and Contemporary Readings**

6. Marcus Braybrooke, **Inter-Faith Organizations, 1893-1979: An Historical Directory**

7. L. William Countryman, **The Rich Christian in the Church of the Early Empire: Contradictions and Accommodations**

8. Irving Hexham, **The Irony of Apartheid: The Struggle for National Independence of Afrikaner Calvinism Against British Imperialism**

9. Michael Ryan, editor, **Human Responses to the Holocaust: Perpetrators and Victims, Bystanders and Resisters**

10. G. Stanley Kane, **Anselm's Doctrine of Freedom and the Will**

11. Bruce Bubacz, **St. Augustine's Theory of Knowledge: A Contemporary Analysis**

12. Anne Barstow, **Married Priests and the Reforming Papacy: The Eleventh-Century Debates**

13. Denis Janz, editor, **Three Reformation Catechisms: Catholic, Anabaptist, Lutheran**

14. David Rausch, **Messianic Judaism: Its History, Theology, and Polity**

15. Ernest E. Best, **Religion and Society in Transition: The Church and Social Change in England, 1560-1850**

16. Donald V. Stump *et al.*, editors, *Hamartia:***The Concept of Error in the Western Tradition**

17. Louis Meyer, **Eminent Hebrew Christians of the Nineteenth Century: Brief Biographical Sketches**, edited by David Rausch

18. J. William Frost, editor, **The Records and Recollections of James Jenkins**

19. Joseph R. Washington, Jr., **Anti-Blackness in English Religion 1500-1800**

20. Joyce E. Salisbury, **Iberian Popular Religion, 600 B.C. to 700 A.D., Celts, Romans and Visigoths**

21. Longinus, **On the Sublime,** translated by James A. Arieti and John M. Crossett

22. James Gollnick, *Flesh* **as Transformation Symbol in the Theology of Anselm of Canterbury,**

23. William Lane Craig, **The Historical Argument for the Resurrection of Jesus During the Deist Controversy**

24. Steven H. Simpler, **Roland H. Bainton: An Examination of His Reformation Historiography**

25. Charles W. Brockwell, **Bishop Reginald Pecock and the Lancastrian Church: Securing the foundations of cultural authority**

26. Sebastian Franck, **280 Paradoxes or Wondrous Sayings,** Translated & Introduced by E. J. Furcha

27. James Heft, **John XXII and Papal Teaching Authority**

28. Shelley Baranowski, **The Confessing Church, Conservative Elites, and the Nazi State**

29. Jan Lindhardt, **Martin Luther: Knowledge and Mediation in the Renaissance**

DATE DUE